ying
itch

Chihiro Ishizuka

3

Contents

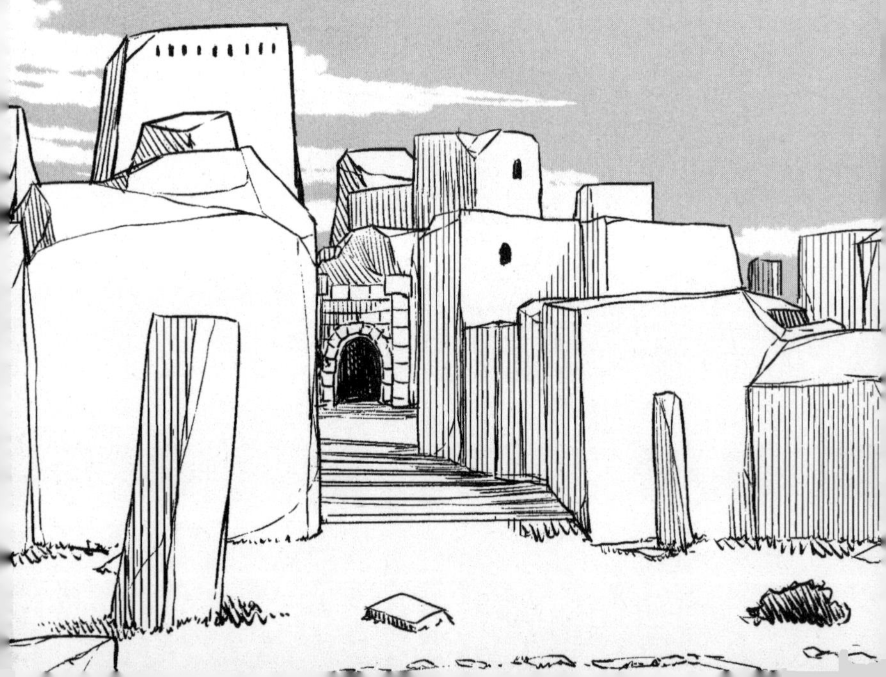

Chapter 13
Café Conclusio

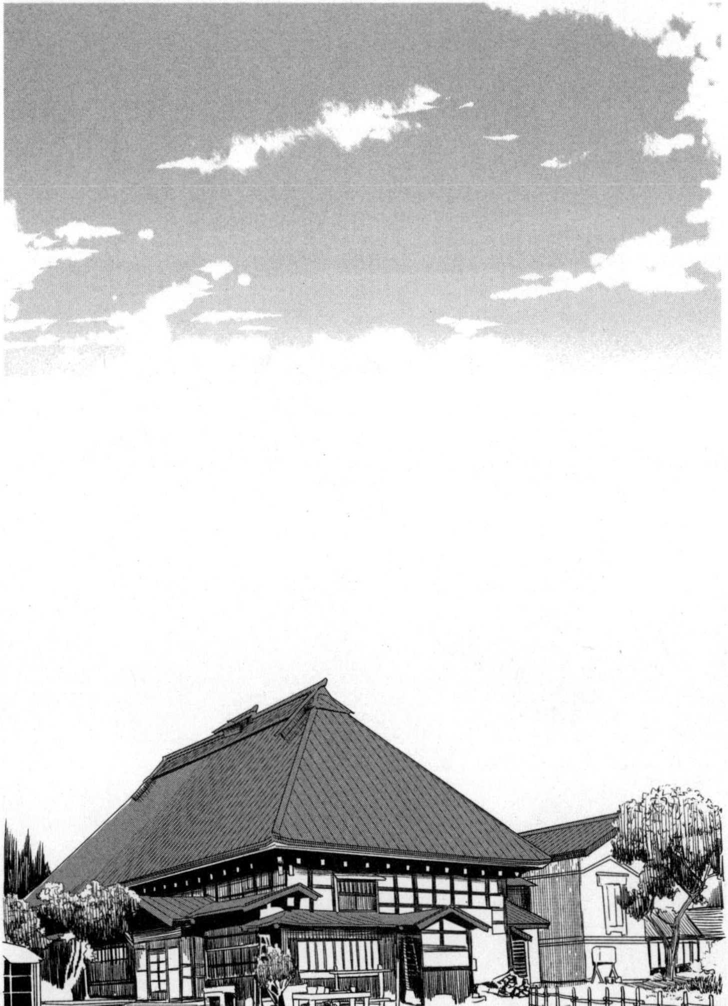

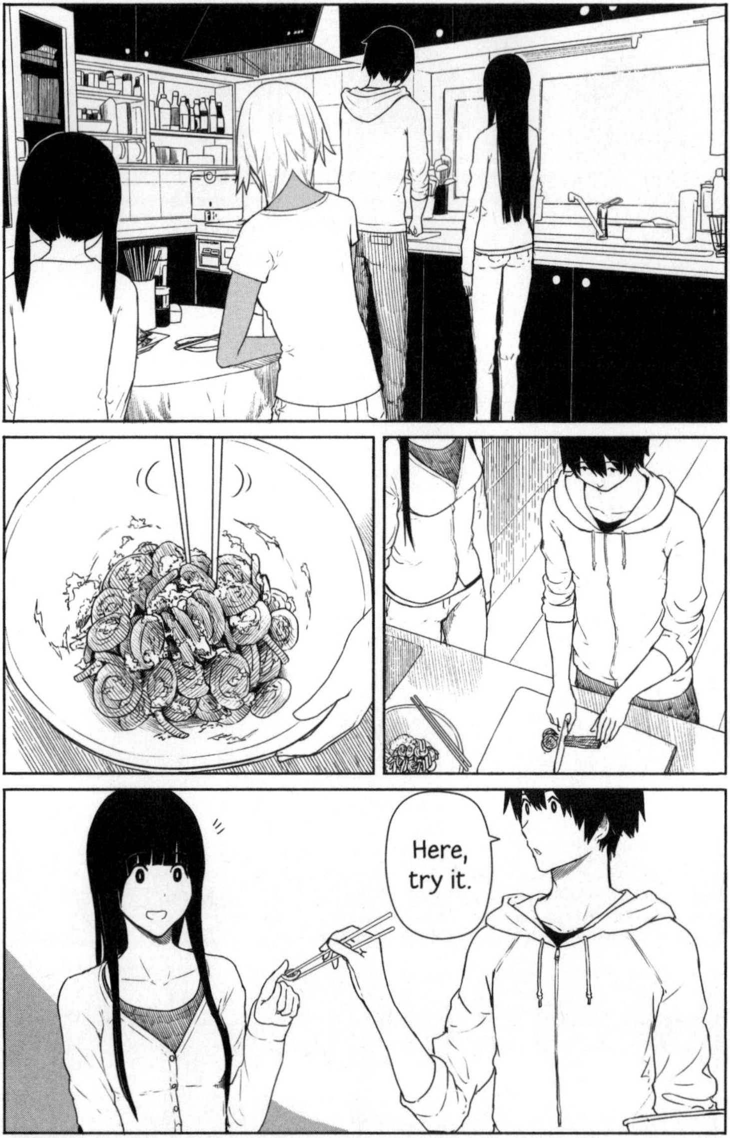
Here, try it.

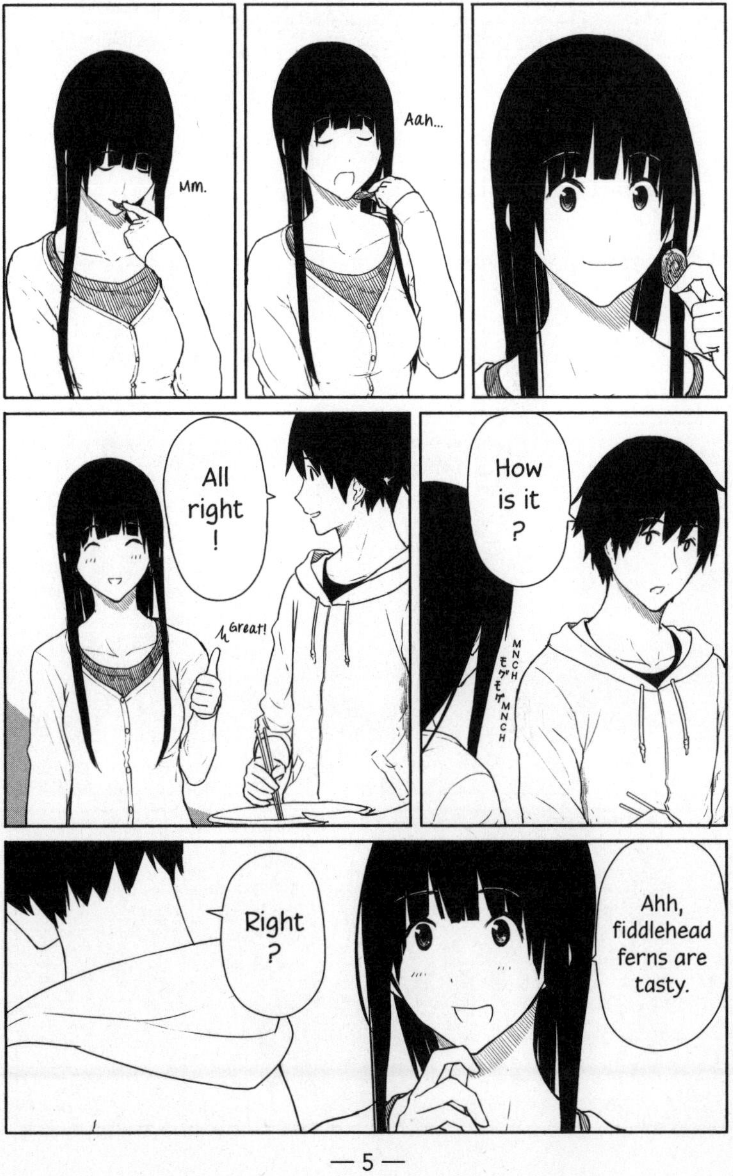
Aah...
Mm.
How is it ?
MNCH MNCH
All right !
Great!
Ahh, fiddlehead ferns are tasty.
Right ?

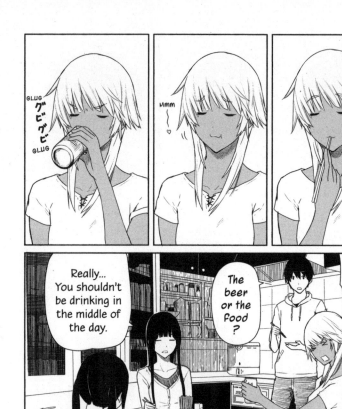

Mmm
~
♡
GLUG
グビグビ
GLUG
Aahh! Good stuff!
The beer or the food?
Really... You shouldn't be drinking in the middle of the day.
Aww, who cares? It's fine!
The immorality of it makes the booze taste better, y'know.
Just wait 'til you're all grown up and then try it.
You sound like an old man.

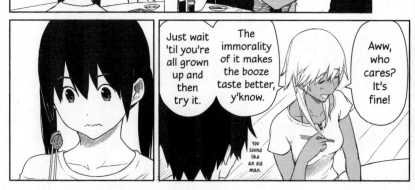

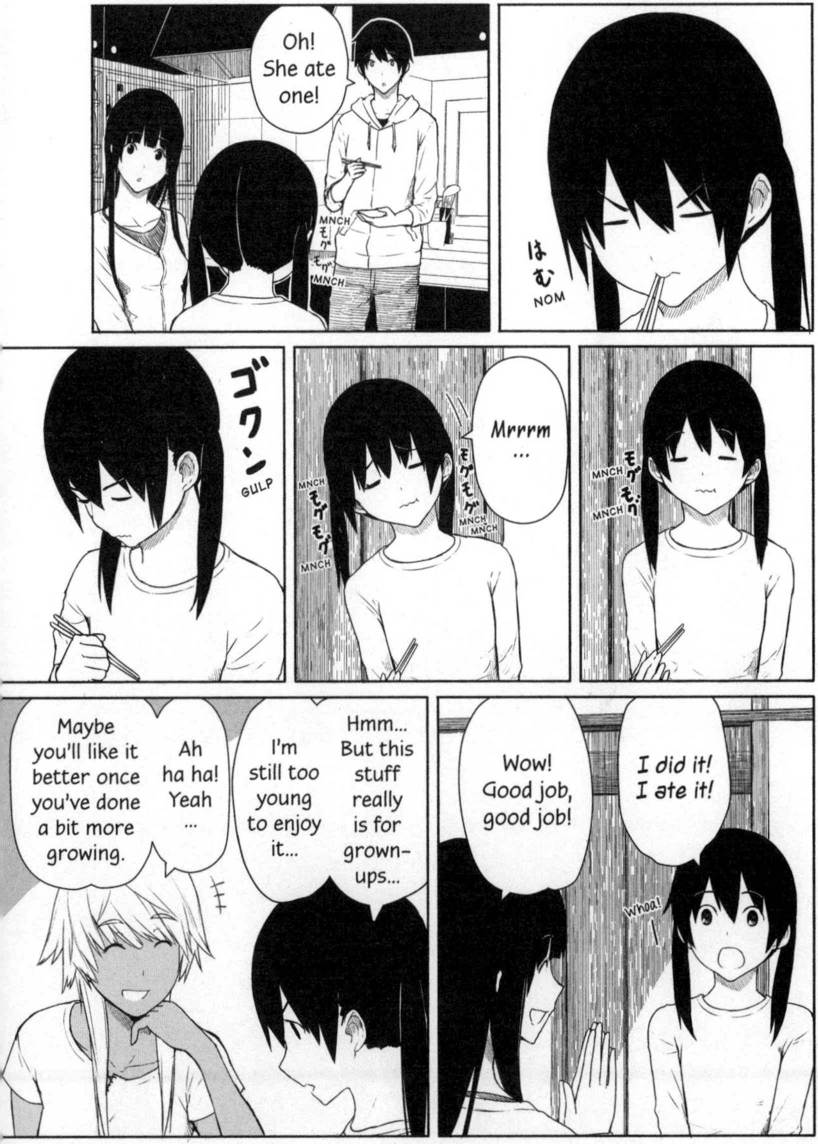
はむ
NOM
Oh! She ate one!
MNCH もぐ
もぐ MNCH
MNCH もぐ もぐ MNCH
Mrrrm ...
もぐもぐ MNCH MNCH
MNCH もぐ もぐ MNCH
ゴクン
GULP
I did it! I ate it!
Wow! Good job, good job!
Whoa!
Hmm... But this stuff really is for grown-ups...
I'm still too young to enjoy it...
Ah ha ha! Yeah ...
Maybe you'll like it better once you've done a bit more growing.

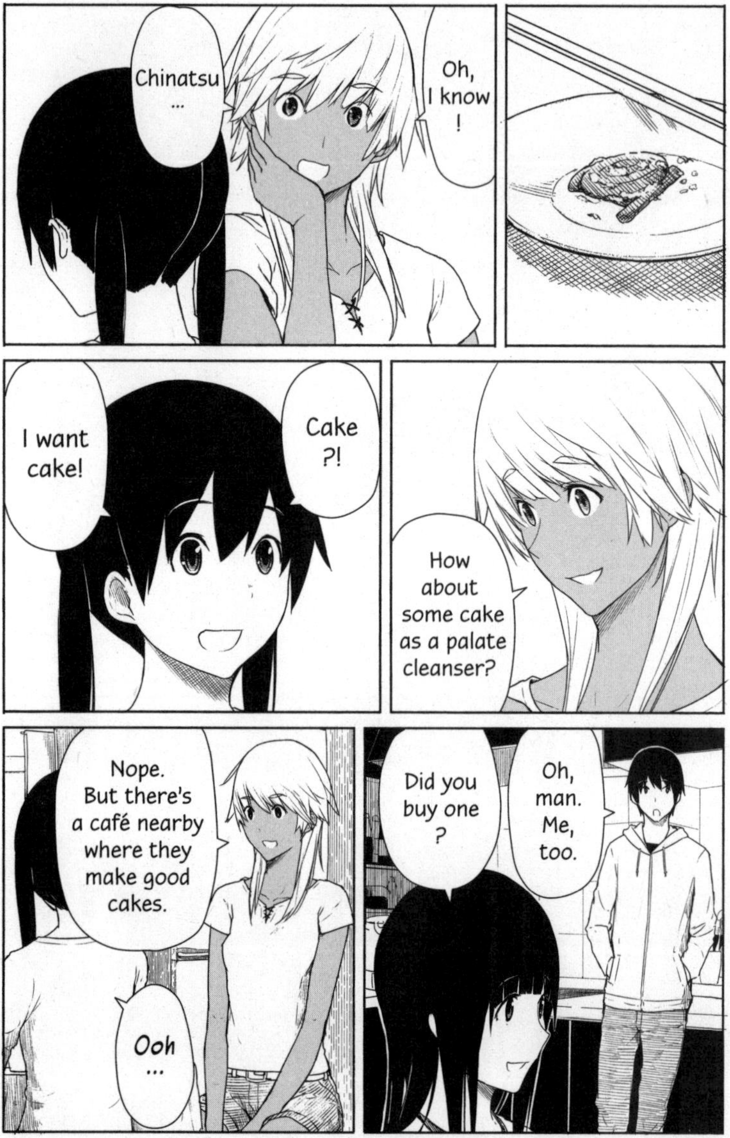
Oh, I know!
Chinatsu...
How about some cake as a palate cleanser?
Cake?!
I want cake!
Oh, man. Me, too.
Did you buy one?
Nope. But there's a café nearby where they make good cakes.
Ooh...

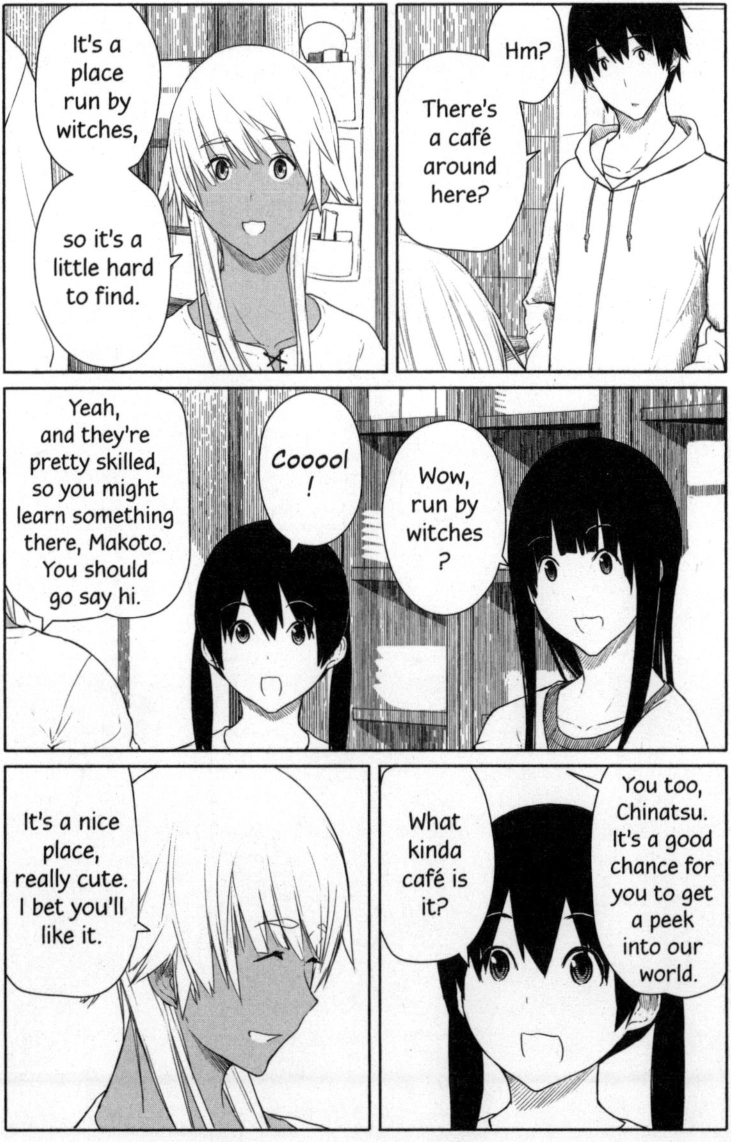
Hm?
There's a café around here?
It's a place run by witches,
so it's a little hard to find.
Wow, run by witches?
Cooool!
Yeah, and they're pretty skilled, so you might learn something there, Makoto. You should go say hi.
You too, Chinatsu. It's a good chance for you to get a peek into our world.
What kinda café is it?
It's a nice place, really cute. I bet you'll like it.

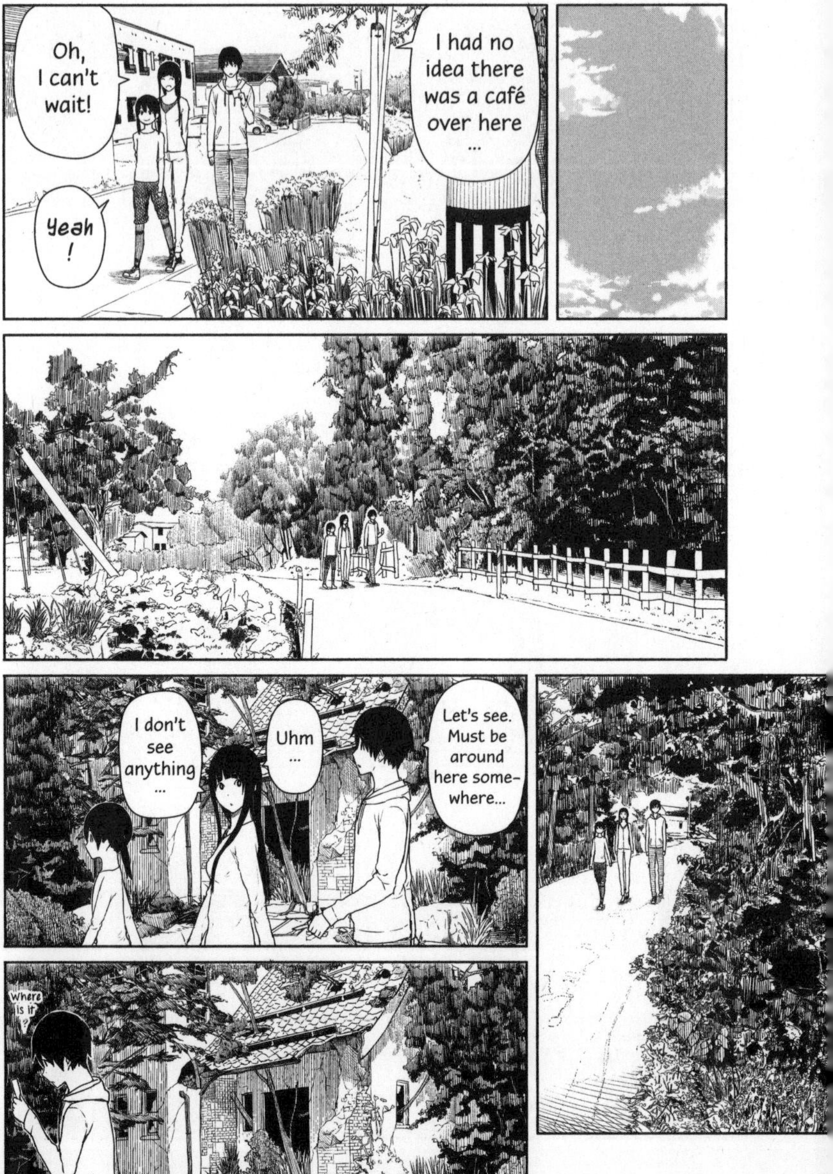
I had no idea there was a café over here ...
Oh, I can't wait!
Yeah!
Let's see. Must be around here some-where...
Uhm ...
I don't see anything ...
Where is it?

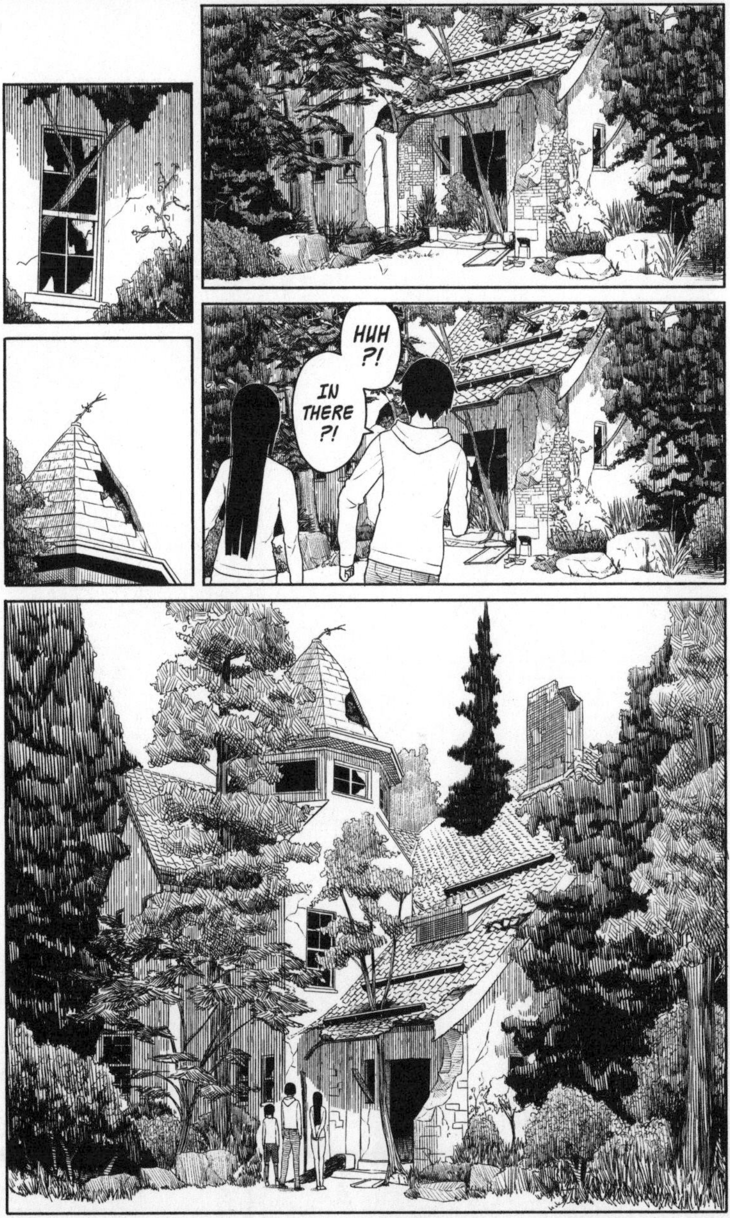
HUH ?!
IN THERE ?!

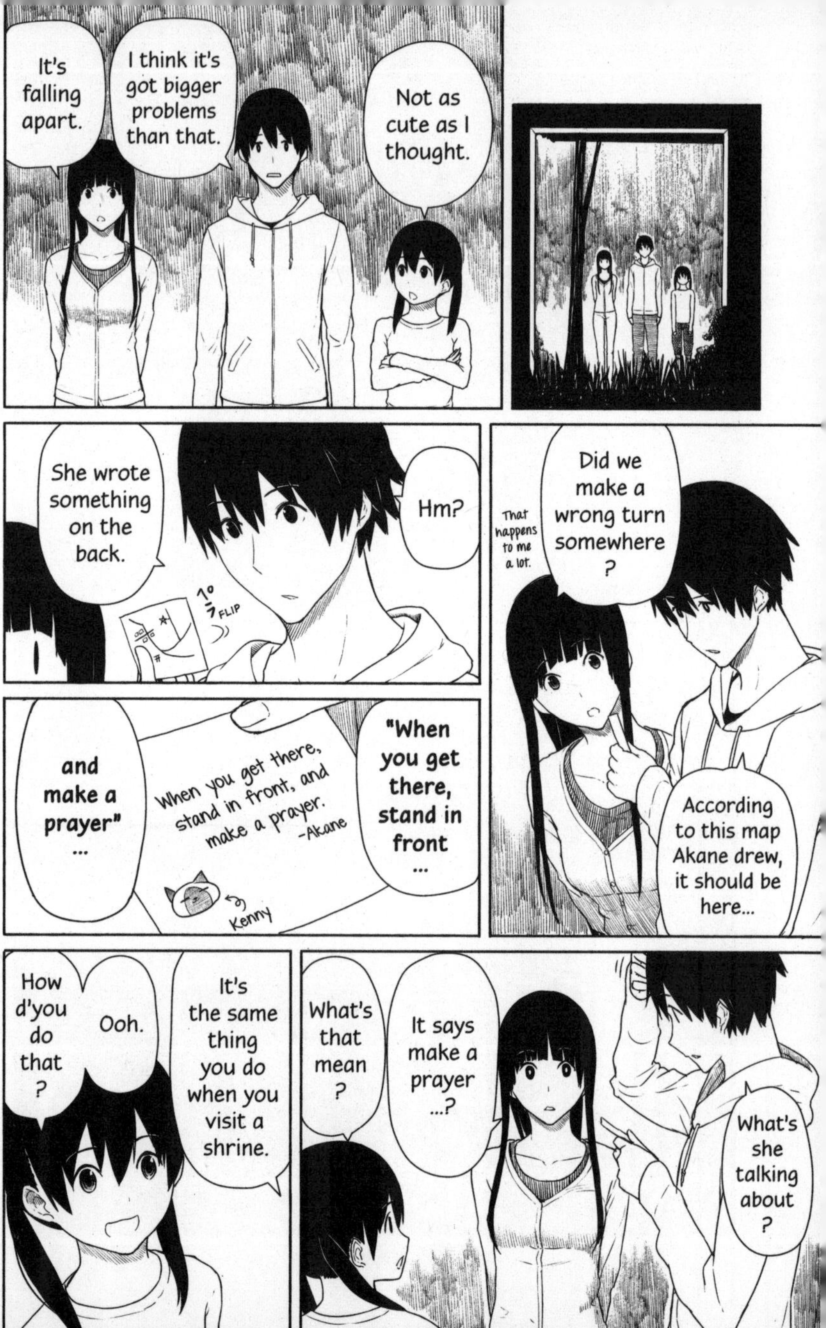
Not as cute as I thought.
I think it's got bigger problems than that.
It's falling apart.
Did we make a wrong turn somewhere?
That happens to me a lot.
According to this map Akane drew, it should be here...
Hm?
She wrote something on the back.
FLIP
"When you get there, stand in front ...
When you get there, stand in front, and make a prayer. -Akane
Kenny
and make a prayer" ...
What's she talking about?
It says make a prayer ...?
What's that mean?
It's the same thing you do when you visit a shrine.
Ooh.
How d'you do that?

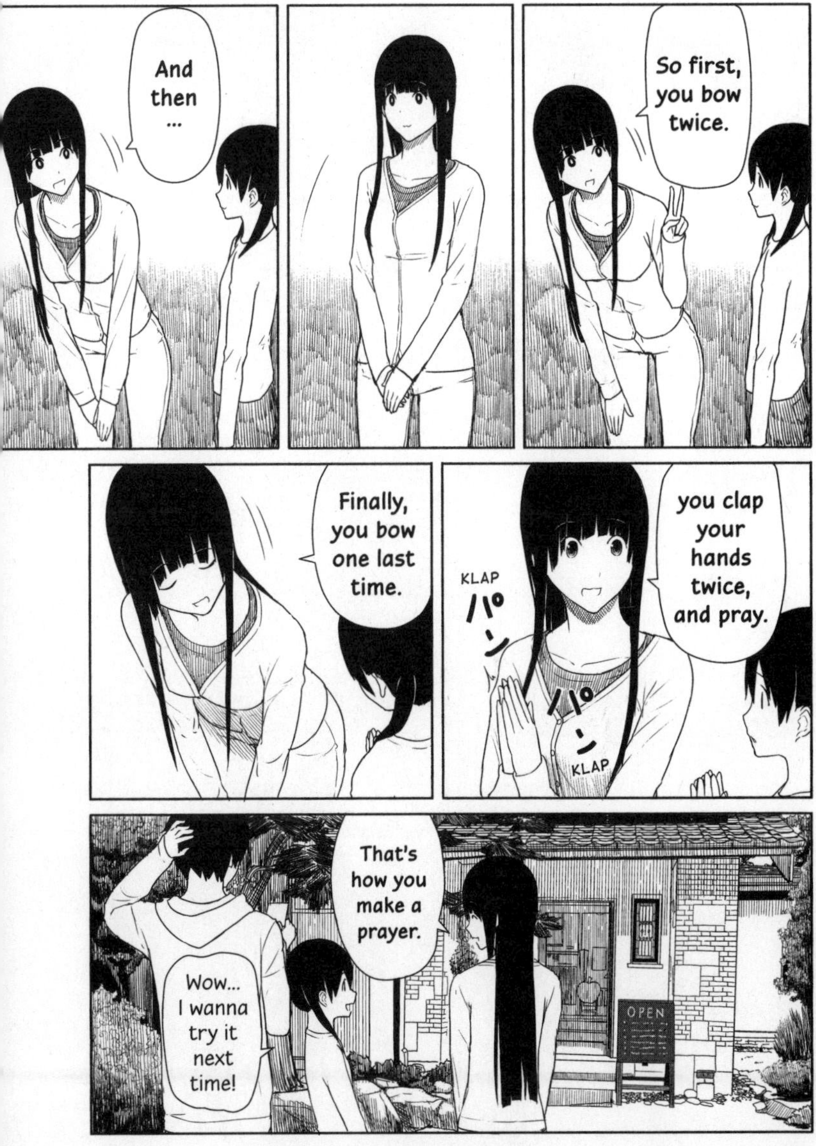
So first, you bow twice.
And then ...
KLAP
パン
you clap your hands twice, and pray.
パン
KLAP
Finally, you bow one last time.
That's how you make a prayer.
OPEN
Wow... I wanna try it next time!

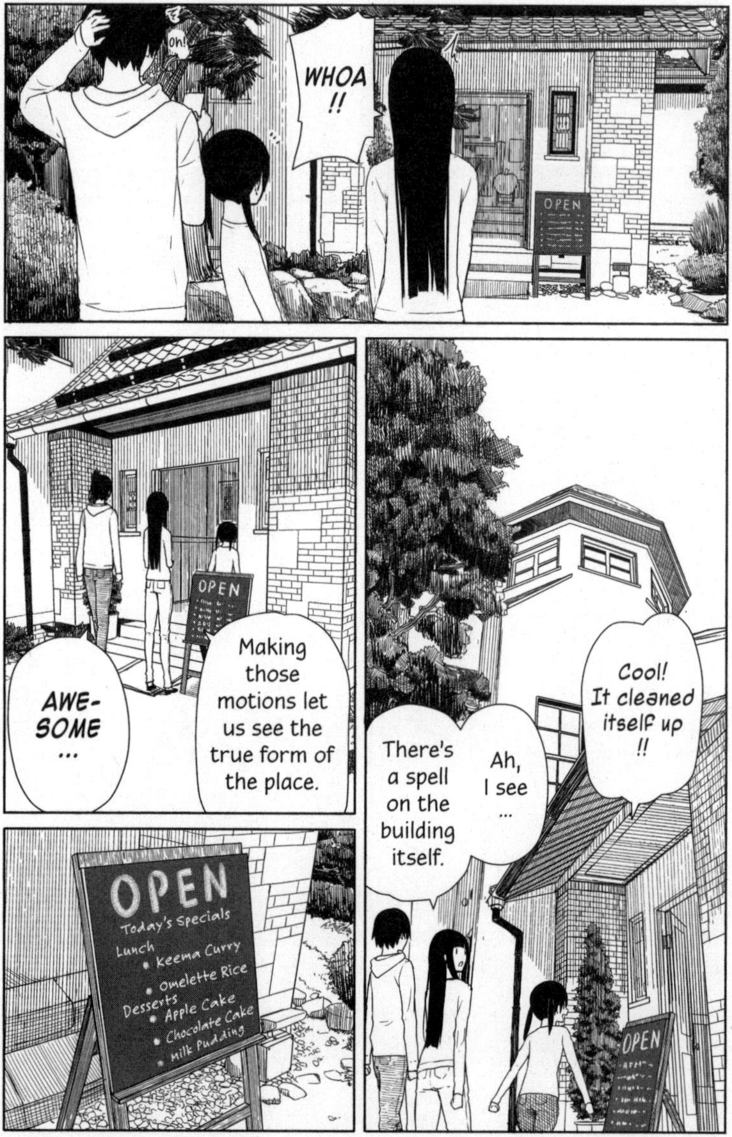
Oh!
WHOA !!
OPEN
Cool! It cleaned itself up !!
Ah, I see ...
There's a spell on the building itself.
OPEN
OPEN
Making those motions let us see the true form of the place.
AWE-SOME ...
OPEN
Today's Specials
Lunch
Keema Curry
Omelette Rice
Desserts
Apple Cake
Chocolate Cake
Milk Pudding

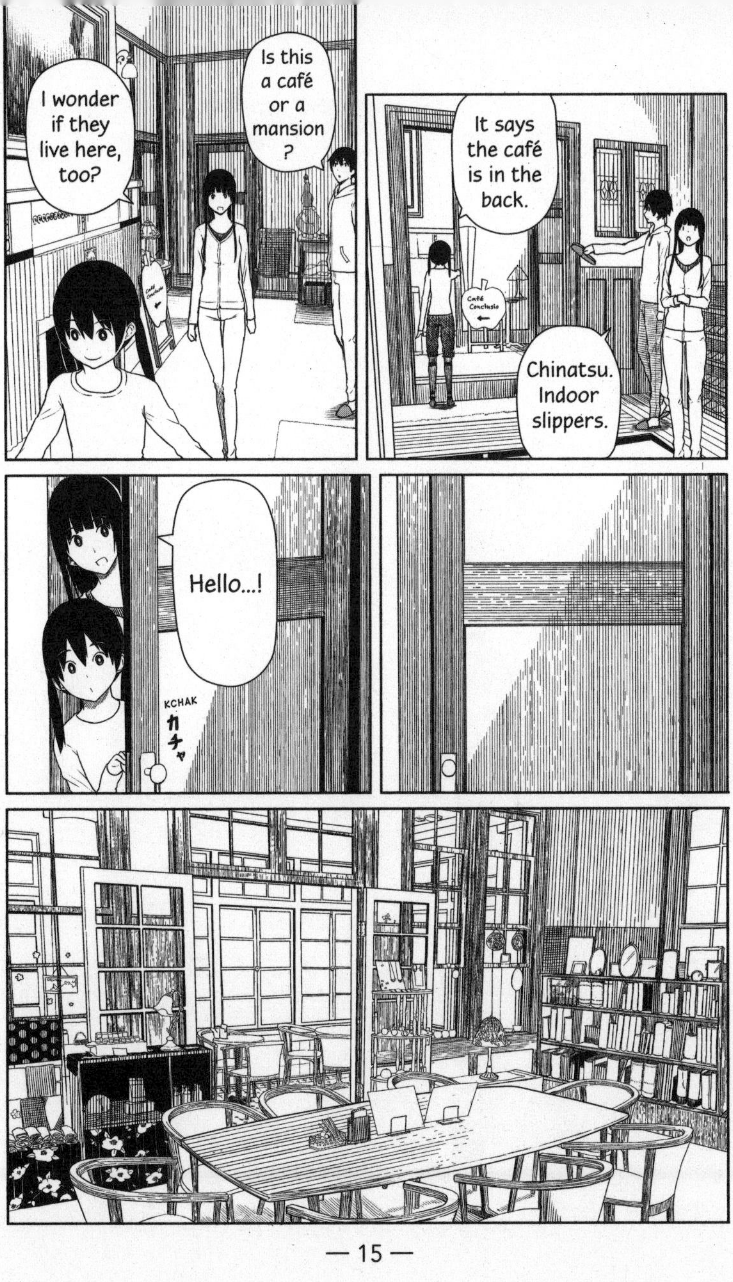
It says the café is in the back.
Café Conclusio
Chinatsu. Indoor slippers.
Is this a café or a mansion?
I wonder if they live here, too?
Hello...!
KCHAK
カチャ

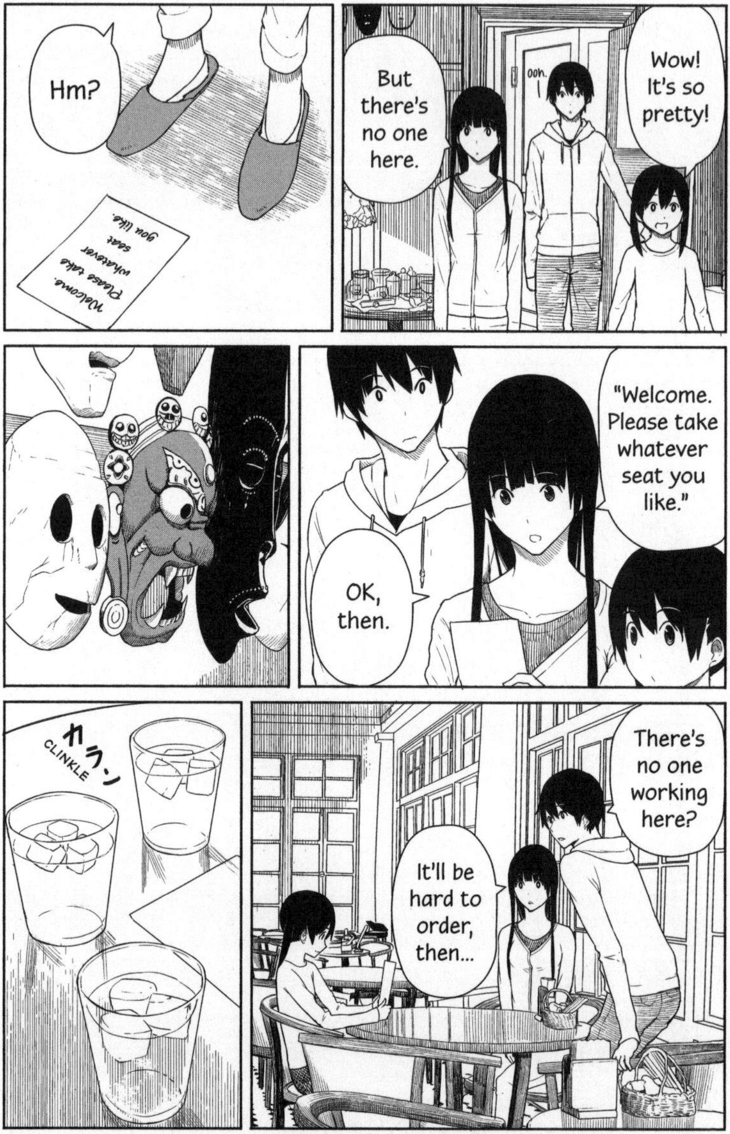
Wow! It's so pretty!
oon.
But there's no one here.
Hm?
Welcome. Please take whatever seat you like.
"Welcome. Please take whatever seat you like."
OK, then.
There's no one working here?
It'll be hard to order, then...
カラン
CLINKLE

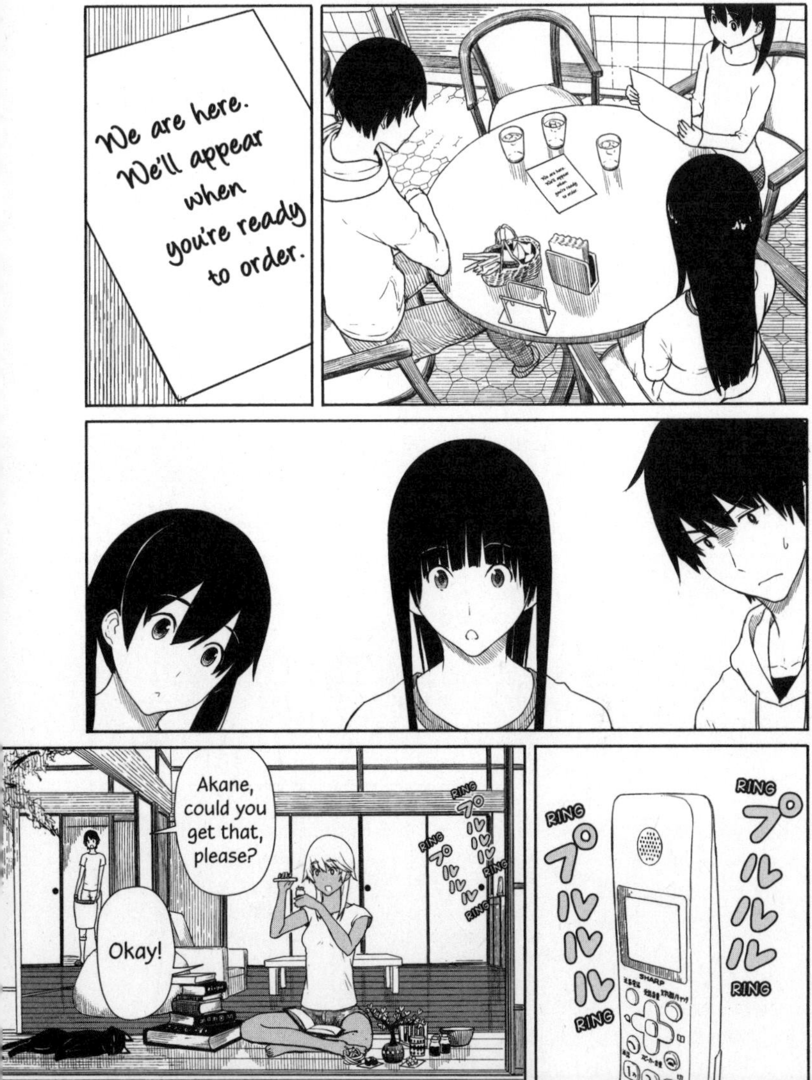
We are here. We'll appear when you're ready to order.
RING
プルルル
RING
RING
プルルル
RING
SHARP
Akane, could you get that, please?
Okay!
RING
プルルル
RING
RING
プルルル
RING

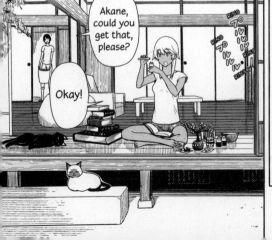

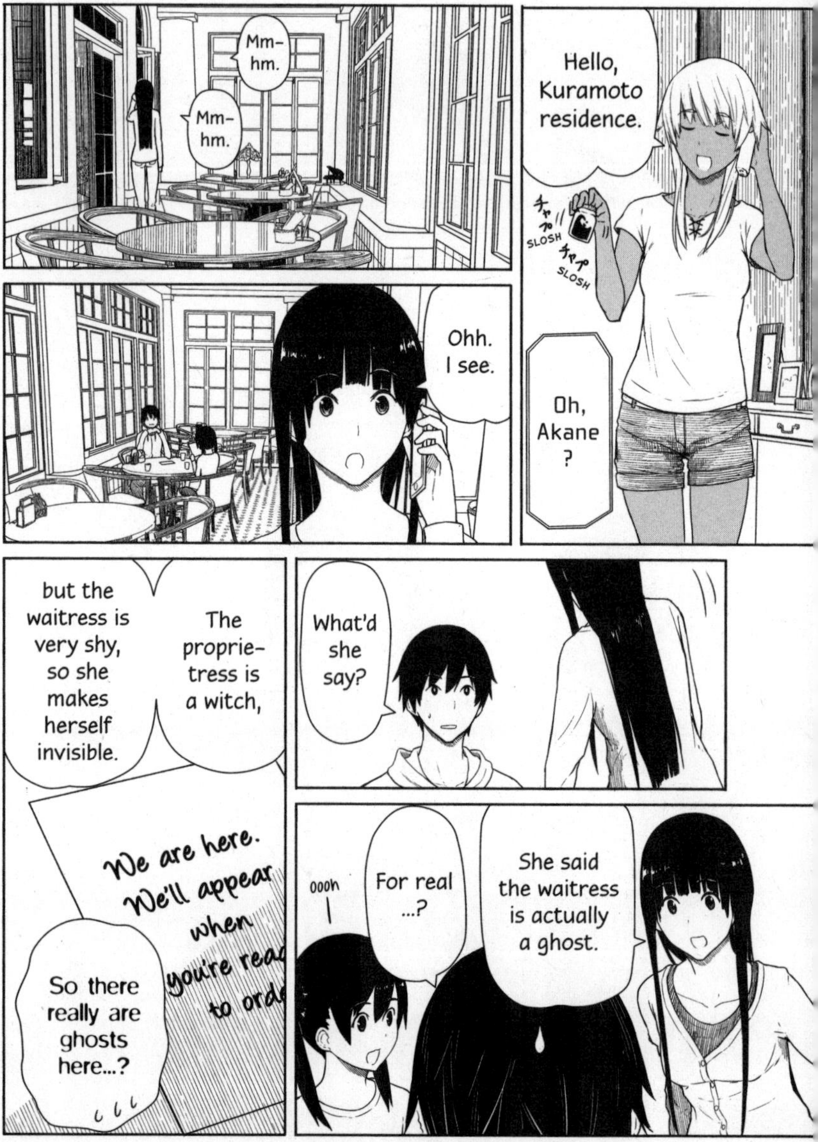
Hello, Kuramoto residence.
チャプ SLOSH
チャプ SLOSH
Oh, Akane?
Mm-hm.
Mm-hm.
Ohh. I see.
What'd she say?
She said the waitress is actually a ghost.
For real ...?
oooh
The proprie-tress is a witch,
but the waitress is very shy, so she makes herself invisible.
We are here. We'll appear when you're rea to ord
So there really are ghosts here...?

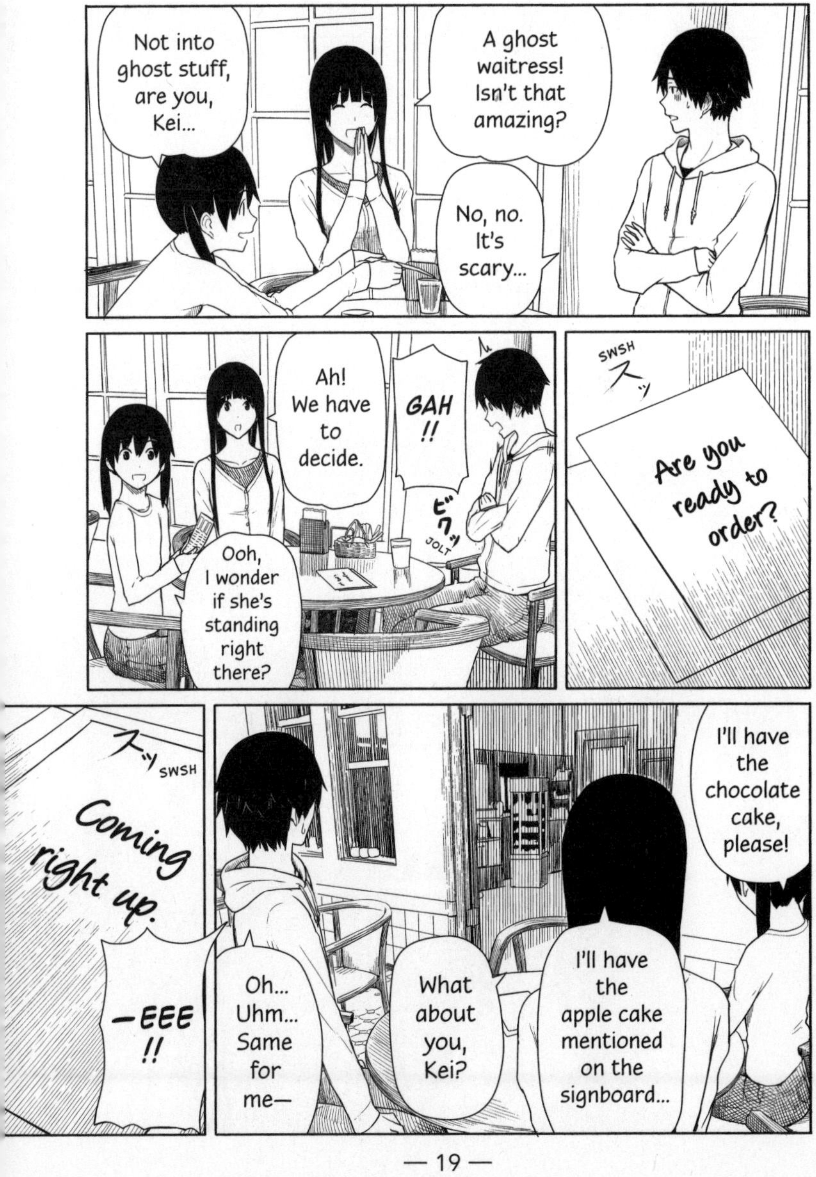
A ghost waitress! Isn't that amazing?
Not into ghost stuff, are you, Kei...
No, no. It's scary...
SWSH
Are you ready to order?
GAH!!
JOLT
Ah! We have to decide.
Ooh, I wonder if she's standing right there?
I'll have the chocolate cake, please!
I'll have the apple cake mentioned on the signboard...
What about you, Kei?
Oh... Uhm... Same for me—
SWSH
Coming right up.
—EEE!!

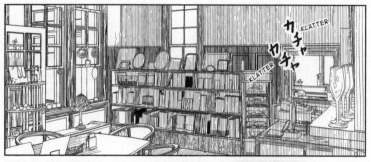

カチャ
KLATTER
カチャ
KLATTER
Whoa... Now it feels like there's someone here...
We're meeting a real ghost. This is so exciting!
I wanna get her autograph!
I wonder what kind of person she was.
Me, too. I'd like to be able to see her.
Kei, it'd be less scary if you could see her, wouldn't it?
Uh... Well...
I guess, but...
Oh! I know!

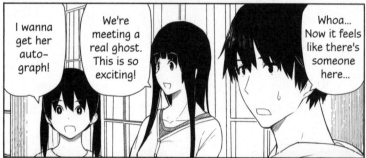

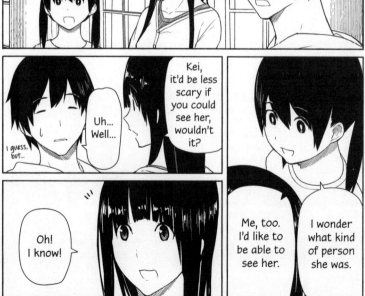

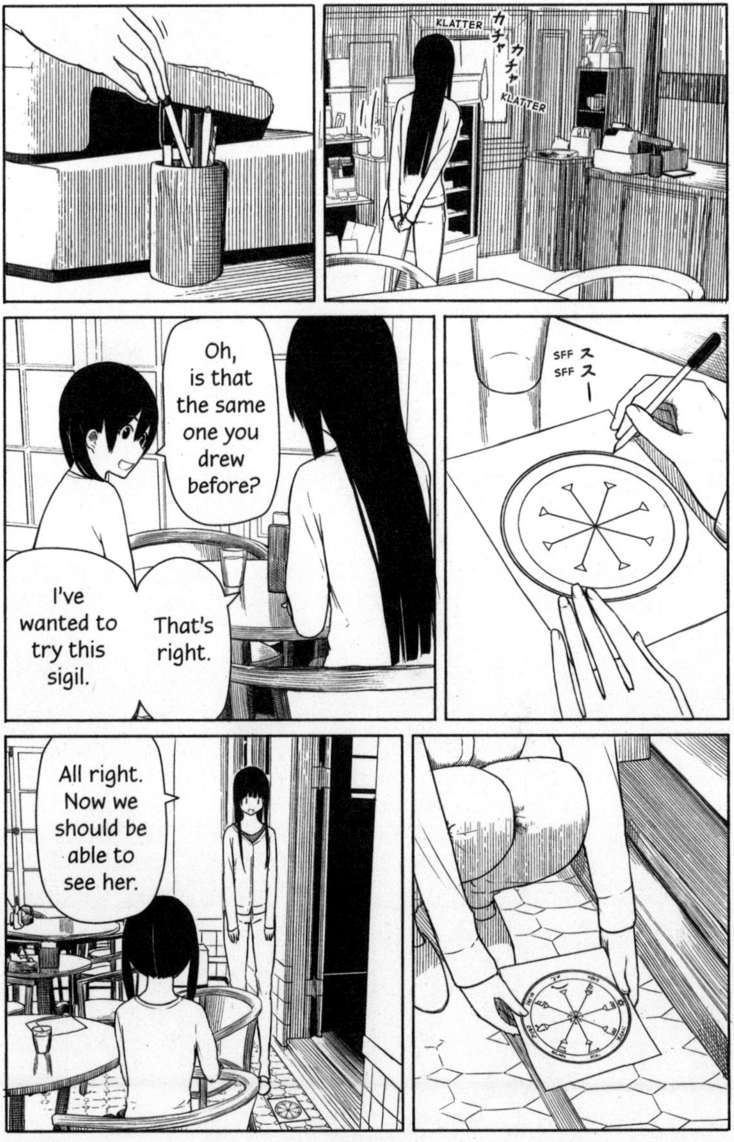
KLATTER カチャ
カチャ KLATTER
SFF SFF スス－
Oh, is that the same one you drew before?
That's right.
I've wanted to try this sigil.
All right. Now we should be able to see her.

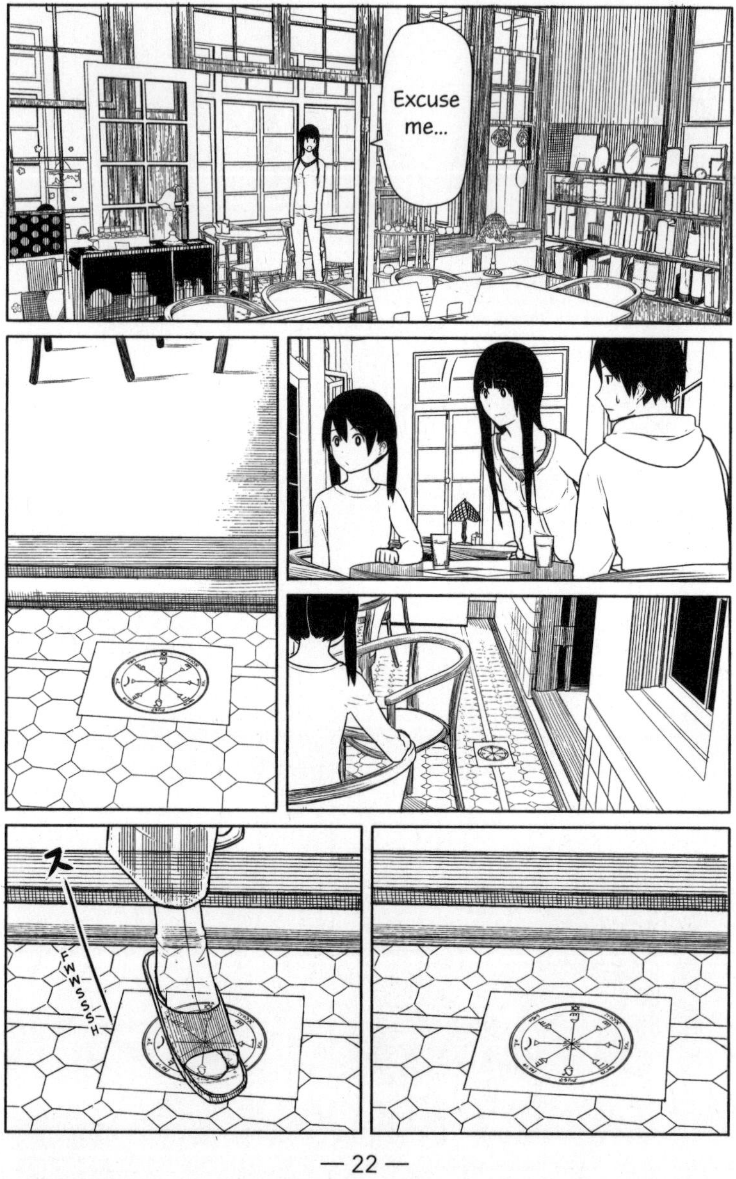
Excuse me...
ス
FWWSSSH

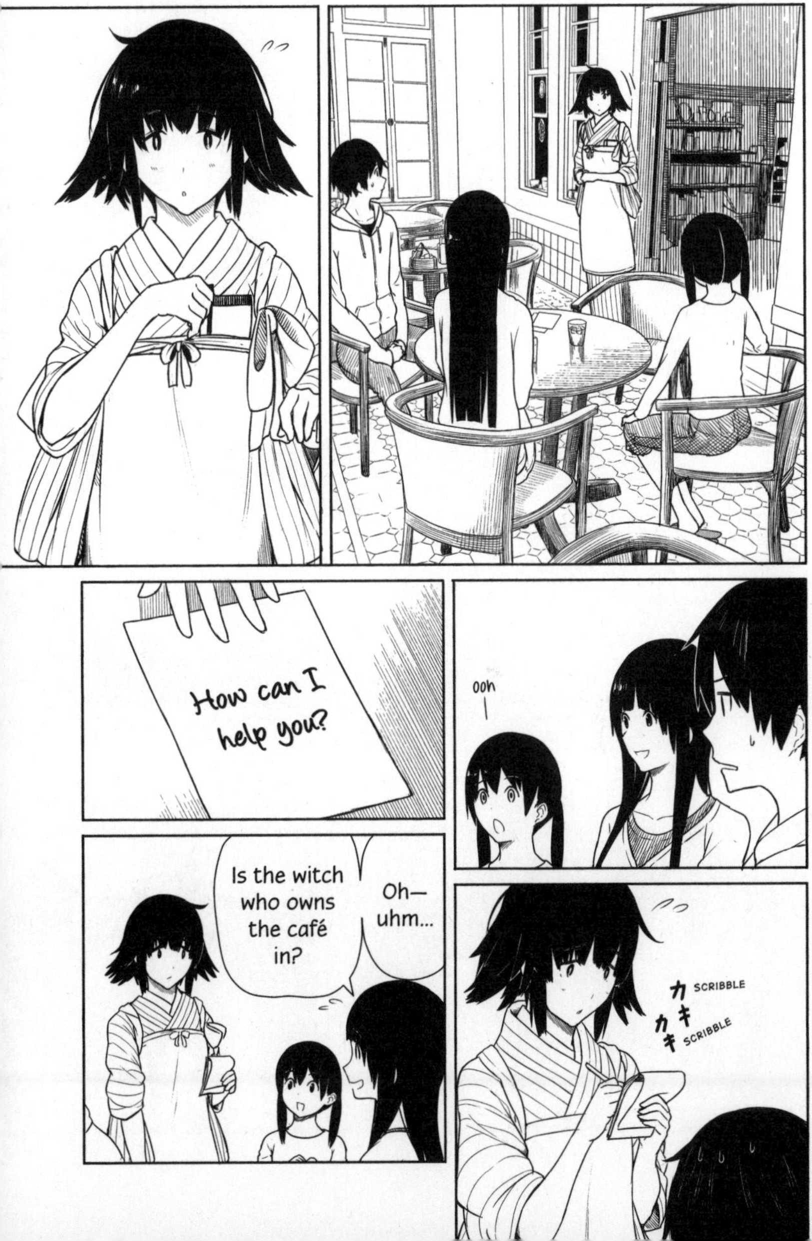

oon
How can I help you?
Oh— uhm...
Is the witch who owns the café in?
カキ SCRIBBLE
カキ SCRIBBLE

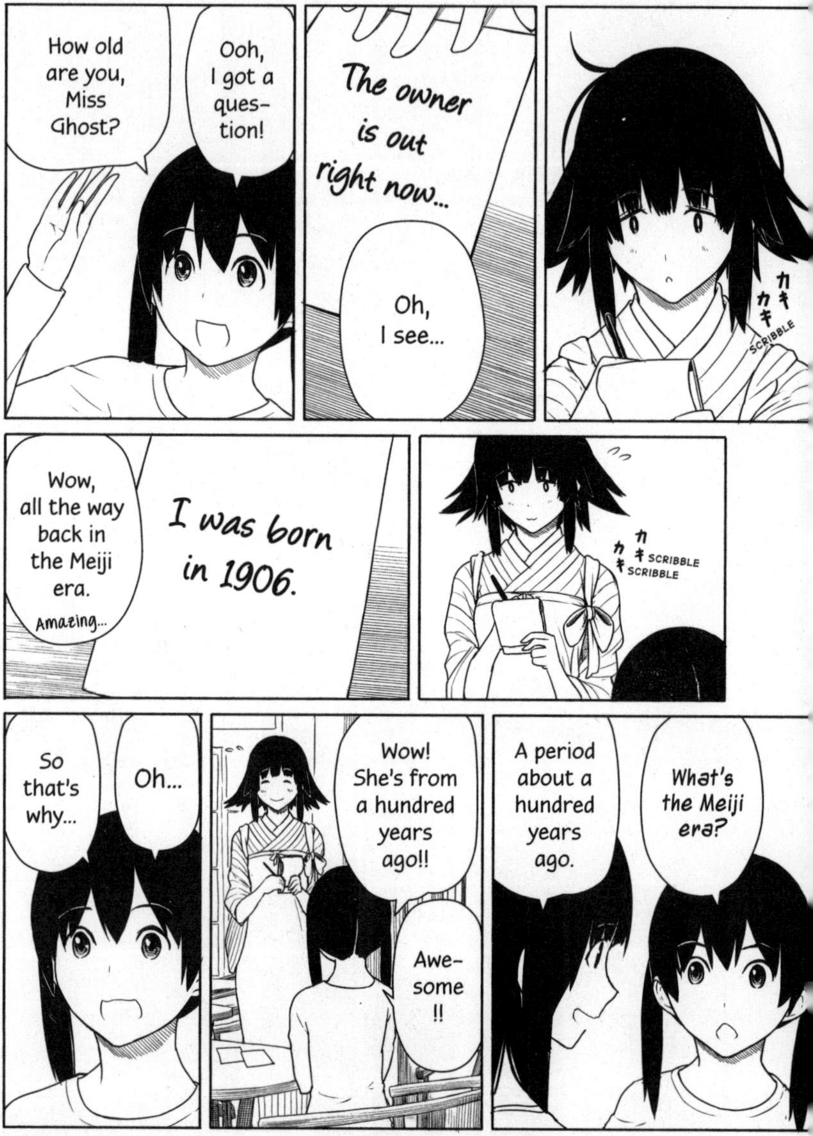
カキ
カキ
SCRIBBLE
The owner is out right now...
Oh, I see...
Ooh, I got a ques-tion!
How old are you, Miss Ghost?
カキ SCRIBBLE
カキ SCRIBBLE
I was born in 1906.
Wow, all the way back in the Meiji era.
Amazing...
What's the Meiji era?
A period about a hundred years ago.
Wow! She's from a hundred years ago!!
Awe-some!!
Oh...
So that's why...

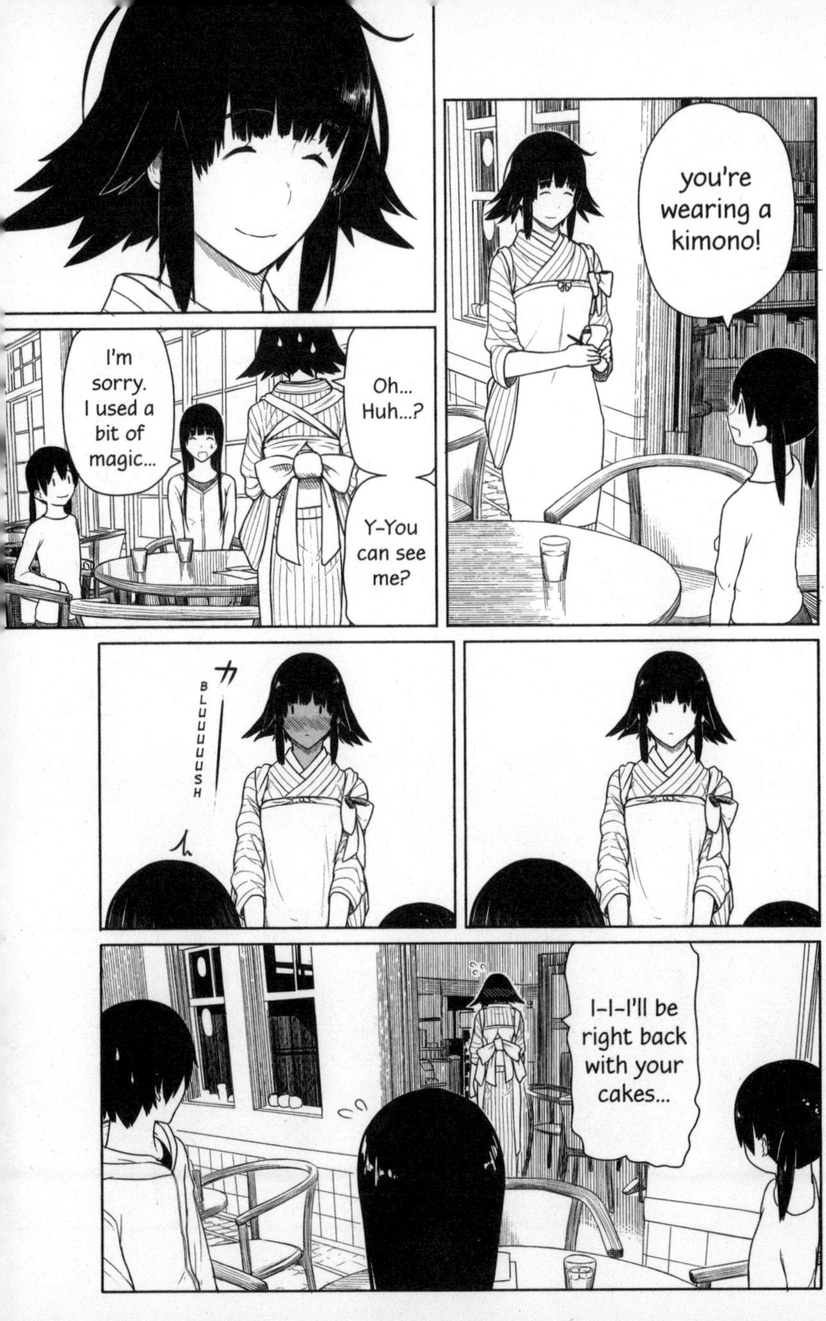

you're wearing a kimono!
Oh... Huh...?
Y-You can see me?
I'm sorry. I used a bit of magic...
カ
BLUUUUUUSH
I-I-I'll be right back with your cakes...

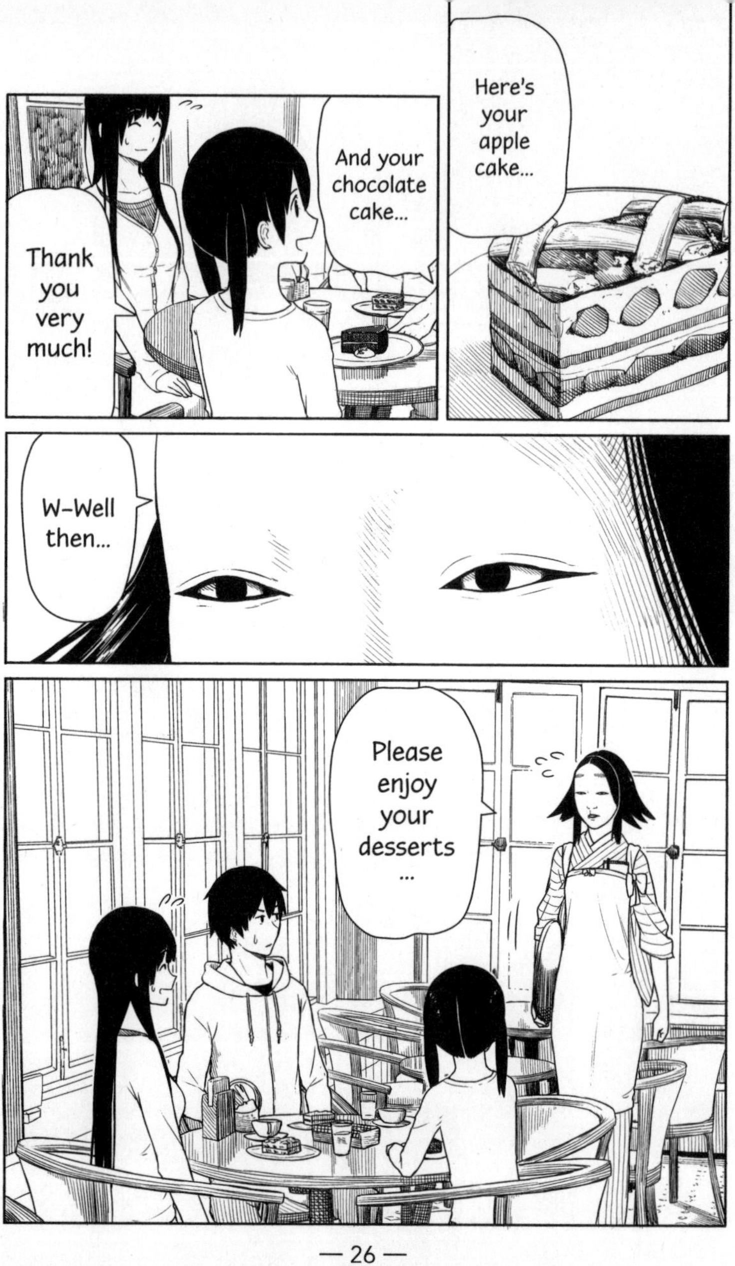
Here's your apple cake...
And your chocolate cake...
Thank you very much!
W-Well then...
Please enjoy your desserts ...

Chapter 14
The Regular's Cry

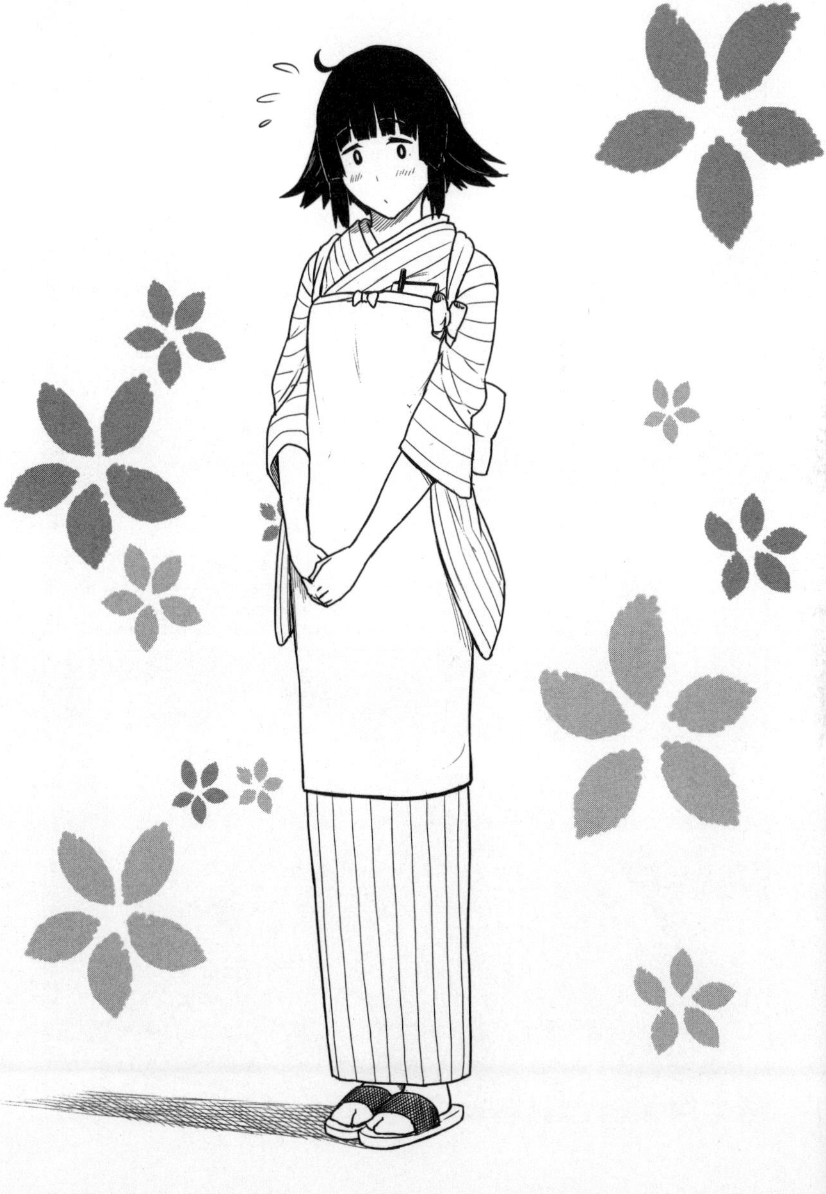

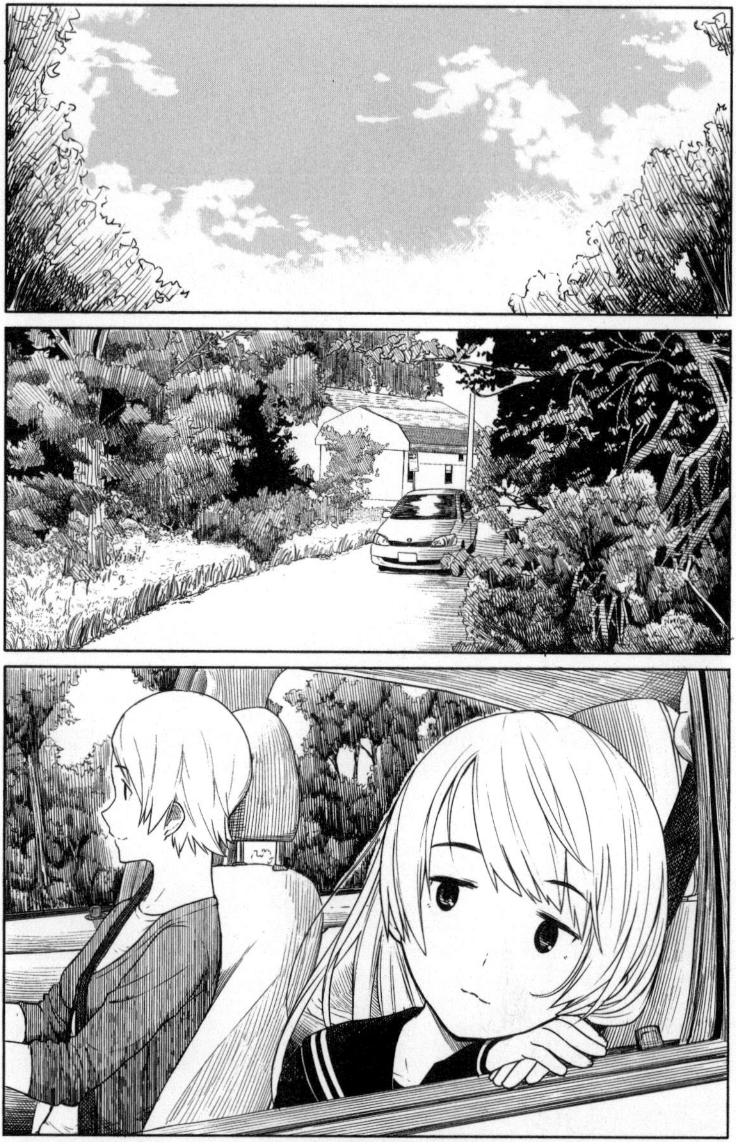

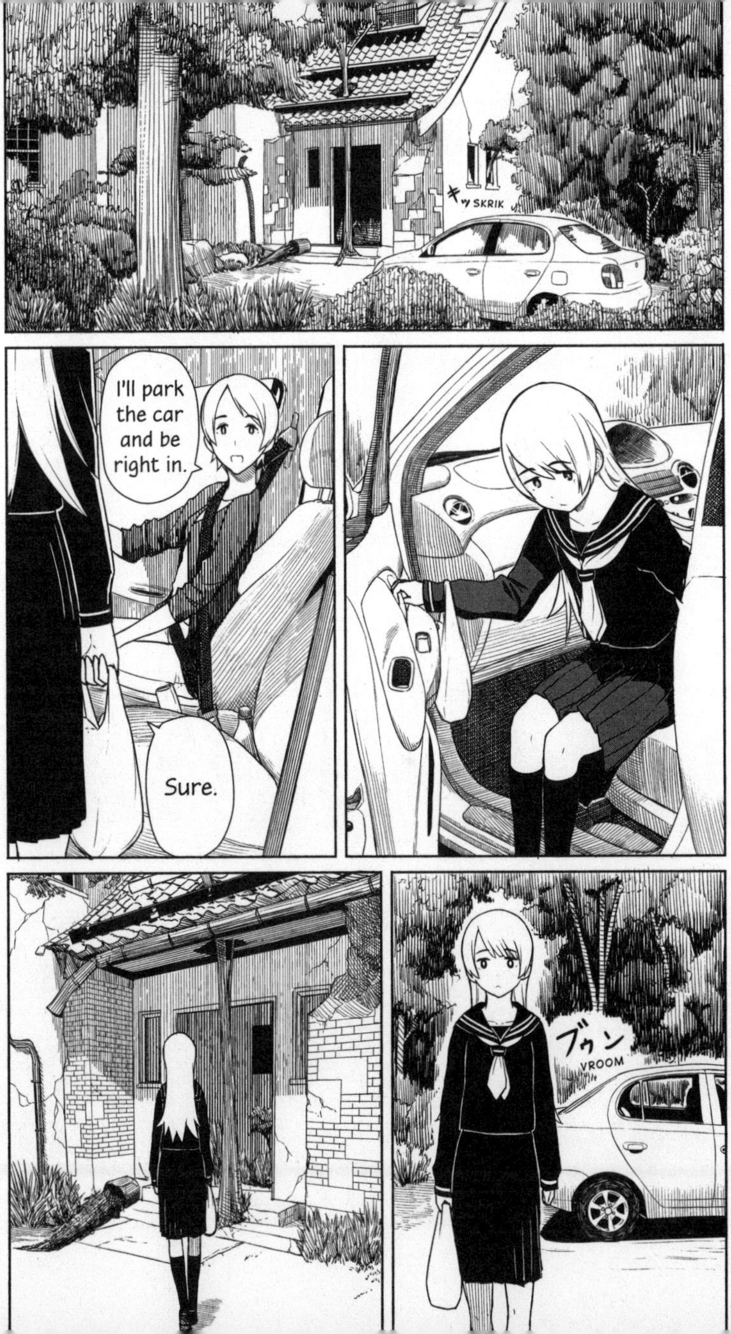
キッ
SKRIK
I'll park the car and be right in.
Sure.
ブゥン
VROOM

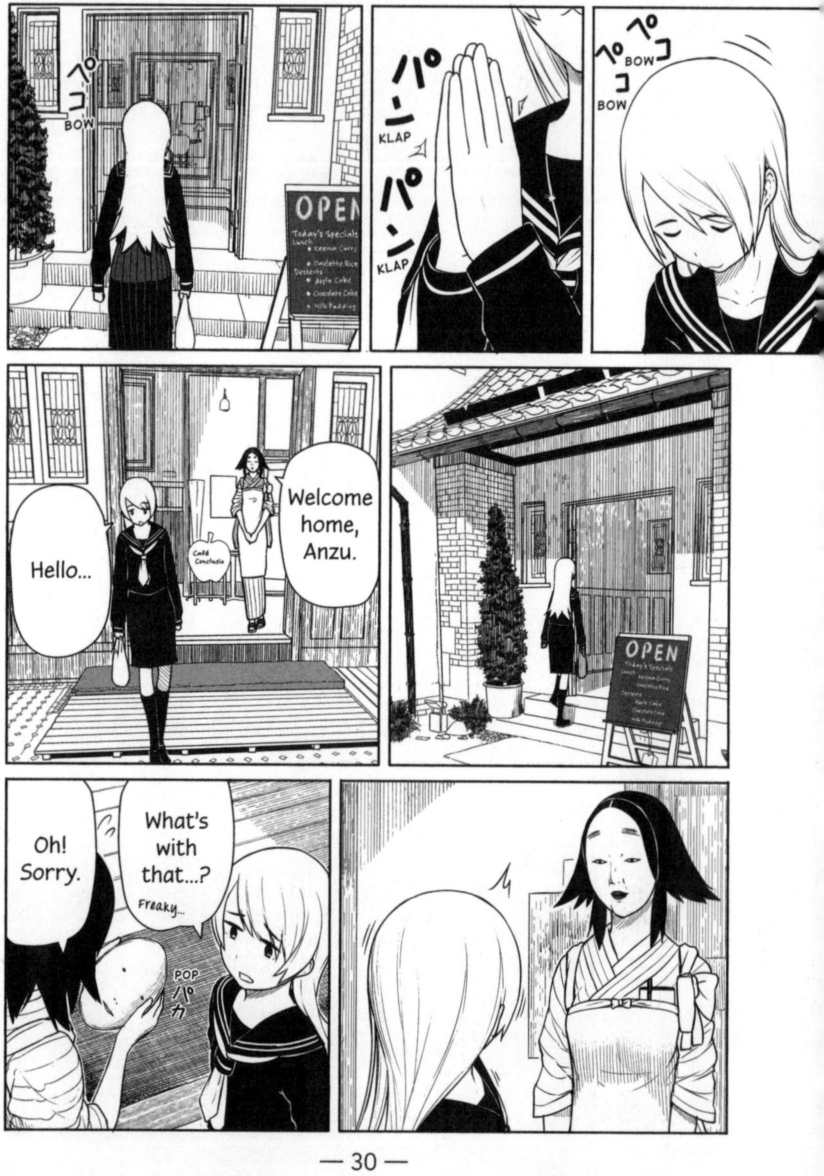
ペコ BOW
ペコ BOW
パン KLAP
パン KLAP
ペコ BOW
OPEN
Today's Specials
Lunch
Keema Curry
Omelette Rice
Desserts
Apple Cake
Chocolate Cake
Milk Pudding
Welcome home, Anzu.
Café Conclusio
Hello...
What's with that...?
Freaky...
Oh! Sorry.
POP パカ

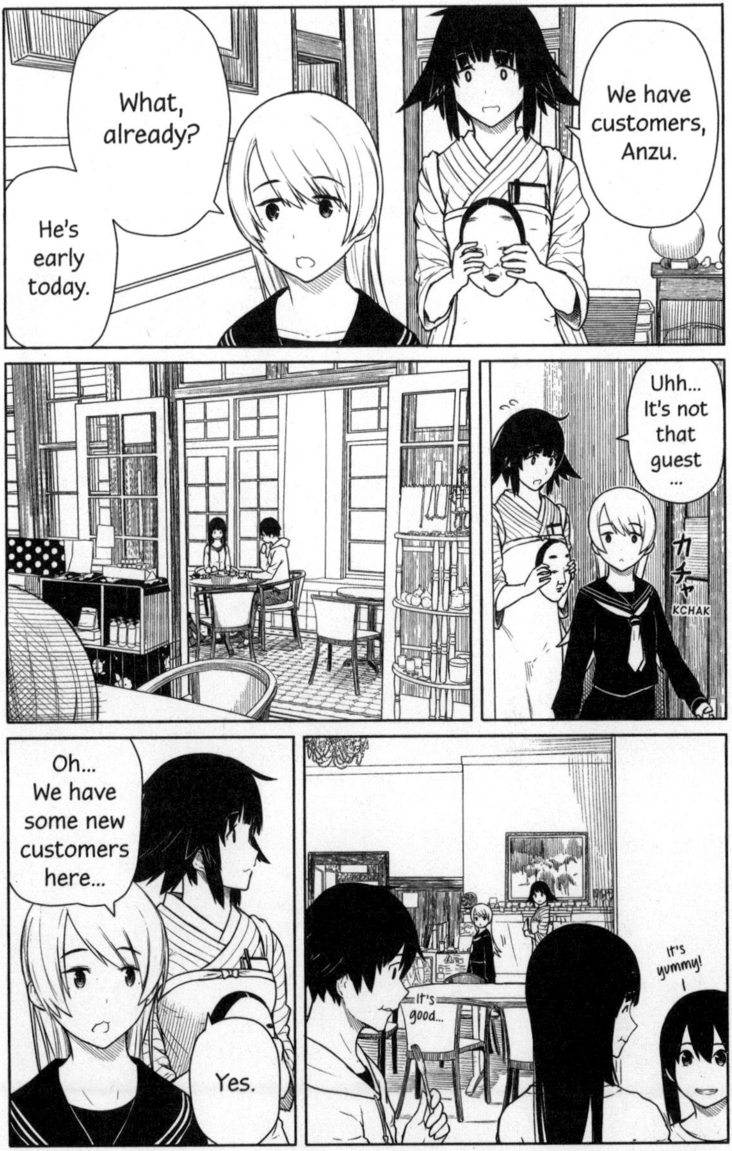
We have customers, Anzu.
What, already?
He's early today.
Uhh... It's not that guest ...
カチャ
KCHAK
It's yummy!
It's good...
Oh... We have some new customers here...
Yes.

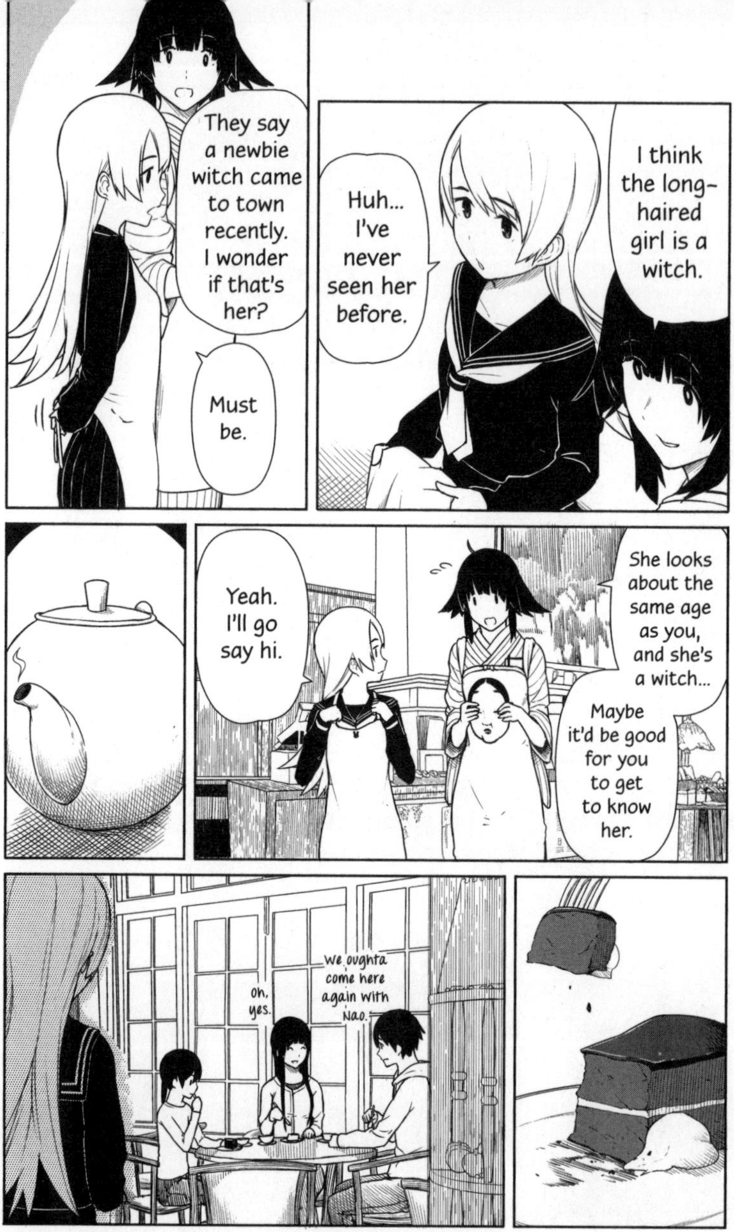
I think the long-haired girl is a witch.
Huh... I've never seen her before.
They say a newbie witch came to town recently. I wonder if that's her?
Must be.
She looks about the same age as you, and she's a witch...
Maybe it'd be good for you to get to know her.
Yeah. I'll go say hi.
We oughta come here again with Nao.
Oh, yes.

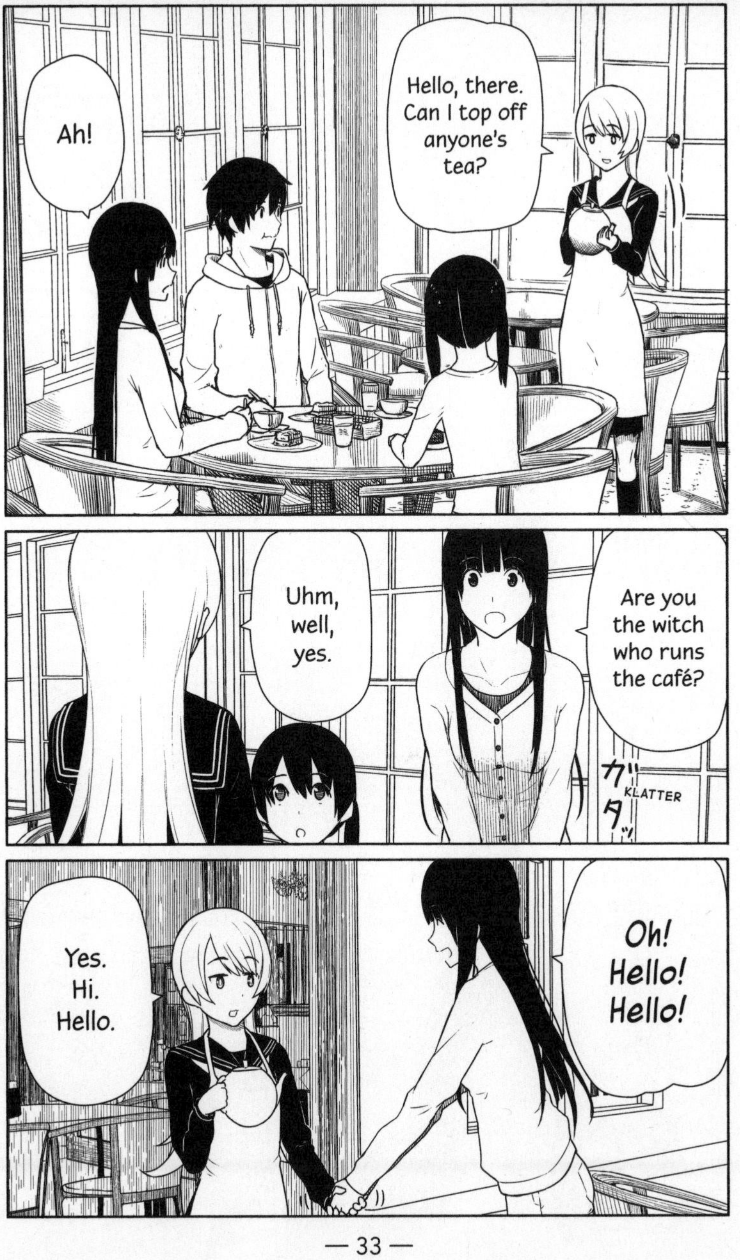

Hello, there. Can I top off anyone's tea?
Ah!
Are you the witch who runs the café?
ガタッ
KLATTER
Uhm, well, yes.
Oh! Hello! Hello!
Yes. Hi. Hello.

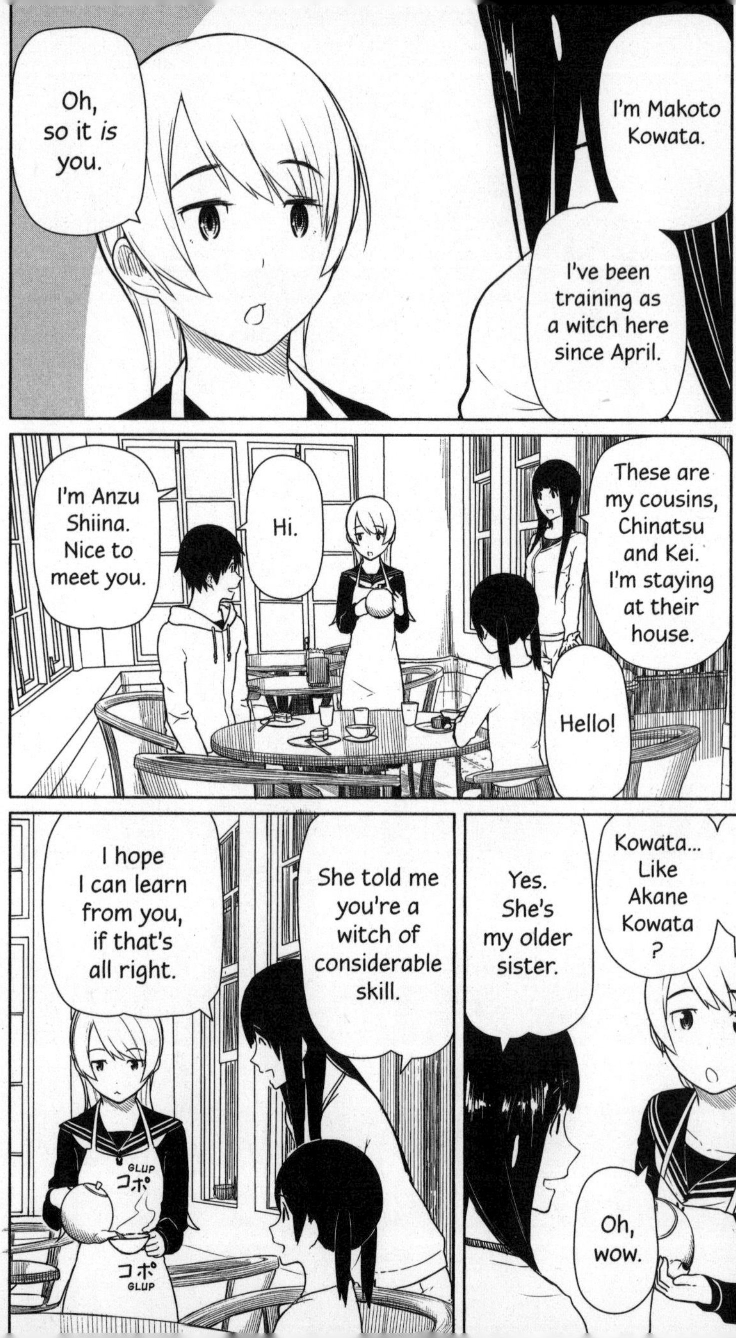
I'm Makoto Kowata.
I've been training as a witch here since April.
Oh, so it *is* you.
These are my cousins, Chinatsu and Kei. I'm staying at their house.
Hello!
Hi.
I'm Anzu Shiina. Nice to meet you.
Huh?
Kowata... Like Akane Kowata?
Yes. She's my older sister.
Oh, wow.
She told me you're a witch of considerable skill.
I hope I can learn from you, if that's all right.
GLUP コポ
コポ GLUP

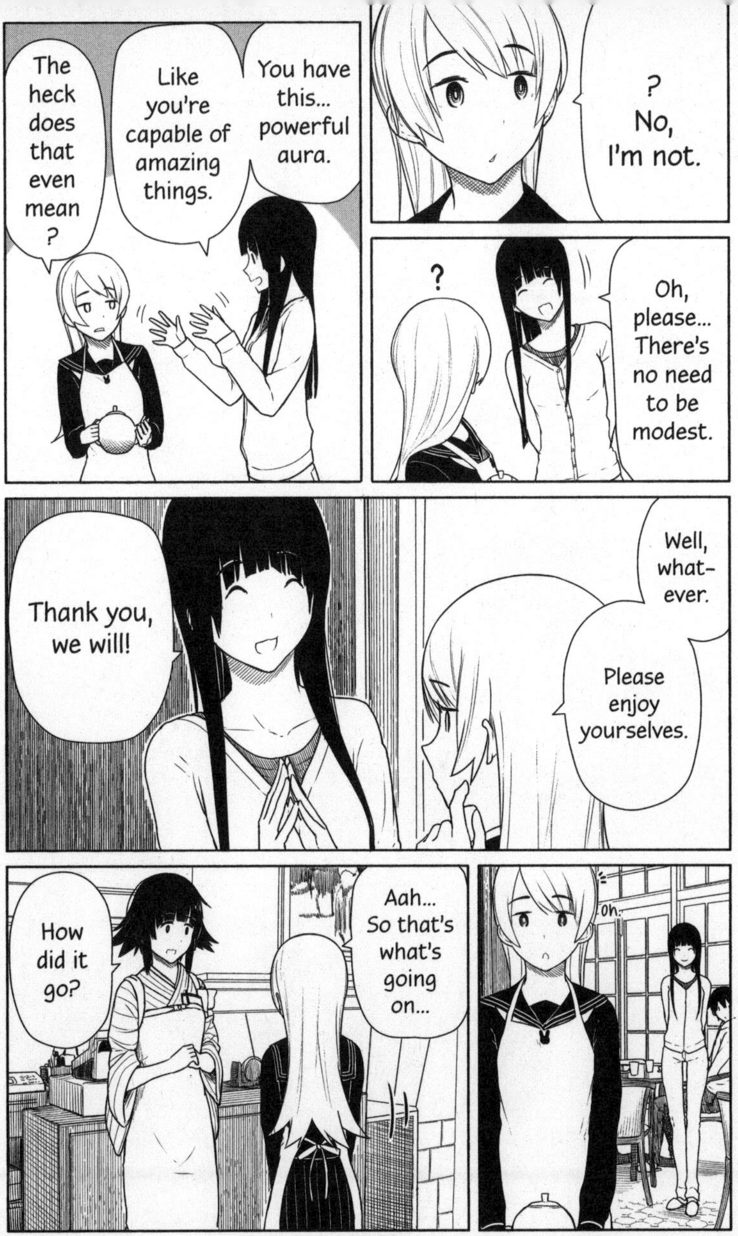
?
No, I'm not.
?
Oh, please... There's no need to be modest.
You have this... powerful aura.
Like you're capable of amazing things.
The heck does that even mean?
Well, whatever.
Please enjoy yourselves.
Thank you, we will!
oh
Aah... So that's what's going on...
How did it go?

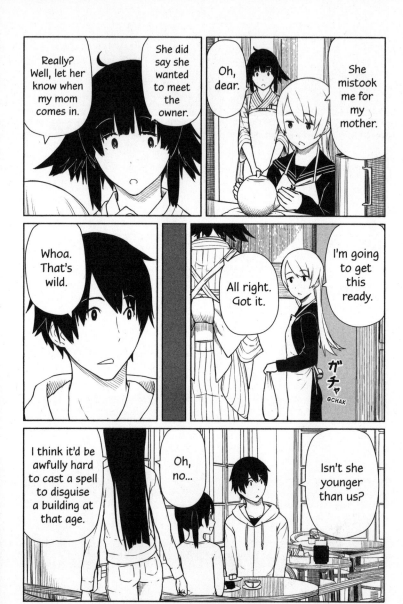

She mistook me for my mother.
Oh, dear.
She did say she wanted to meet the owner.
Really? Well, let her know when my mom comes in.
I'm going to get this ready.
All right. Got it.
ガチャ
GCHAK
Whoa. That's wild.
Isn't she younger than us?
Oh, no...
I think it'd be awfully hard to cast a spell to disguise a building at that age.

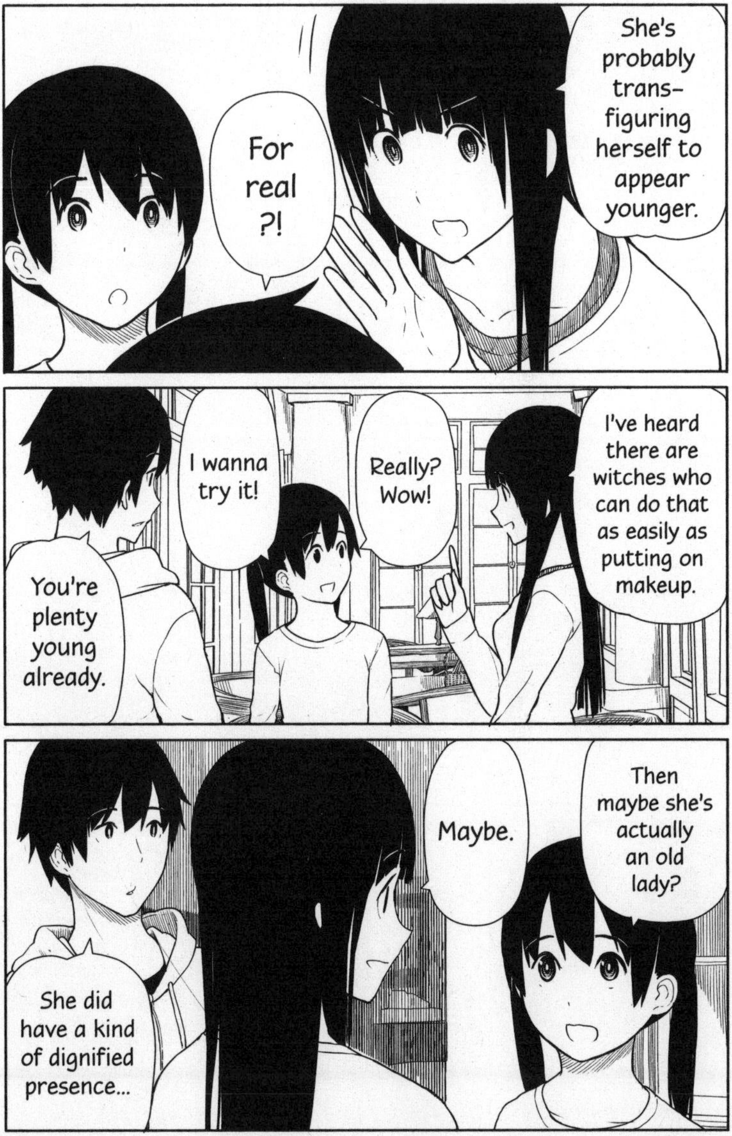
She's probably trans-figuring herself to appear younger.
For real ?!
I've heard there are witches who can do that as easily as putting on makeup.
Really? Wow!
I wanna try it!
You're plenty young already.
Then maybe she's actually an old lady?
Maybe.
She did have a kind of dignified presence...

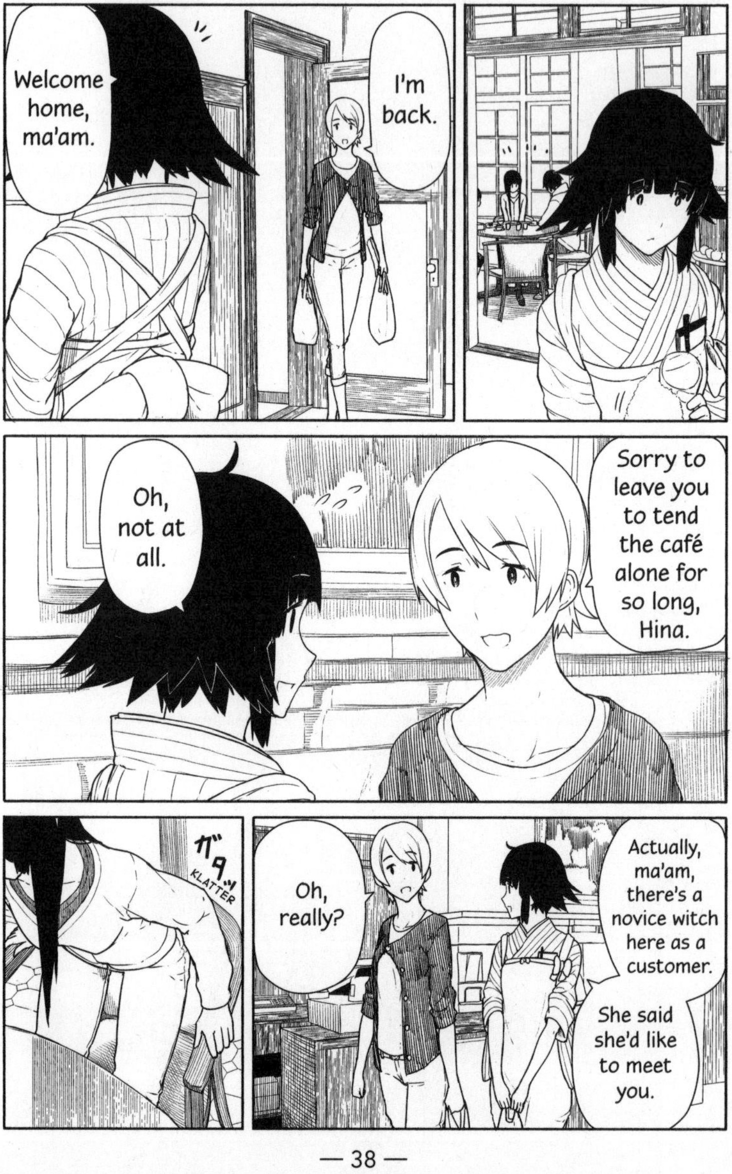
I'm back.
Welcome home, ma'am.
Sorry to leave you to tend the café alone for so long, Hina.
Oh, not at all.
Actually, ma'am, there's a novice witch here as a customer.
She said she'd like to meet you.
Oh, really?
ガタッ
KLATTER

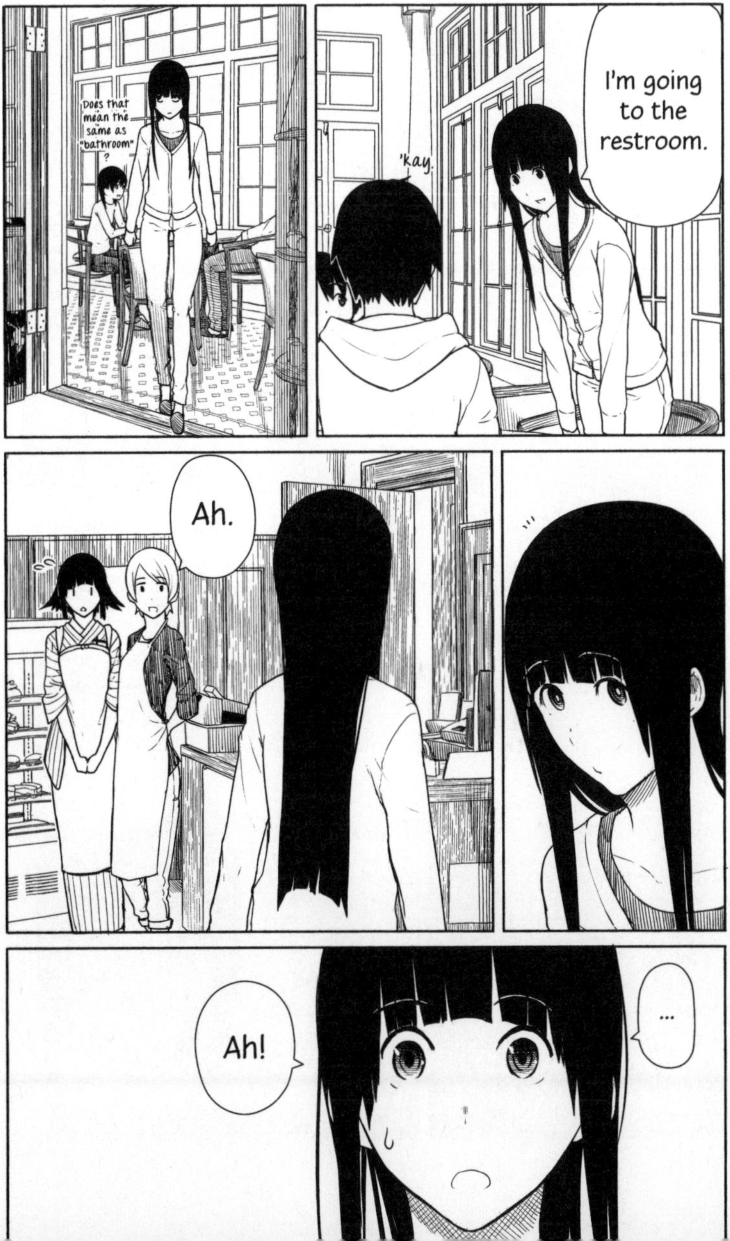
I'm going to the restroom.
'kay.
Does that mean the same as "bathroom"?
Ah.
...
Ah!

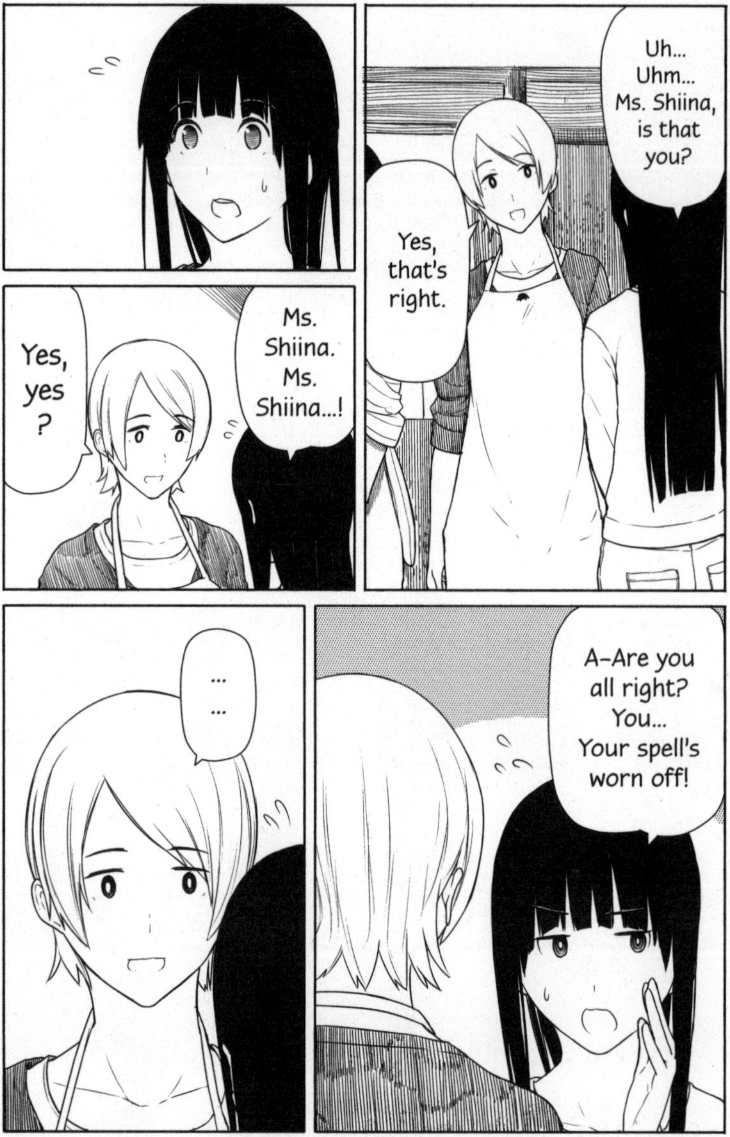
Uh... Uhm... Ms. Shiina, is that you?
Yes, that's right.
Ms. Shiina. Ms. Shiina...!
Yes, yes ?
A-Are you all right? You... Your spell's worn off!
... ...

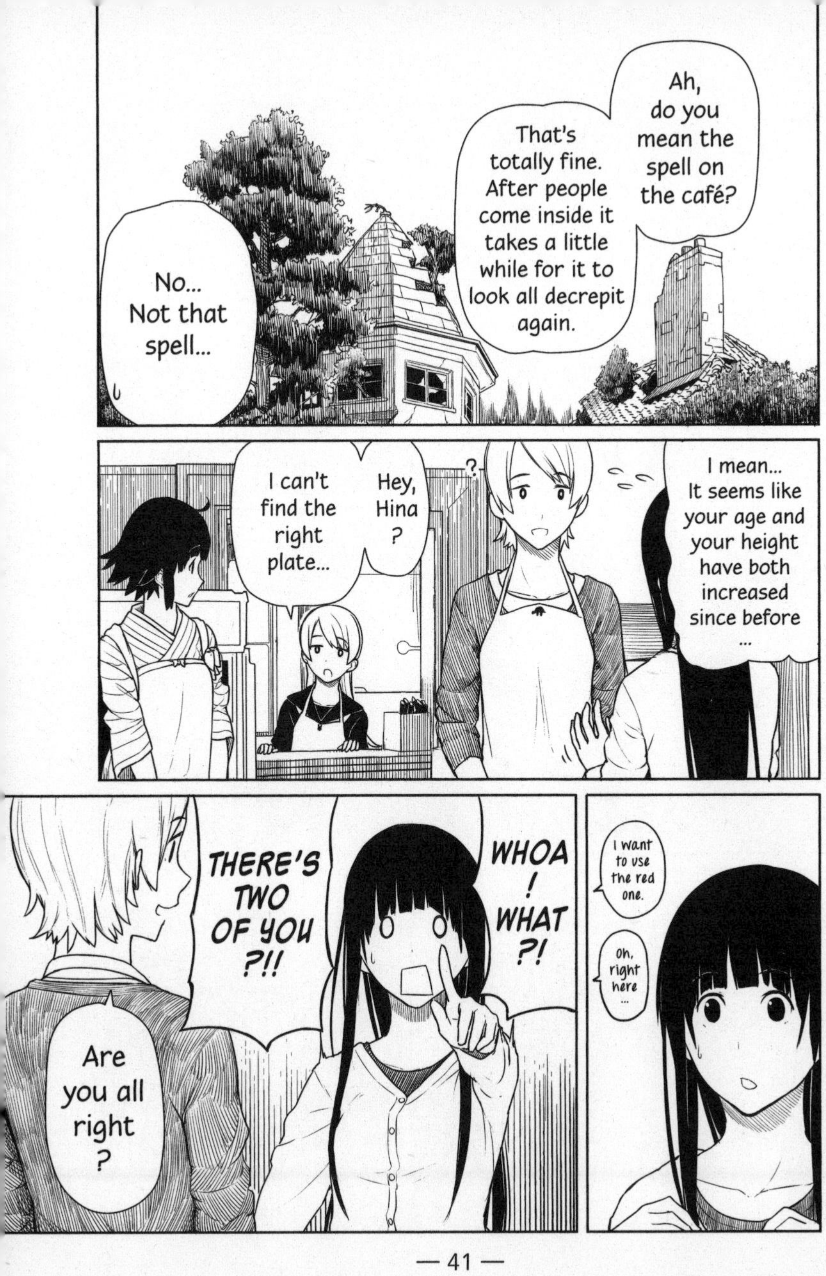

Ah, do you mean the spell on the café?
That's totally fine. After people come inside it takes a little while for it to look all decrepit again.
No... Not that spell...
I mean... It seems like your age and your height have both increased since before ...
Hey, Hina ?
I can't find the right plate...
I want to use the red one.
Oh, right here ...
WHOA ! WHAT ?!
THERE'S TWO OF YOU ?!!
Are you all right ?

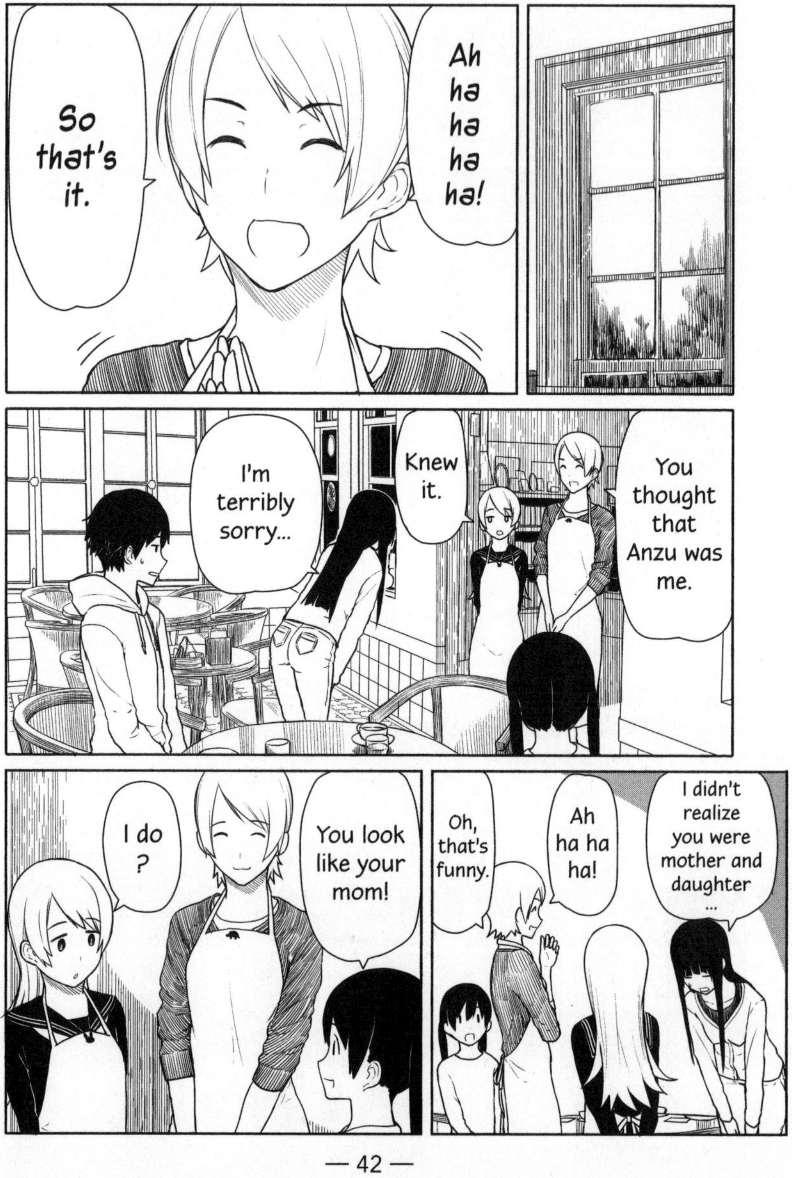
Ah ha ha ha ha!
So that's it.
You thought that Anzu was me.
Knew it.
I'm terribly sorry...
I didn't realize you were mother and daughter ...
Ah ha ha ha!
Oh, that's funny.
You look like your mom!
I do ?

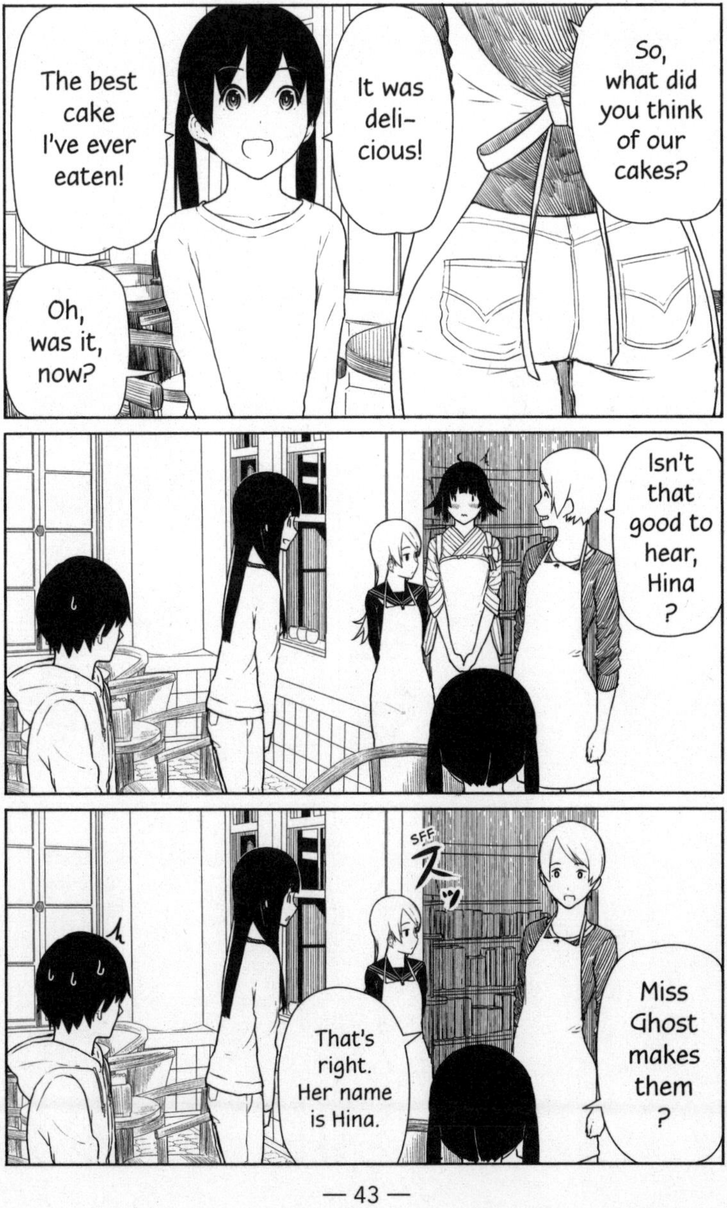

So, what did you think of our cakes?
It was deli- cious!
The best cake I've ever eaten!
Oh, was it, now?
Isn't that good to hear, Hina?
SFF
スッ
Miss Ghost makes them?
That's right. Her name is Hina.

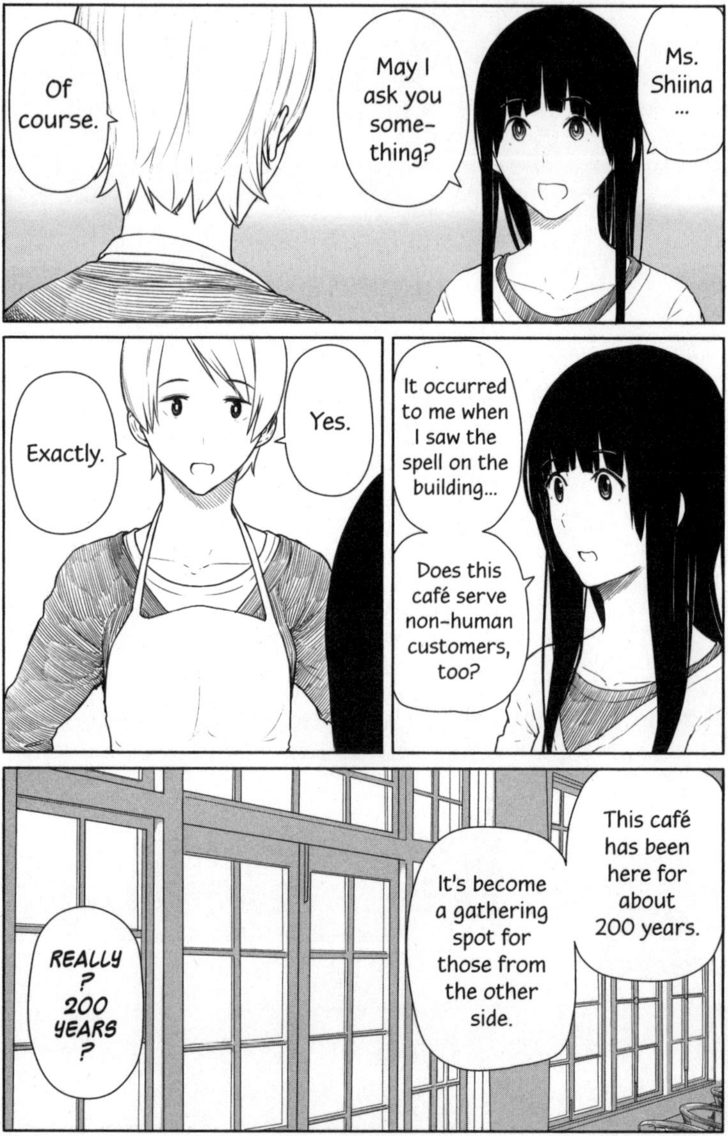
Ms. Shiina ...
May I ask you some-thing?
Of course.
It occurred to me when I saw the spell on the building...
Does this café serve non-human customers, too?
Yes.
Exactly.
This café has been here for about 200 years.
It's become a gathering spot for those from the other side.
REALLY? 200 YEARS?

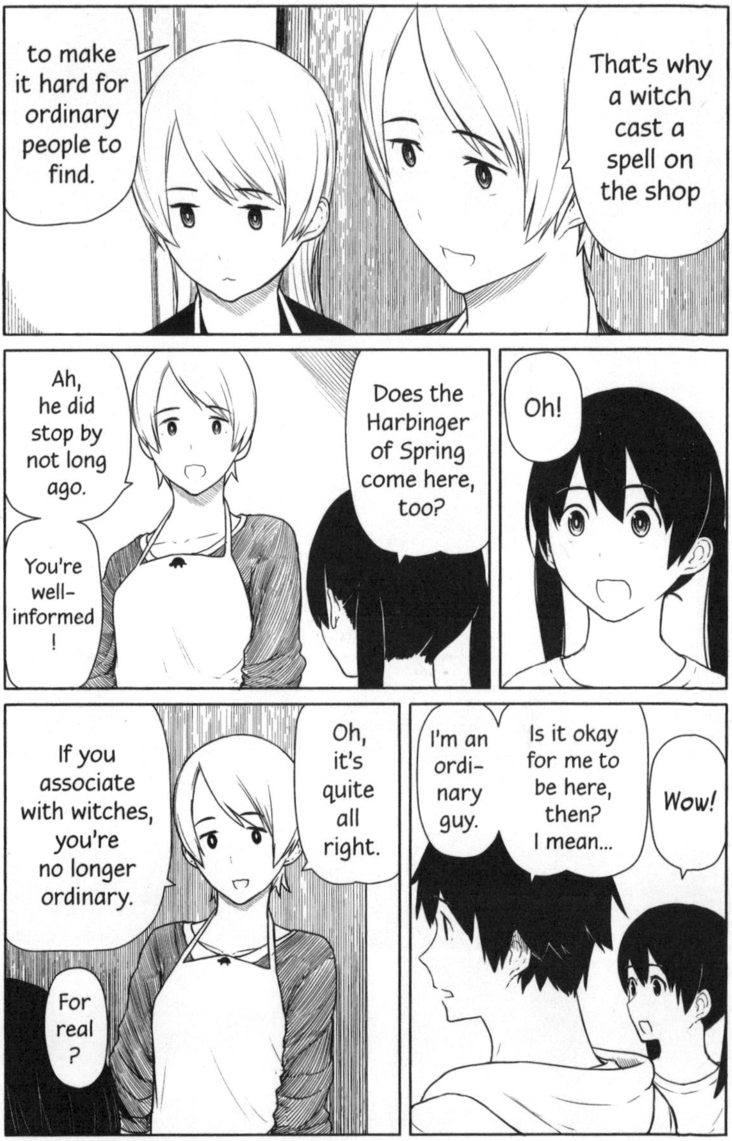
That's why a witch cast a spell on the shop
to make it hard for ordinary people to find.
Oh!
Does the Harbinger of Spring come here, too?
Ah, he did stop by not long ago.
You're well-informed!
Wow!
Is it okay for me to be here, then? I mean...
I'm an ordi-nary guy.
Oh, it's quite all right.
If you associate with witches, you're no longer ordinary.
For real?

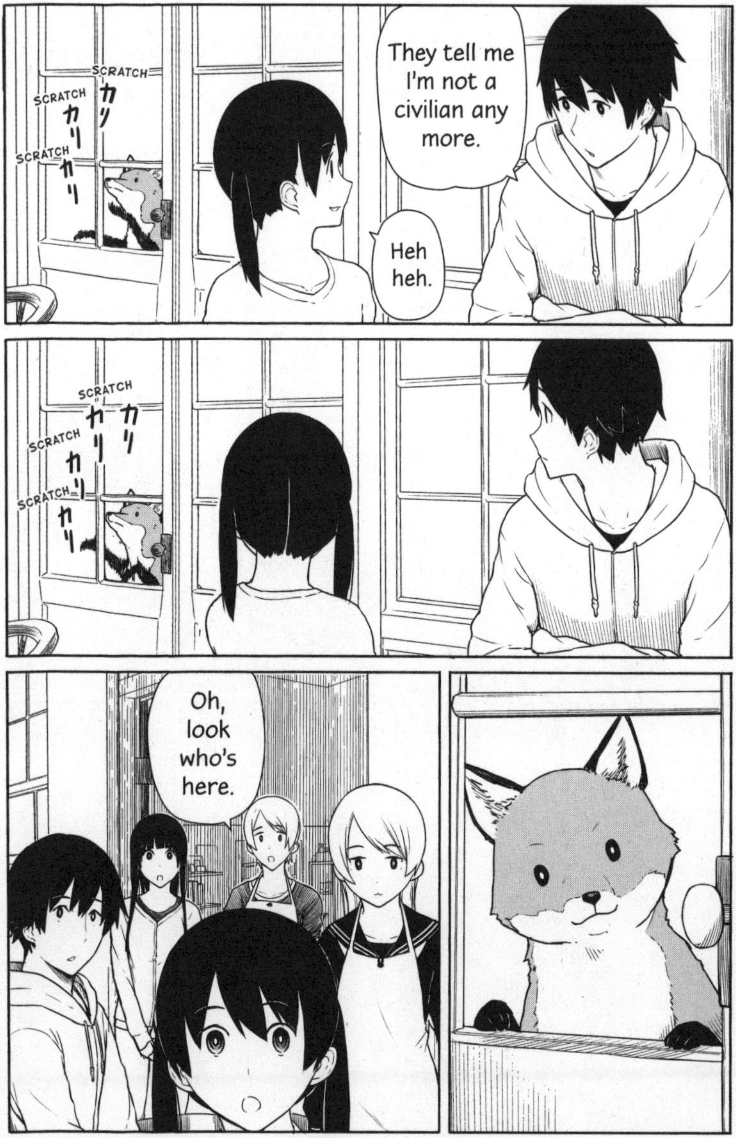
They tell me I'm not a civilian any more.
Heh heh.
SCRATCH カリ
SCRATCH カリ
SCRATCH カリ
SCRATCH カリ
SCRATCH カリ
SCRATCH カリ
Oh, look who's here.

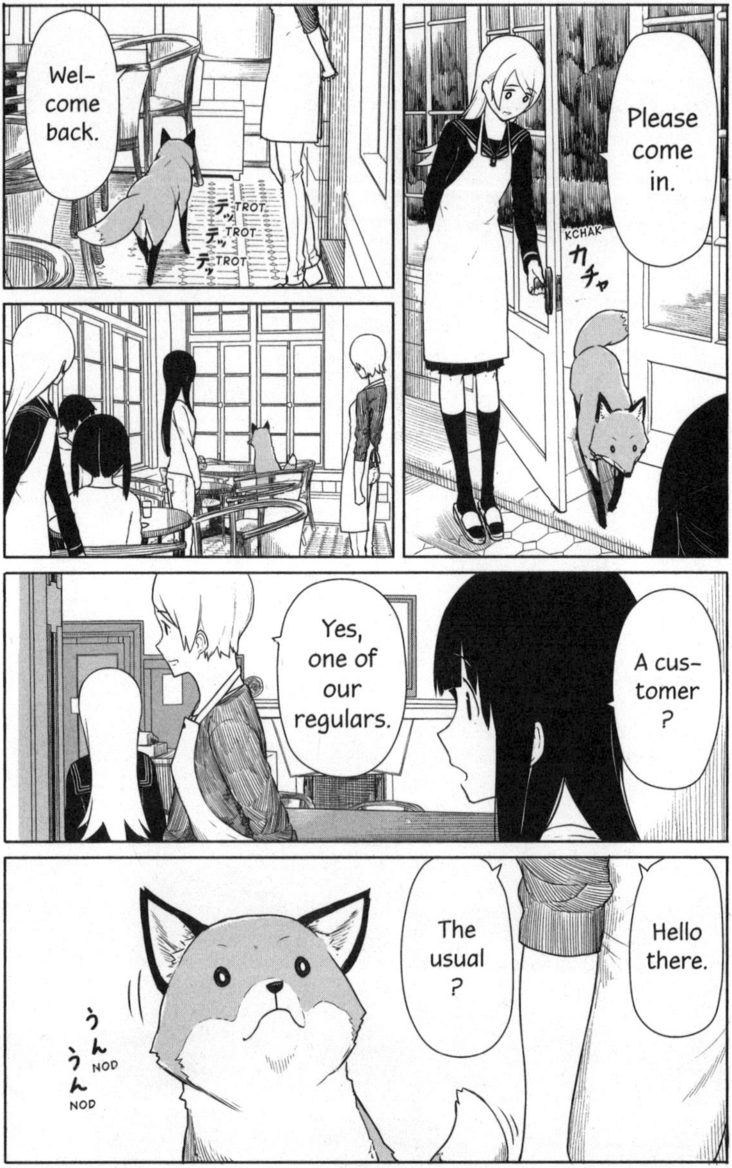
Please come in.
KCHAK
カチャ
Wel-come back.
テッ TROT
テッ TROT
テッ TROT
A cus-tomer?
Yes, one of our regulars.
Hello there.
The usual?
うん NOD
うん NOD

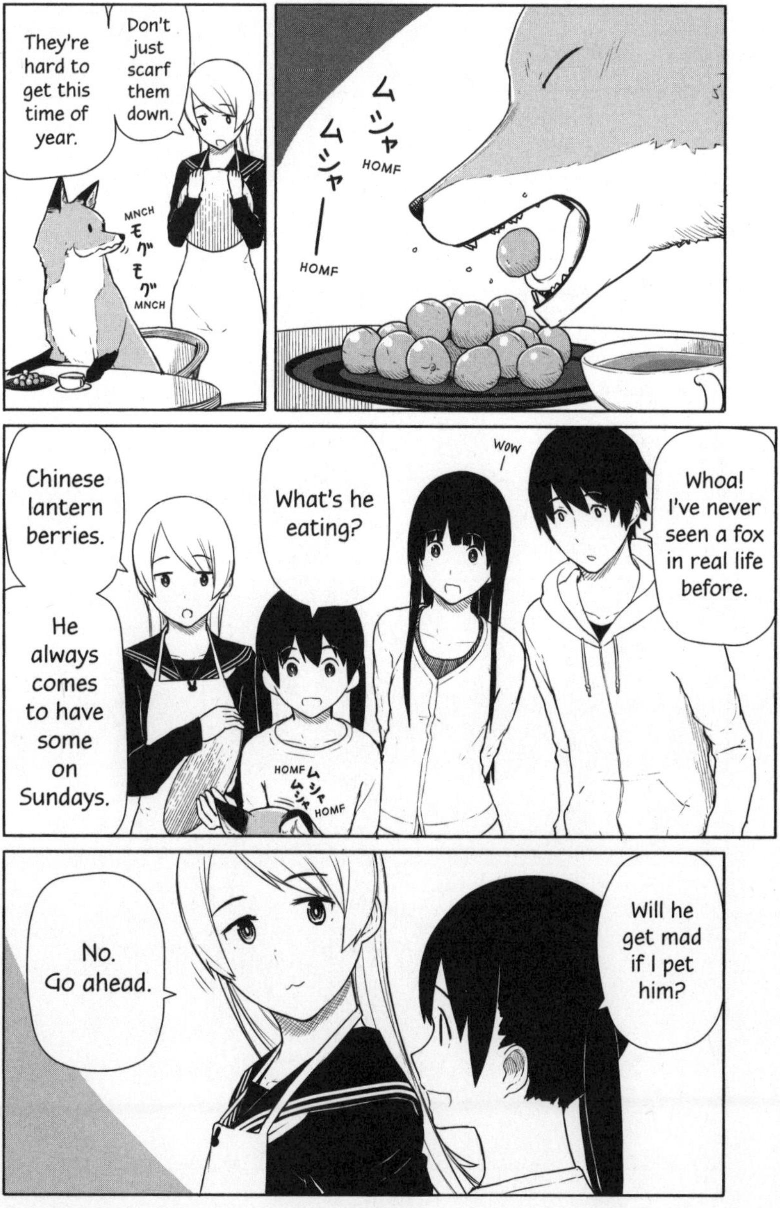
ムシャ
HOMF
ムシャー
HOMF
Don't just scarf them down.
They're hard to get this time of year.
MNCH
モグ
モグ
MNCH
Whoa! I've never seen a fox in real life before.
WOW
What's he eating?
Chinese lantern berries.
He always comes to have some on Sundays.
HOMF
ムシャ
ムシャ
HOMF
Will he get mad if I pet him?
No. Go ahead.

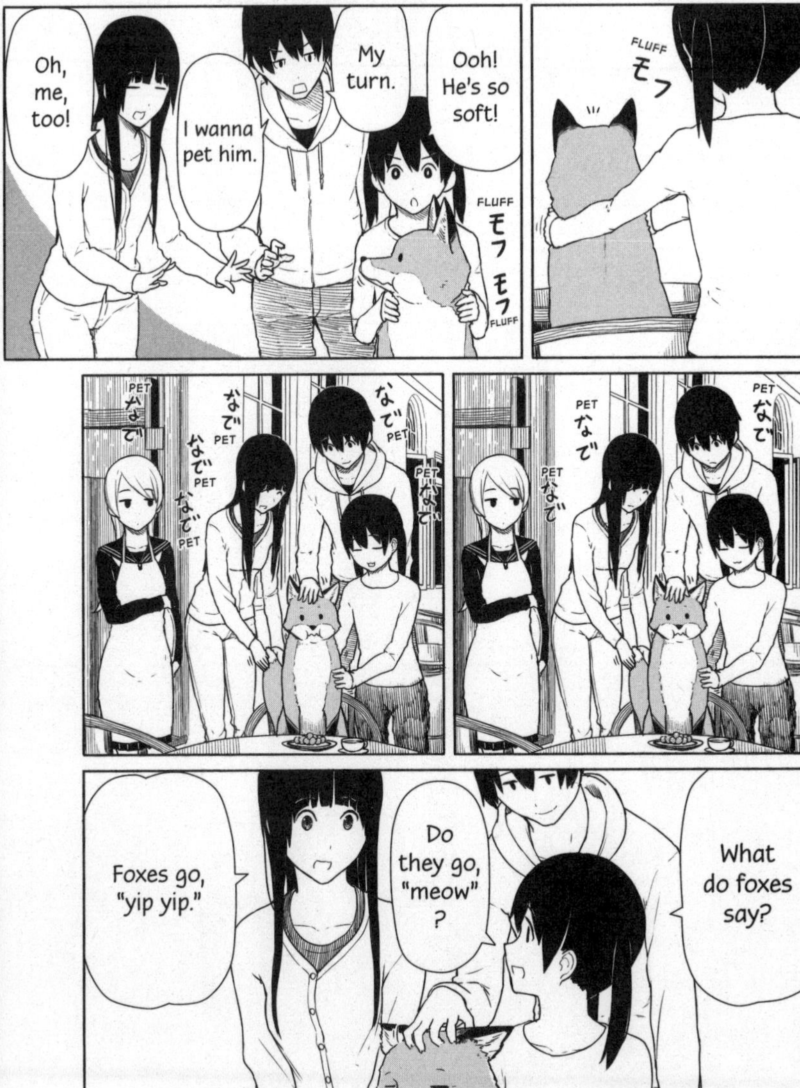
FLUFF
モフ
Ooh! He's so soft!
FLUFF モフ
モフ FLUFF
My turn.
I wanna pet him.
Oh, me, too!
PET なで
PET なで
PET なで
なで PET
PET なで
なで PET
なで PET
PET なで
What do foxes say?
Do they go, "meow"?
Foxes go, "yip yip."

I wanna hear it.

Wow !

It's yip-yip?

ARF !

Flying
Witch

Chapter 15
Tomorrow's Tomorrow is Right Now

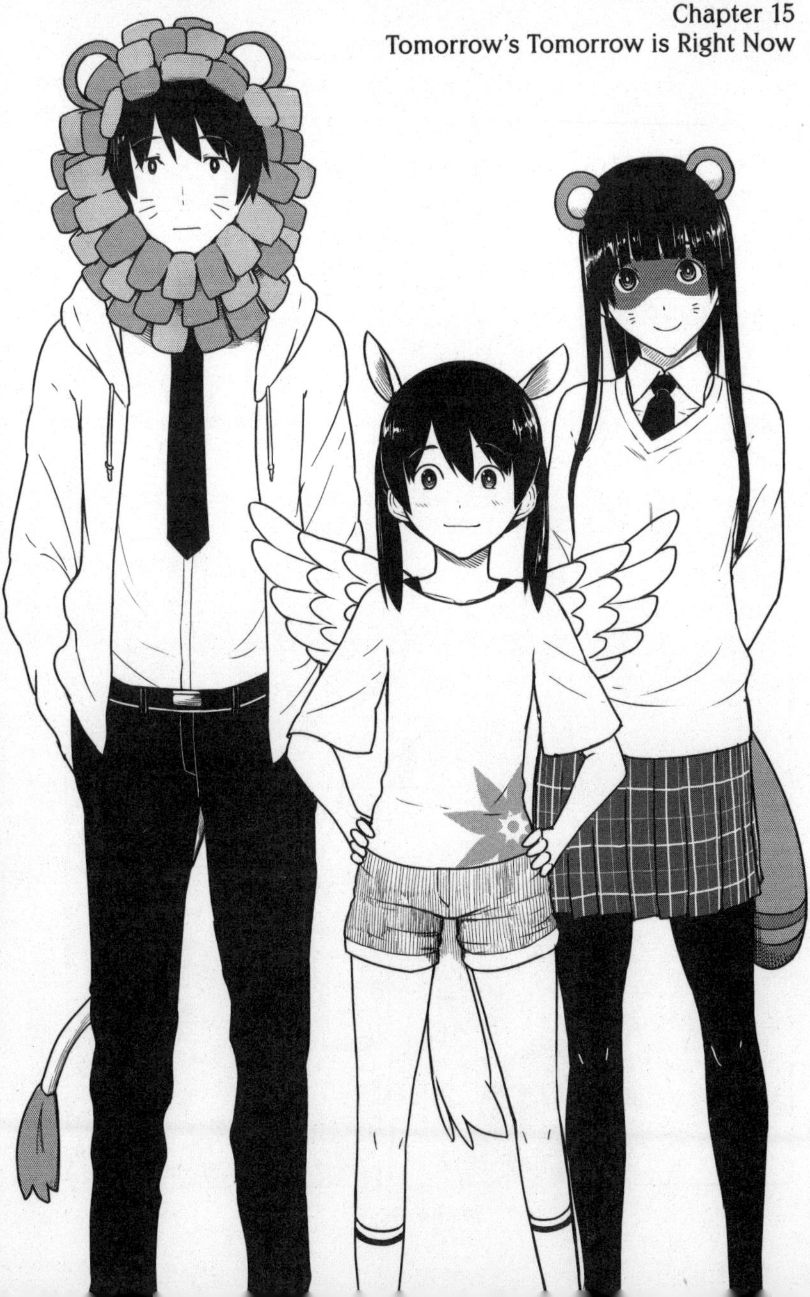

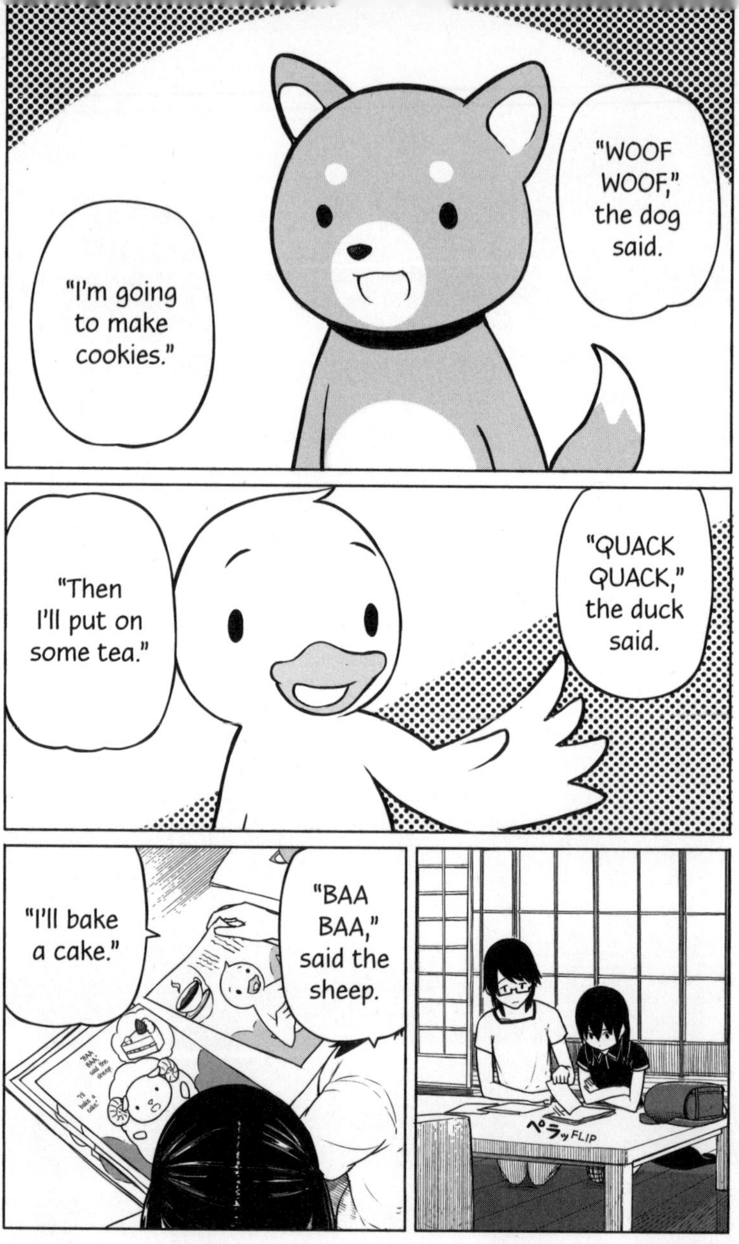
"WOOF WOOF," the dog said.
"I'm going to make cookies."
"QUACK QUACK," the duck said.
"Then I'll put on some tea."
ペラッ FLIP
"BAA BAA," said the sheep.
"I'll bake a cake."

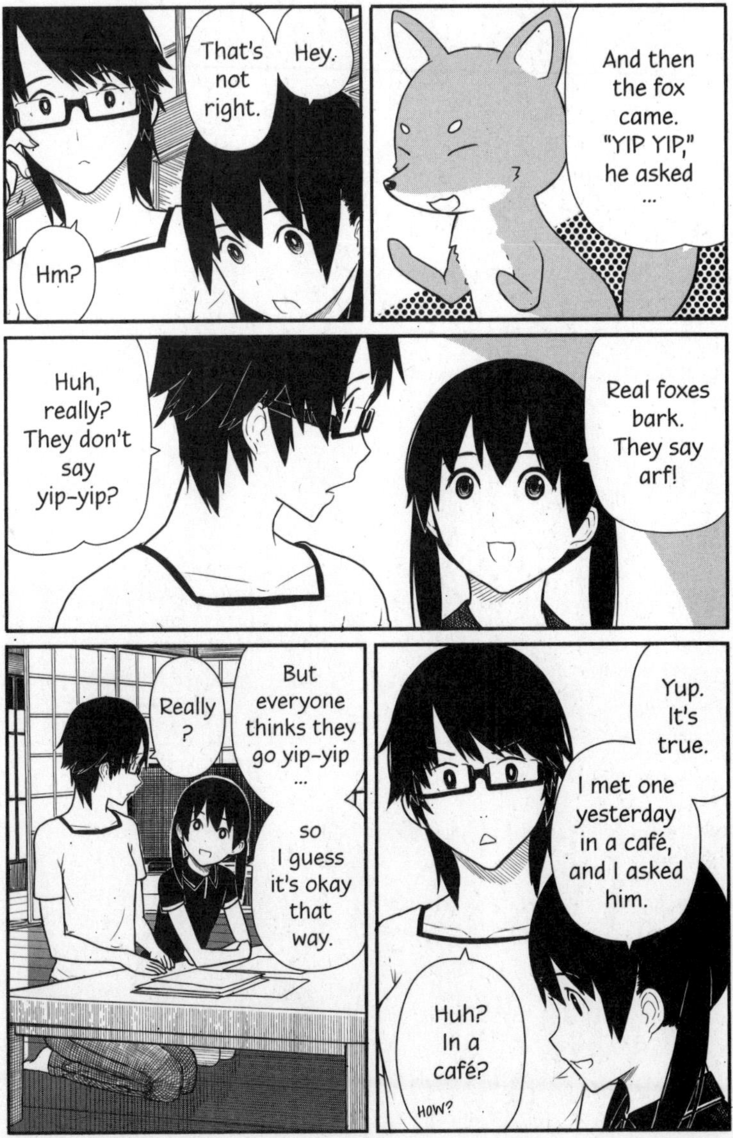
And then the fox came. "YIP YIP," he asked ...
Hey.
That's not right.
Hm?
Real foxes bark. They say arf!
Huh, really? They don't say yip-yip?
Yup. It's true.
I met one yesterday in a café, and I asked him.
Huh? In a café?
HOW?
But everyone thinks they go yip-yip ...
Really ?
so I guess it's okay that way.

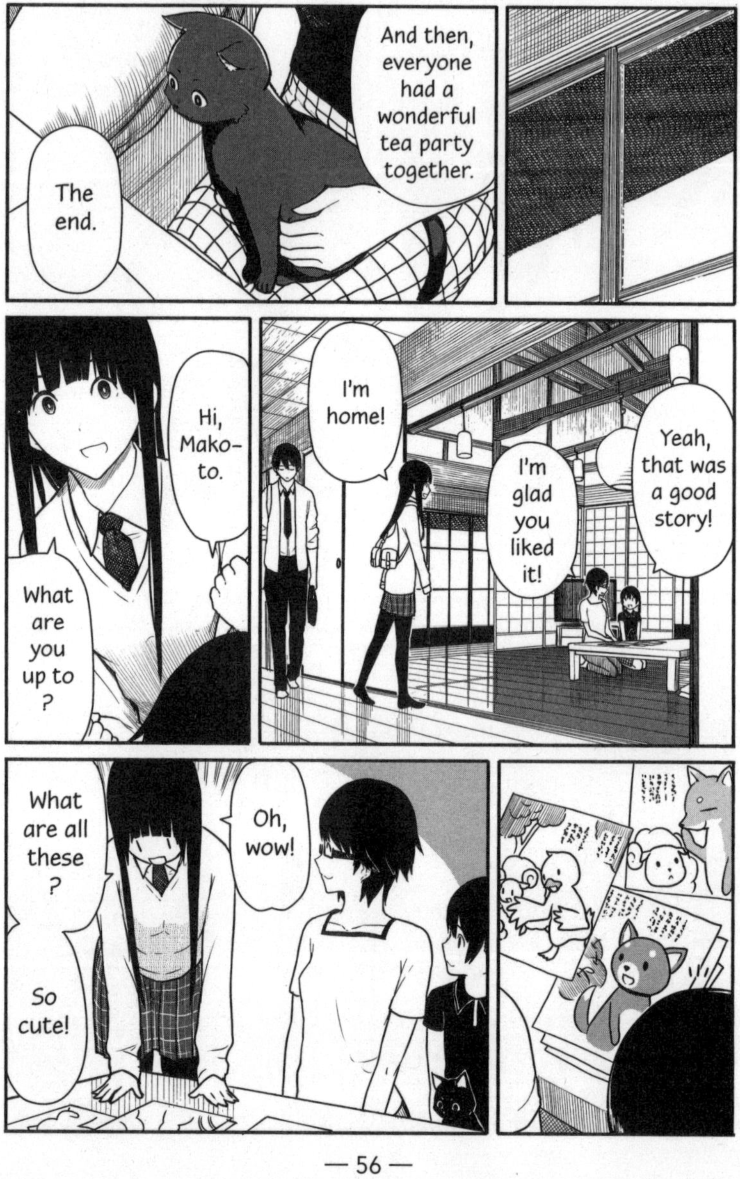
And then, everyone had a wonderful tea party together.
The end.
Yeah, that was a good story!
I'm glad you liked it!
I'm home!
Hi, Mako-to.
What are you up to?
Oh, wow!
What are all these?
So cute!

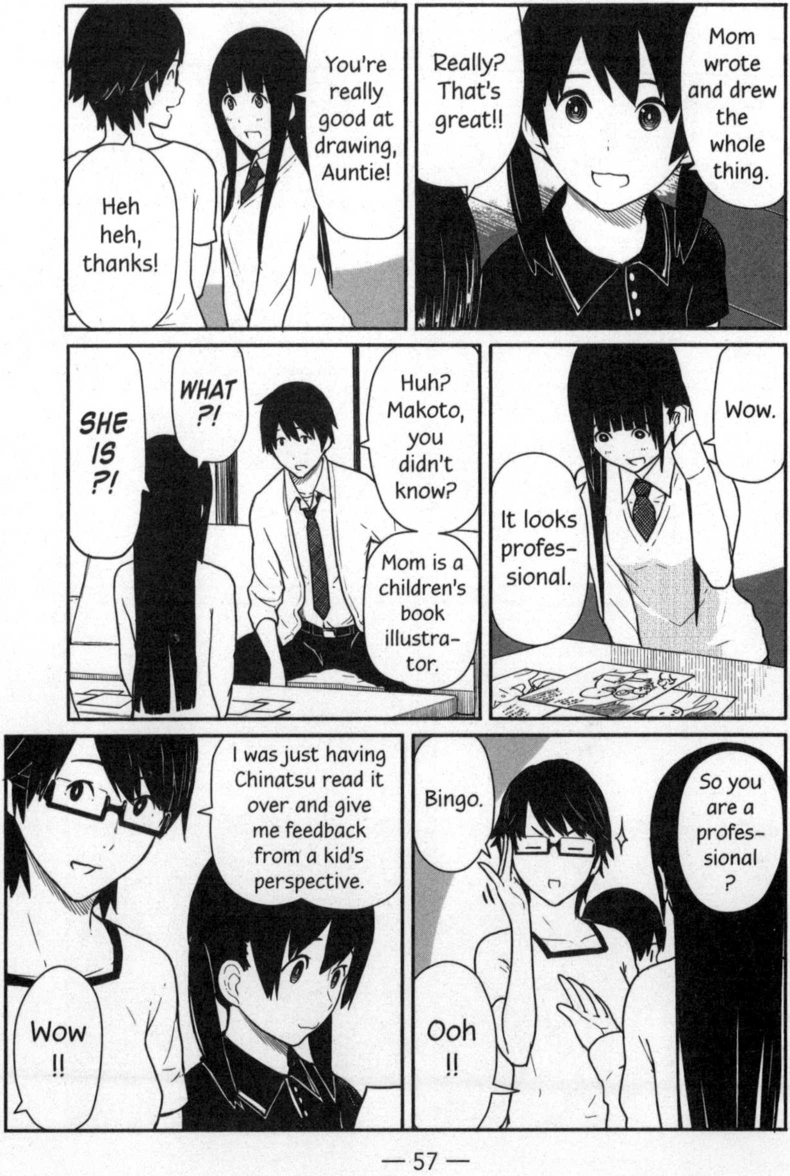
Mom wrote and drew the whole thing.
Really? That's great!!
You're really good at drawing, Auntie!
Heh heh, thanks!
Wow.
It looks profes-sional.
Huh? Makoto, you didn't know?
Mom is a children's book illustra-tor.
WHAT ?!
SHE IS ?!
So you are a profes-sional ?
Bingo.
Ooh !!
I was just having Chinatsu read it over and give me feedback from a kid's perspective.
Wow !!

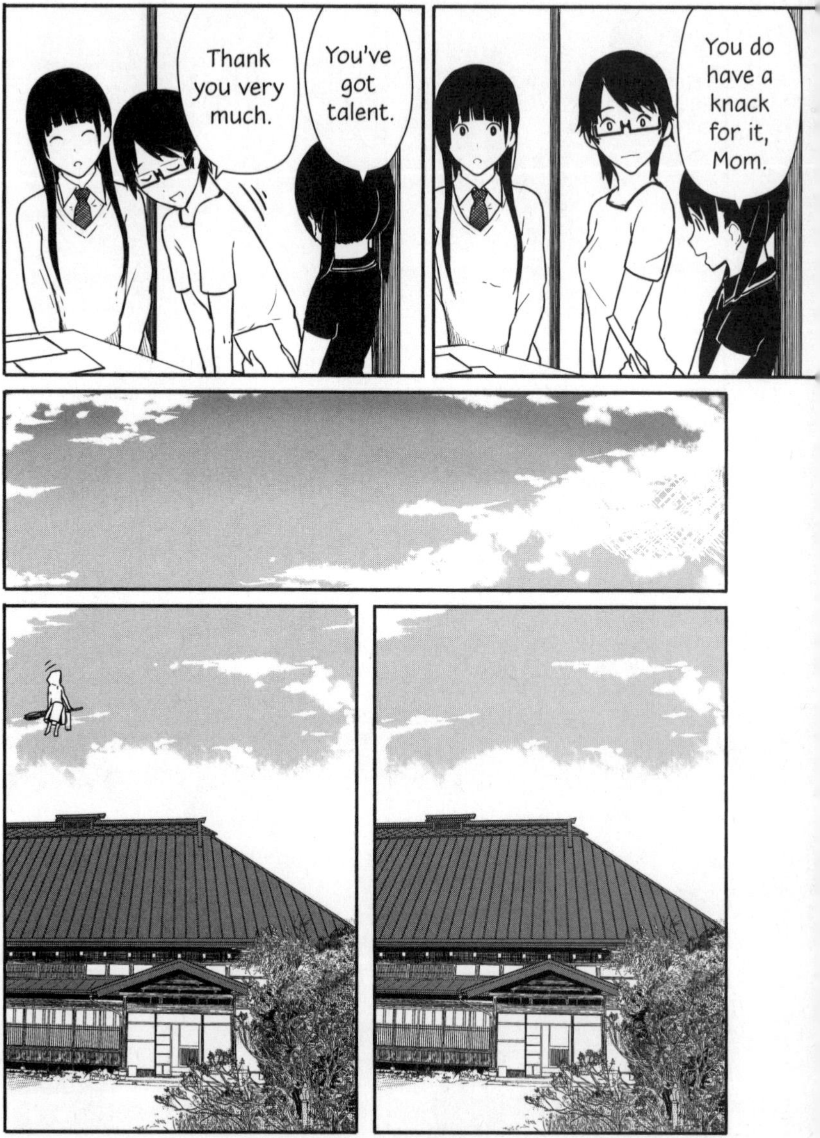
You do have a knack for it, Mom.
You've got talent.
Thank you very much.

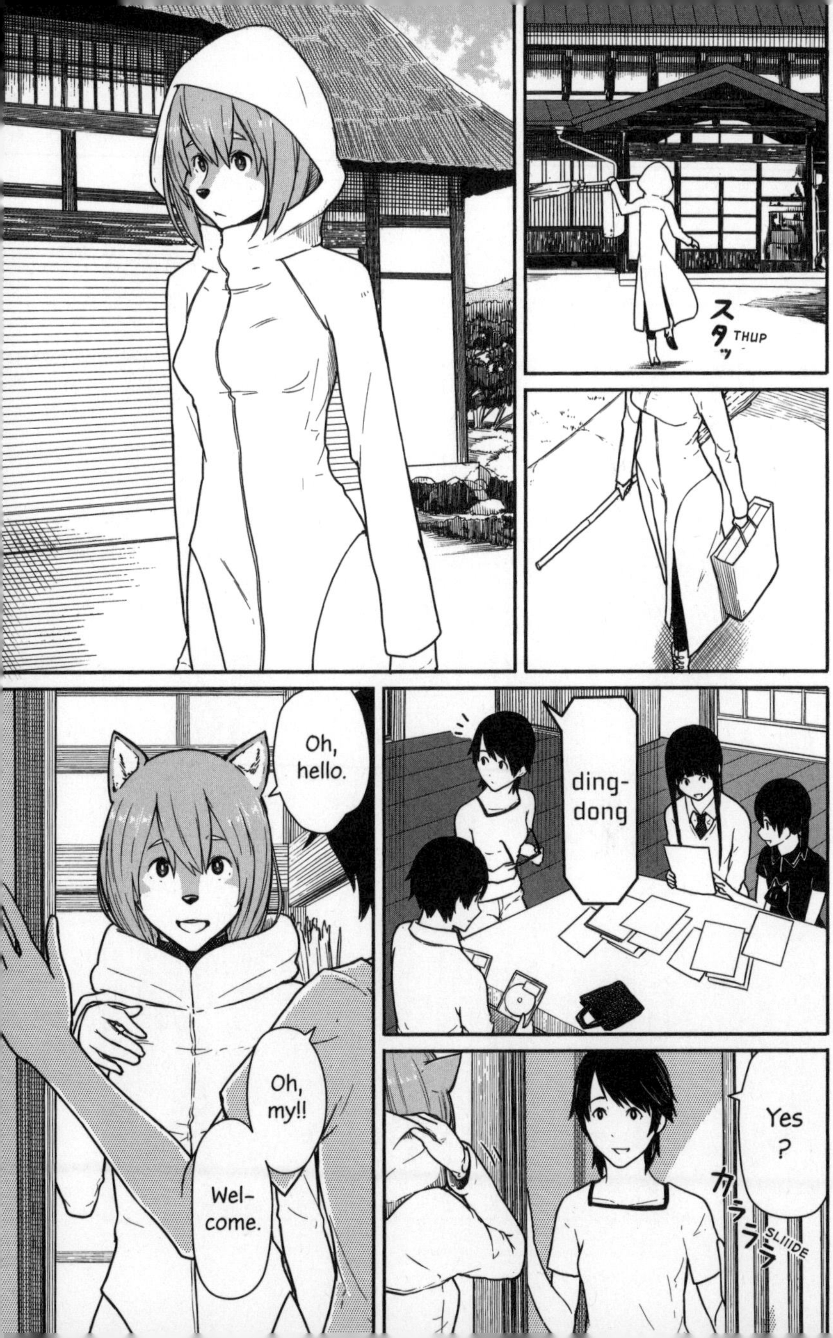
スタッ
THUP
ding-dong
Yes?
カラララ
SLIIIDE
Oh, hello.
Oh, my!!
Wel-come.

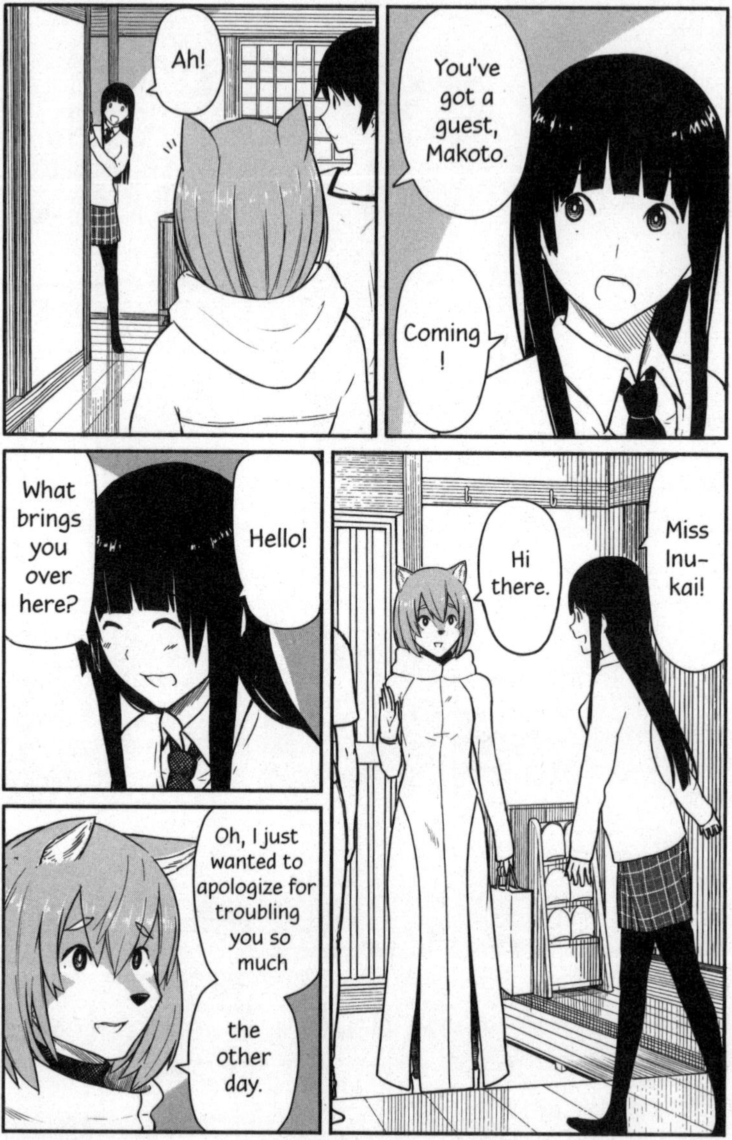
You've got a guest, Makoto.
Coming!
Ah!
Miss Inu-kai!
Hi there.
Hello!
What brings you over here?
Oh, I just wanted to apologize for troubling you so much
the other day.

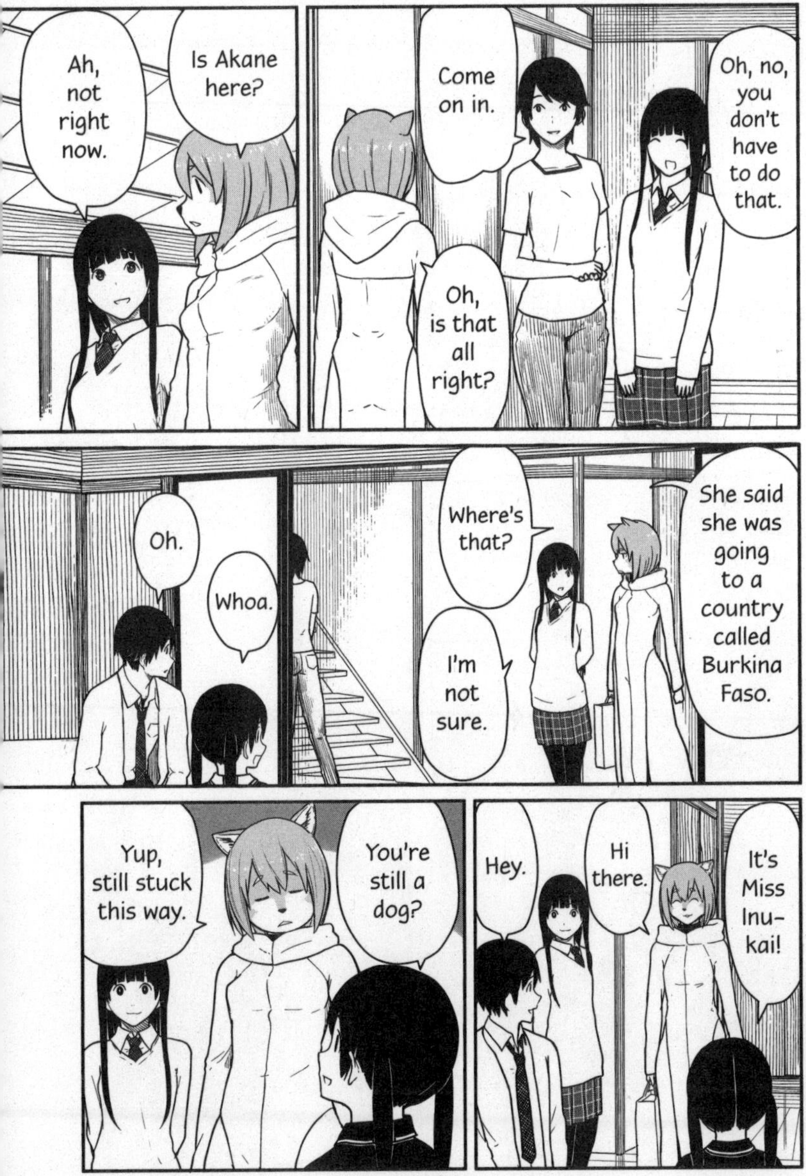

Oh, no, you don't have to do that.
Come on in.
Oh, is that all right?
Is Akane here?
Ah, not right now.
She said she was going to a country called Burkina Faso.
Where's that?
I'm not sure.
Whoa.
Oh.
It's Miss Inu-kai!
Hi there.
Hey.
You're still a dog?
Yup, still stuck this way.

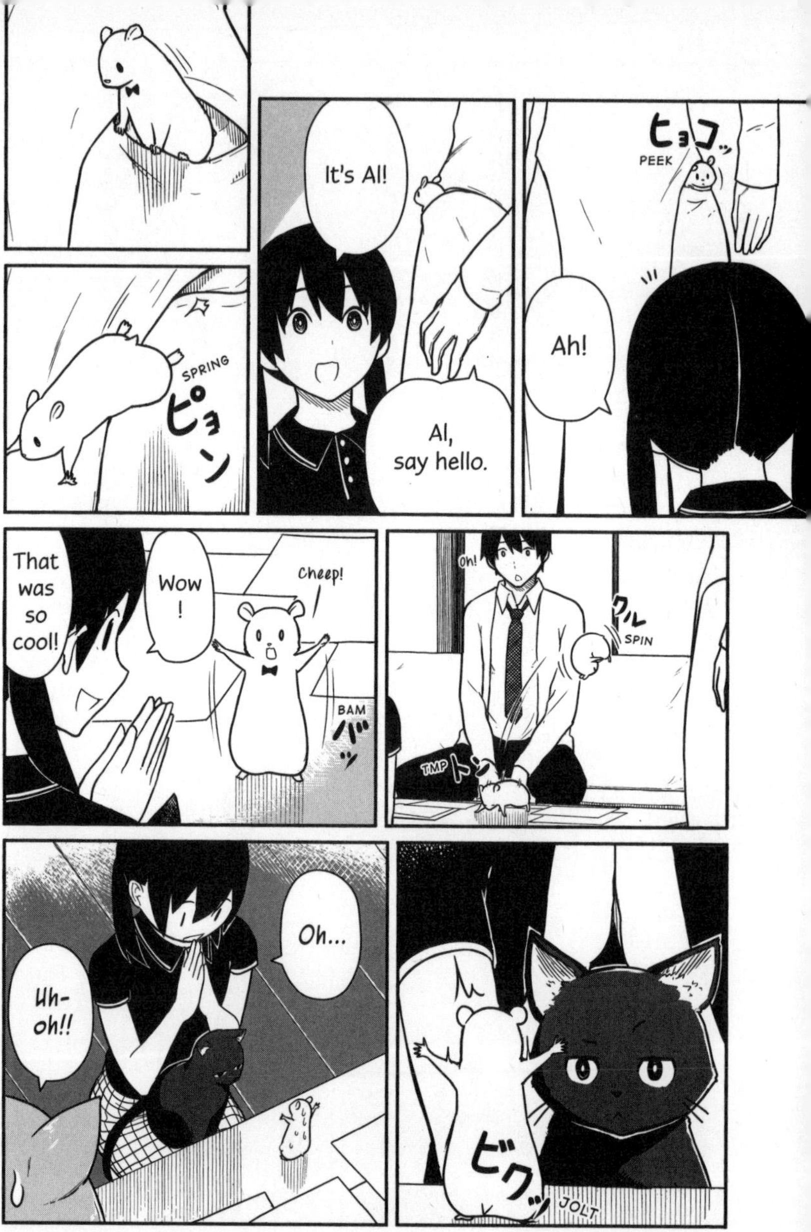
ヒョコッ
PEEK
Ah!
It's Al!
Al, say hello.
SPRING
ピョン
Oh!
クル
SPIN
TMP
トン
Cheep!
Wow!
That was so cool!
BAM
バッ
ビクッ
JOLT
Oh...
Uh-oh!!

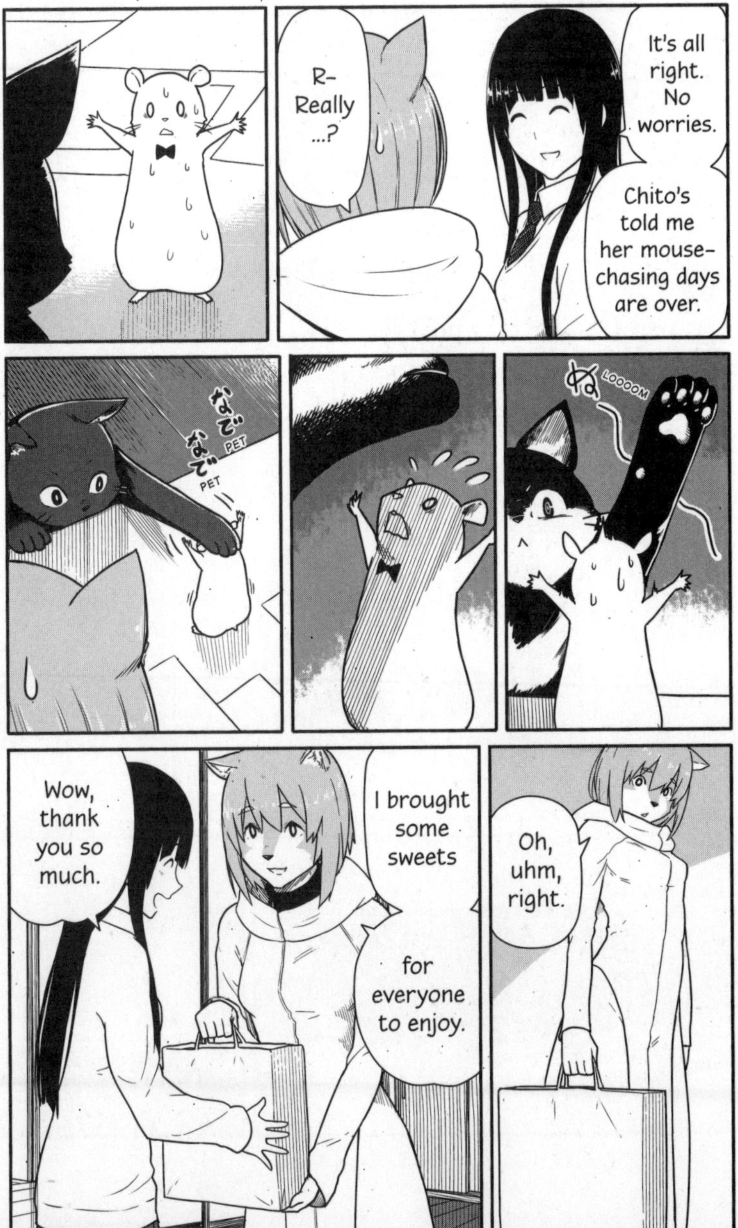
It's all right. No worries.
Chito's told me her mouse-chasing days are over.
R-Really ...?
ぬ
LOOOOM
なで
PET
なで
PET
Oh, uhm, right.
I brought some sweets
for everyone to enjoy.
Wow, thank you so much.

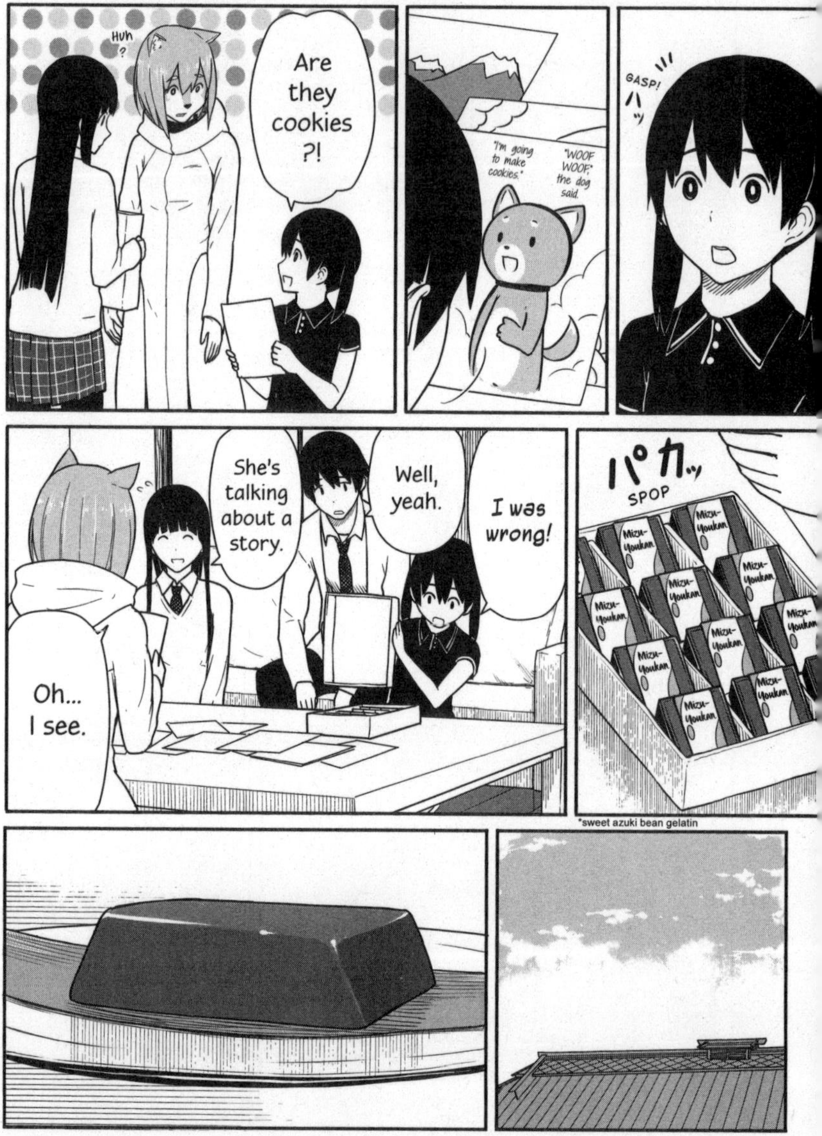
GASP!
ハッ
"I'm going to make cookies."
"WOOF WOOF," the dog said.
Are they cookies ?!
Huh ?
パカッ
SPOP
Mizu-Youkan
I was wrong!
Well, yeah.
She's talking about a story.
Oh... I see.
*sweet azuki bean gelatin

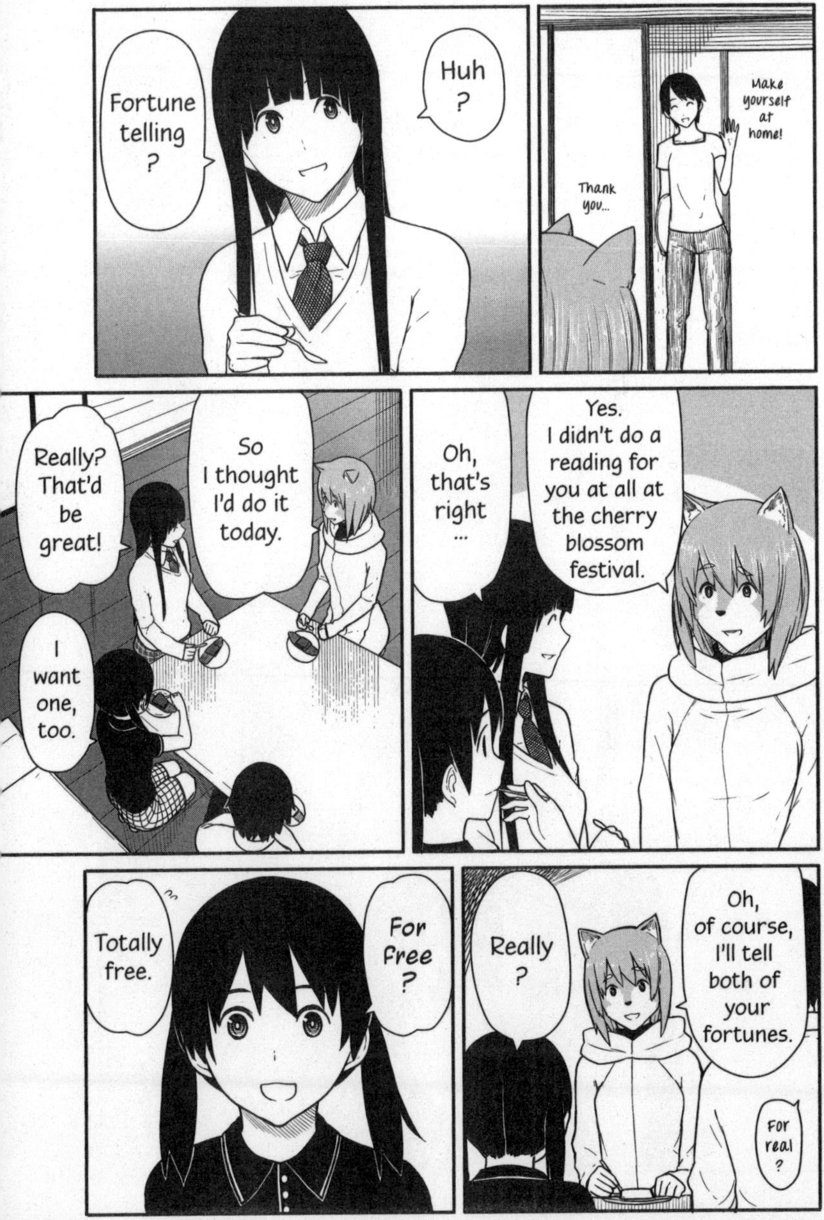
Make yourself at home!
Thank you...
Huh?
Fortune telling?
Yes. I didn't do a reading for you at all at the cherry blossom festival.
Oh, that's right...
So I thought I'd do it today.
Really? That'd be great!
I want one, too.
Oh, of course, I'll tell both of your fortunes.
Really?
For real?
For free?
Totally free.

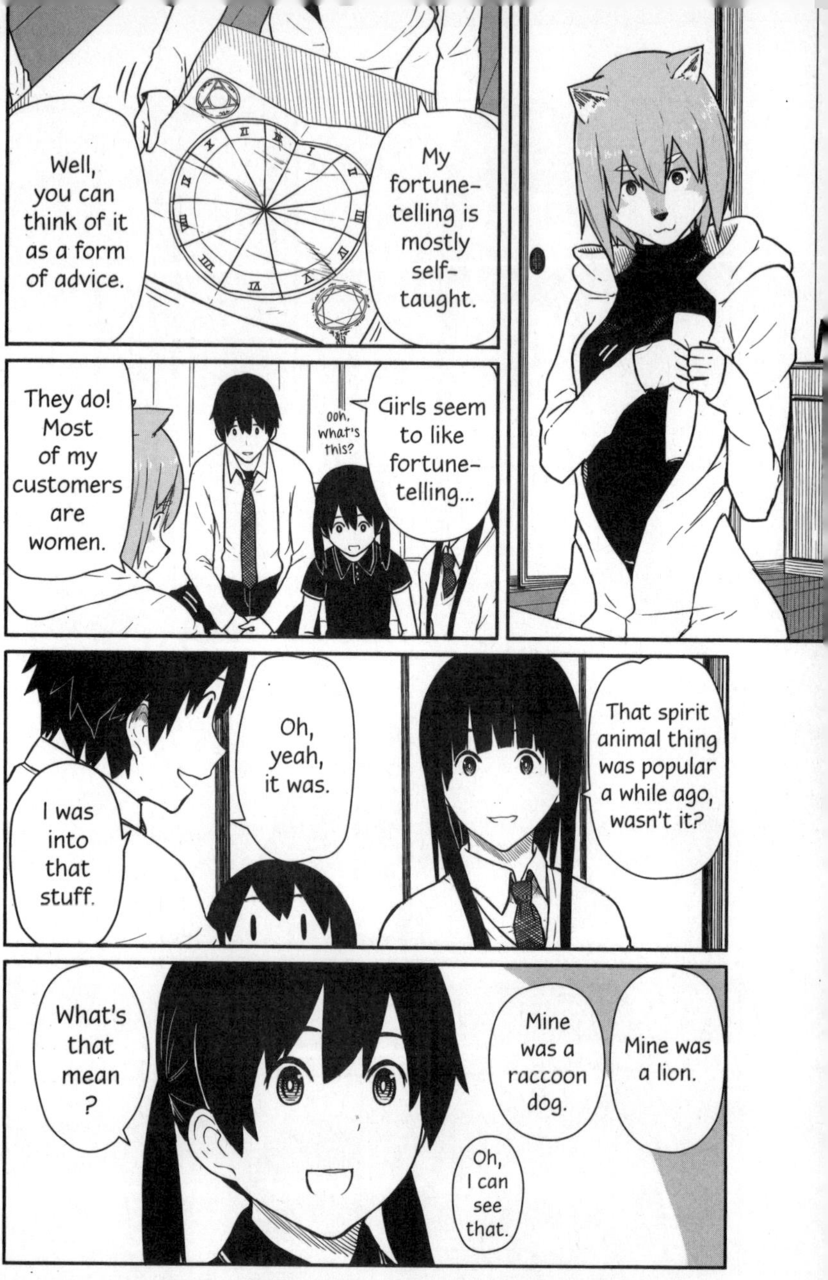
My fortune-telling is mostly self-taught.
Well, you can think of it as a form of advice.
Girls seem to like fortune-telling...
Ooh, what's this?
They do! Most of my customers are women.
That spirit animal thing was popular a while ago, wasn't it?
Oh, yeah, it was.
I was into that stuff.
Mine was a lion.
Mine was a raccoon dog.
Oh, I can see that.
What's that mean?

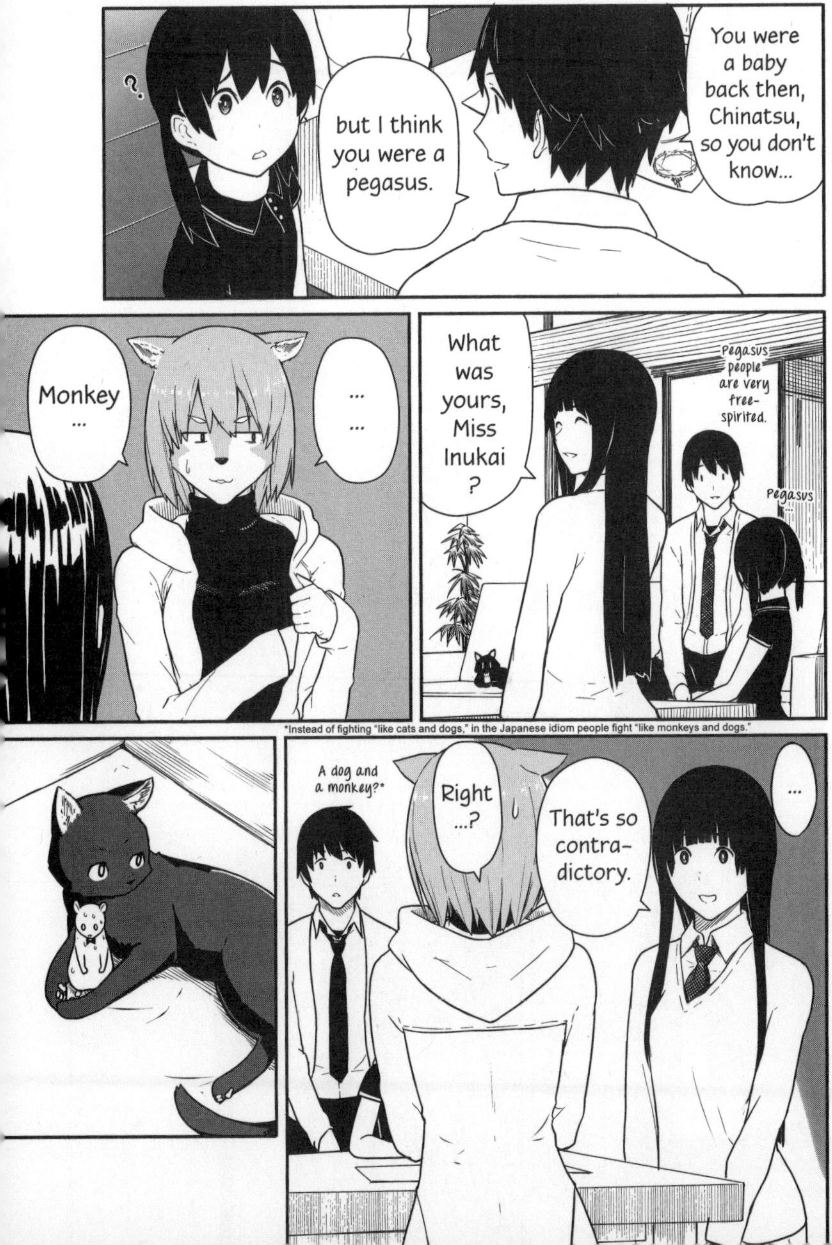
You were a baby back then, Chinatsu, so you don't know...
but I think you were a pegasus.
Pegasus people are very free-spirited.
What was yours, Miss Inukai?
Pegasus...
......
Monkey...
...
That's so contra-dictory.
Right...?
A dog and a monkey?*

*Instead of fighting "like cats and dogs," in the Japanese idiom people fight "like monkeys and dogs."

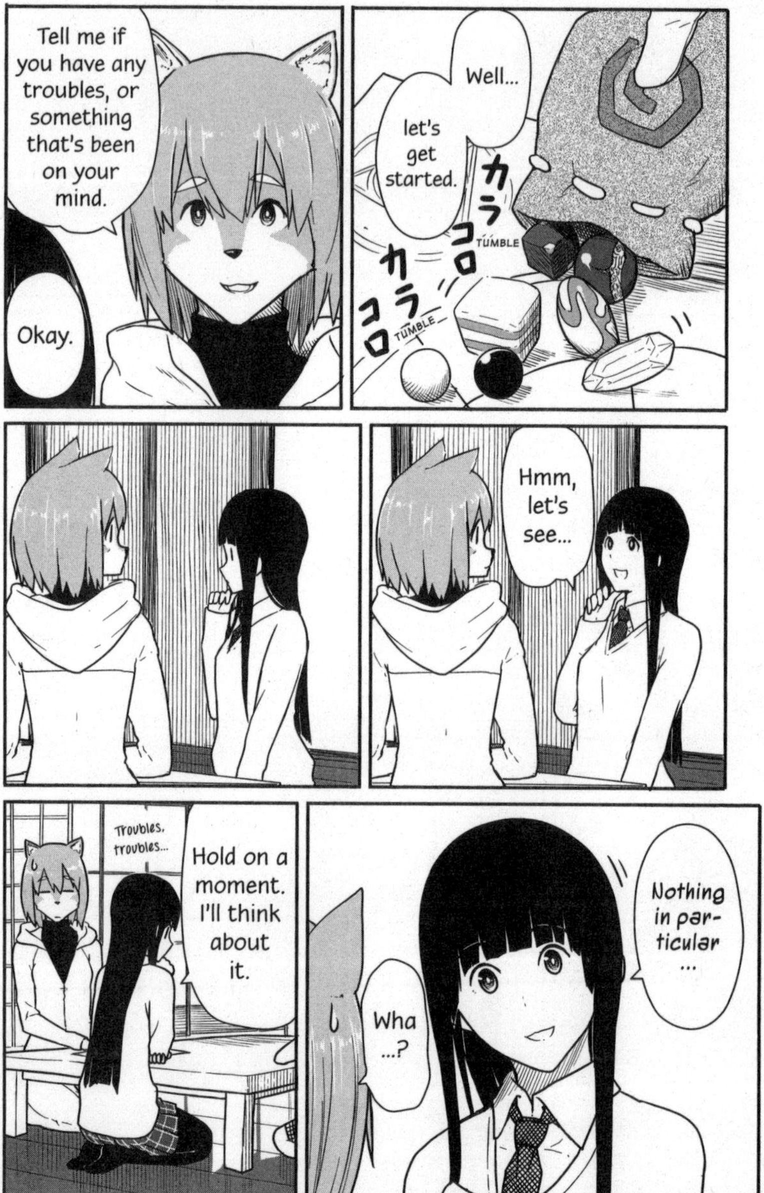
Well...
let's get started.
カラコロ
TUMBLE
カラコロ
TUMBLE
Tell me if you have any troubles, or something that's been on your mind.
Okay.
Hmm, let's see...
Nothing in particular ...
Wha ...?
Hold on a moment. I'll think about it.
Troubles, troubles...

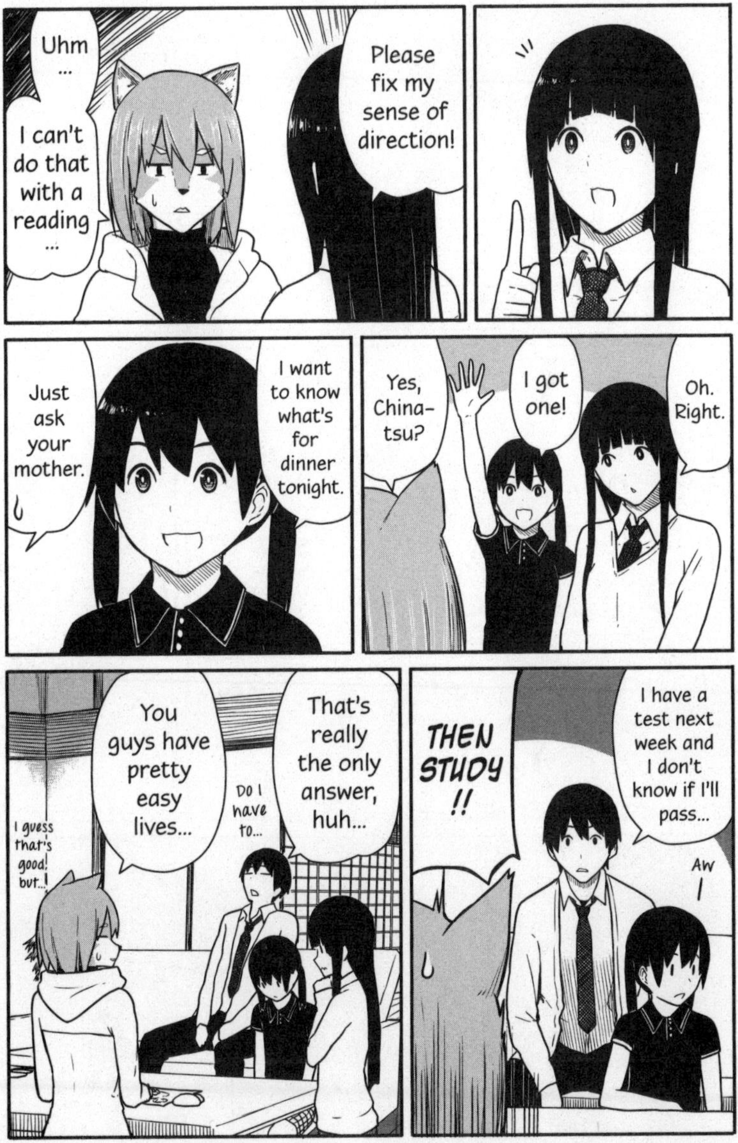
Please fix my sense of direction!
Uhm ...
I can't do that with a reading ...
Oh. Right.
I got one!
Yes, China-tsu?
I want to know what's for dinner tonight.
Just ask your mother.
I have a test next week and I don't know if I'll pass...
AW
THEN STUDY !!
That's really the only answer, huh...
Do I have to...
You guys have pretty easy lives...
I guess that's good! but...!

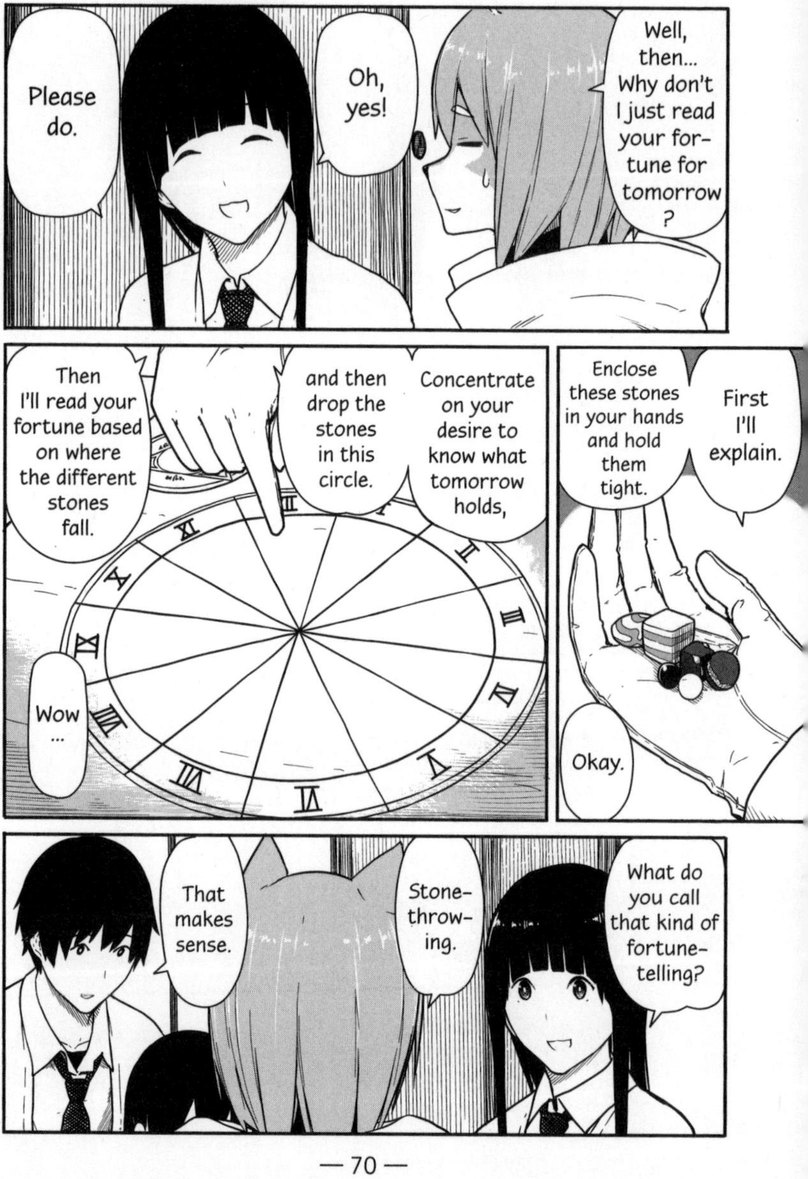
Well, then... Why don't I just read your for-tune for tomorrow?
Oh, yes!
Please do.
First I'll explain.
Enclose these stones in your hands and hold them tight.
Okay.
Concentrate on your desire to know what tomorrow holds,
and then drop the stones in this circle.
Then I'll read your fortune based on where the different stones fall.
Wow...
What do you call that kind of fortune-telling?
Stone-throwing.
That makes sense.

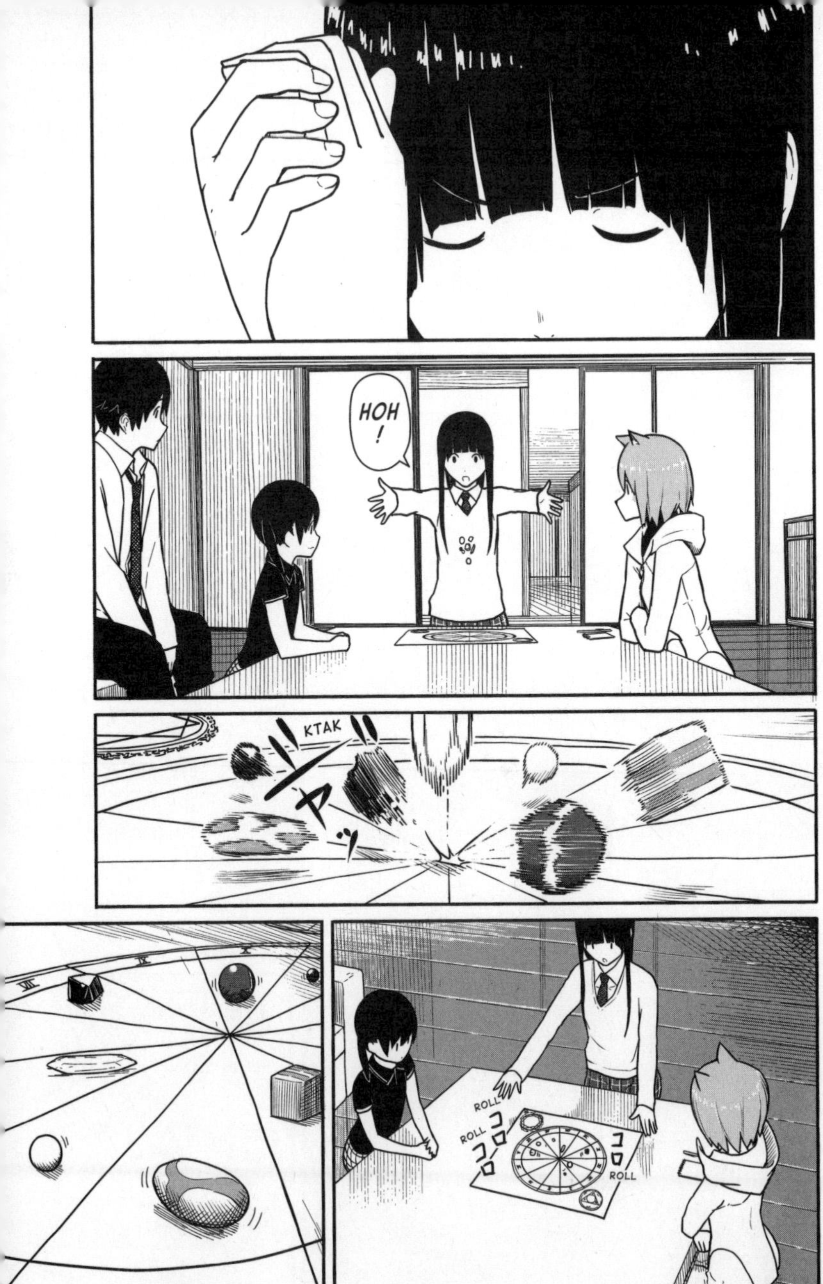

HOH!
KTAK
ジャッ
ROLL
コロ
ROLL
コロ
コロ
ROLL

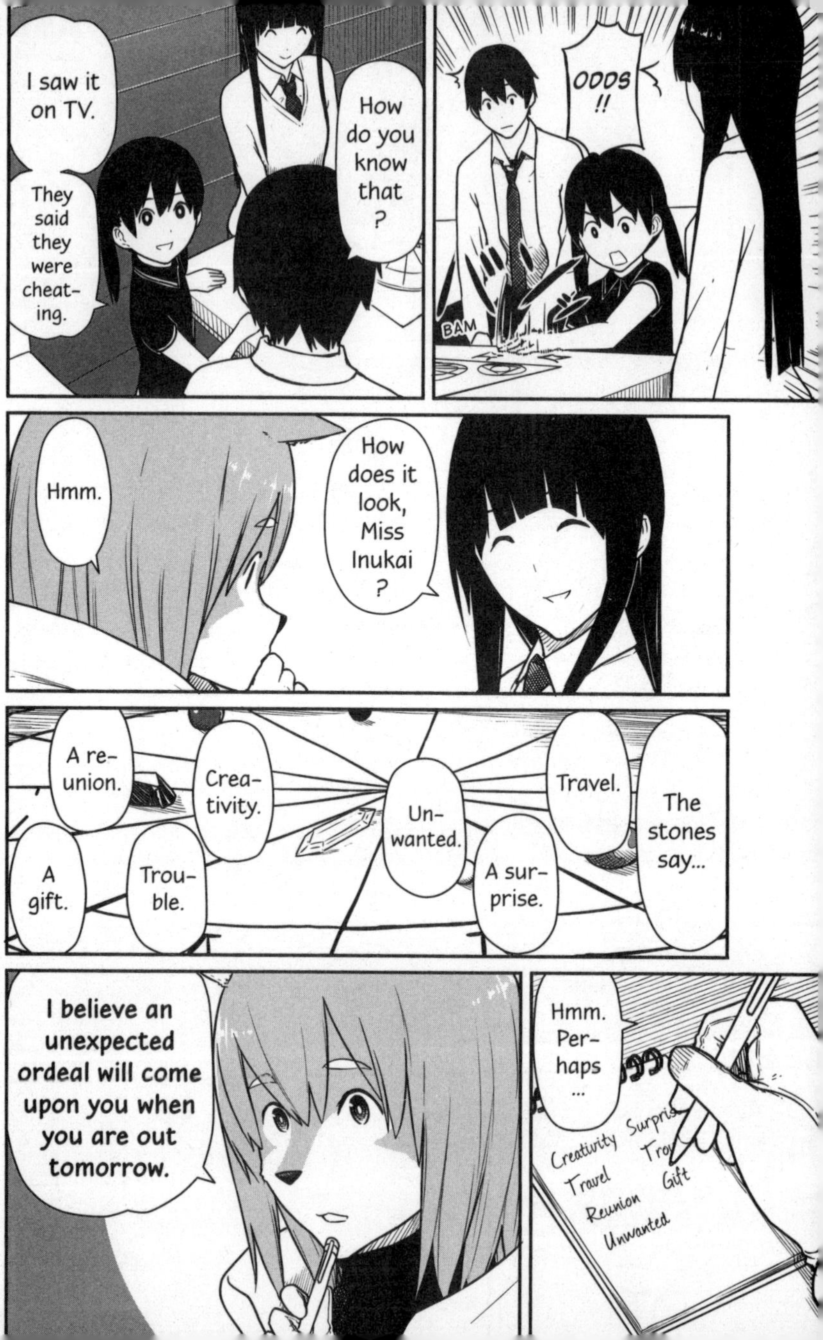
ODDS !!
BAM
How do you know that?
I saw it on TV.
They said they were cheating.
How does it look, Miss Inukai?
Hmm.
The stones say...
Travel.
A surprise.
Unwanted.
Creativity.
Trouble.
A reunion.
A gift.
Hmm. Perhaps ...
Creativity Surpris
Travel Tro
Reunion Gift
Unwanted
I believe an unexpected ordeal will come upon you when you are out tomorrow.

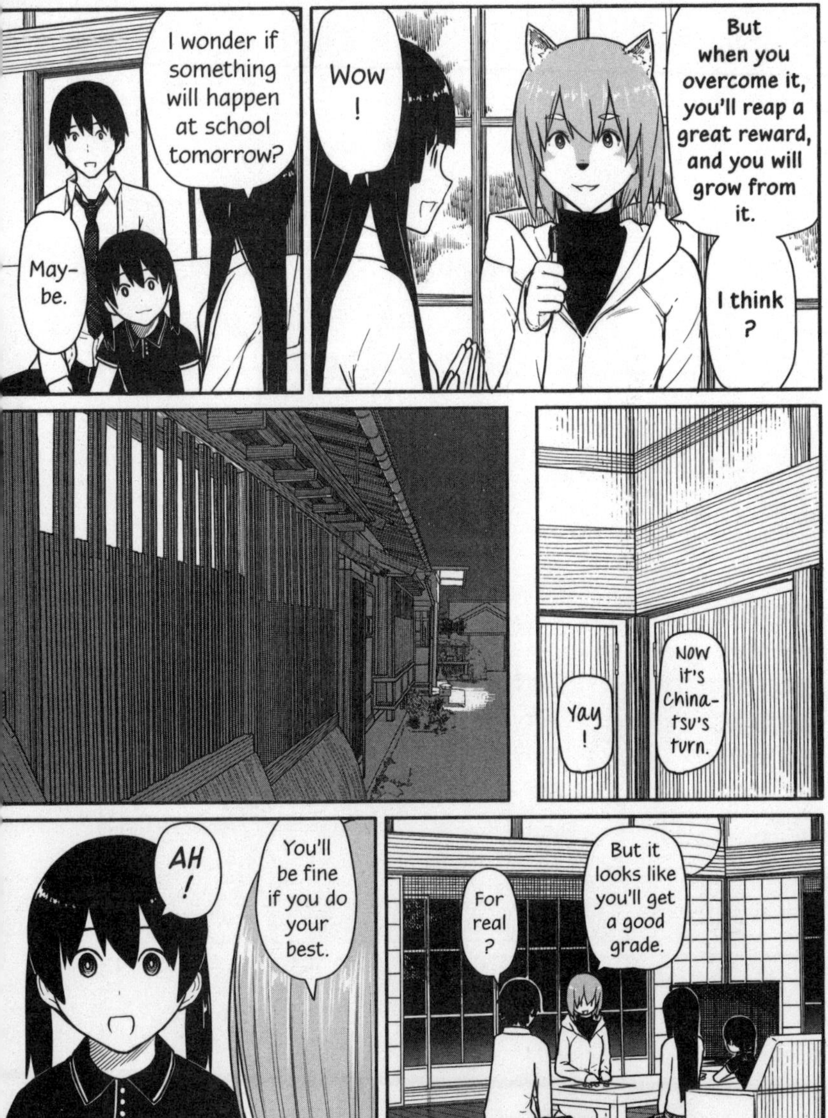
But when you overcome it, you'll reap a great reward, and you will grow from it.
I think?
Wow!
I wonder if something will happen at school tomorrow?
May-be.
Now it's China-tsu's turn.
Yay!
But it looks like you'll get a good grade.
For real?
You'll be fine if you do your best.
AH!

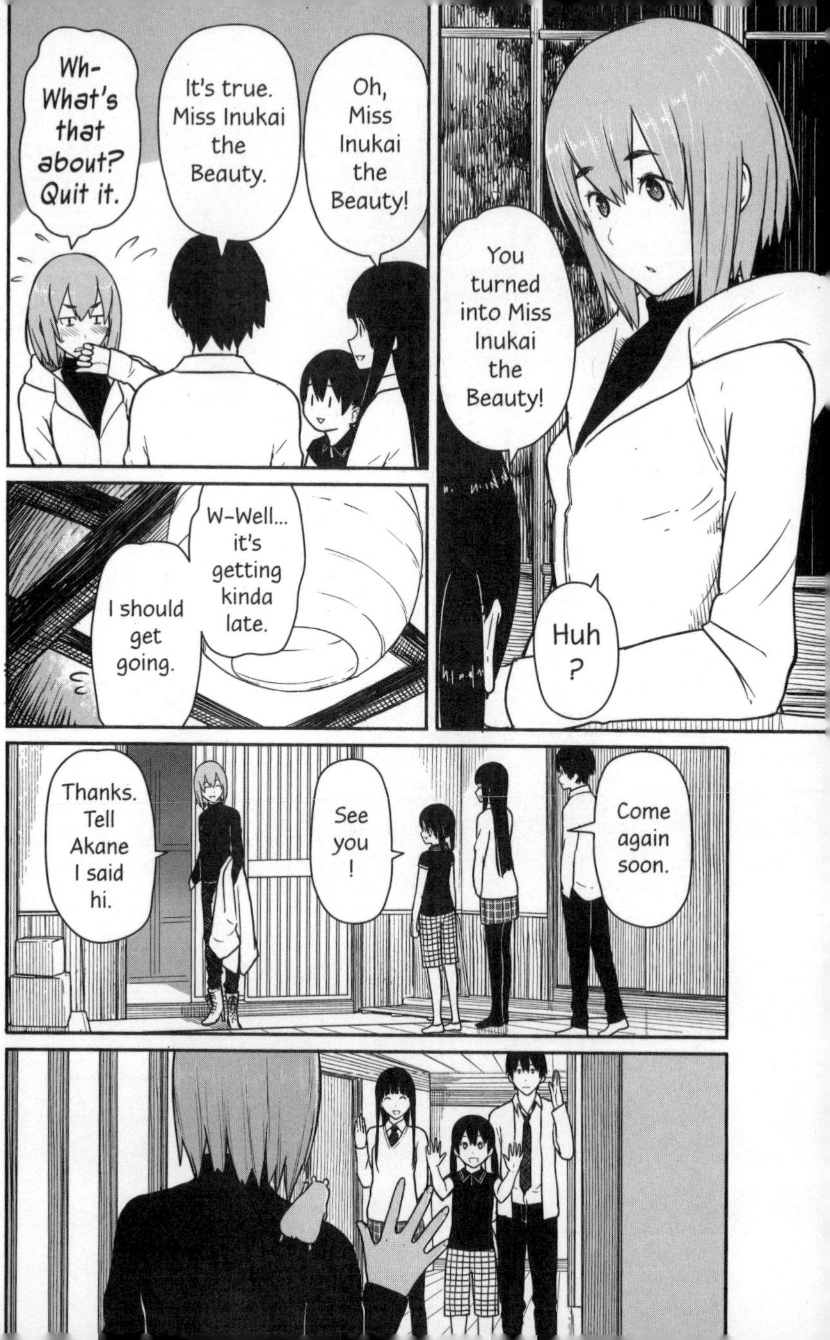

You turned into Miss Inukai the Beauty!
Huh?
Oh, Miss Inukai the Beauty!
It's true. Miss Inukai the Beauty.
Wh- What's that about? Quit it.
W-Well... it's getting kinda late.
I should get going.
Come again soon.
See you!
Thanks. Tell Akane I said hi.

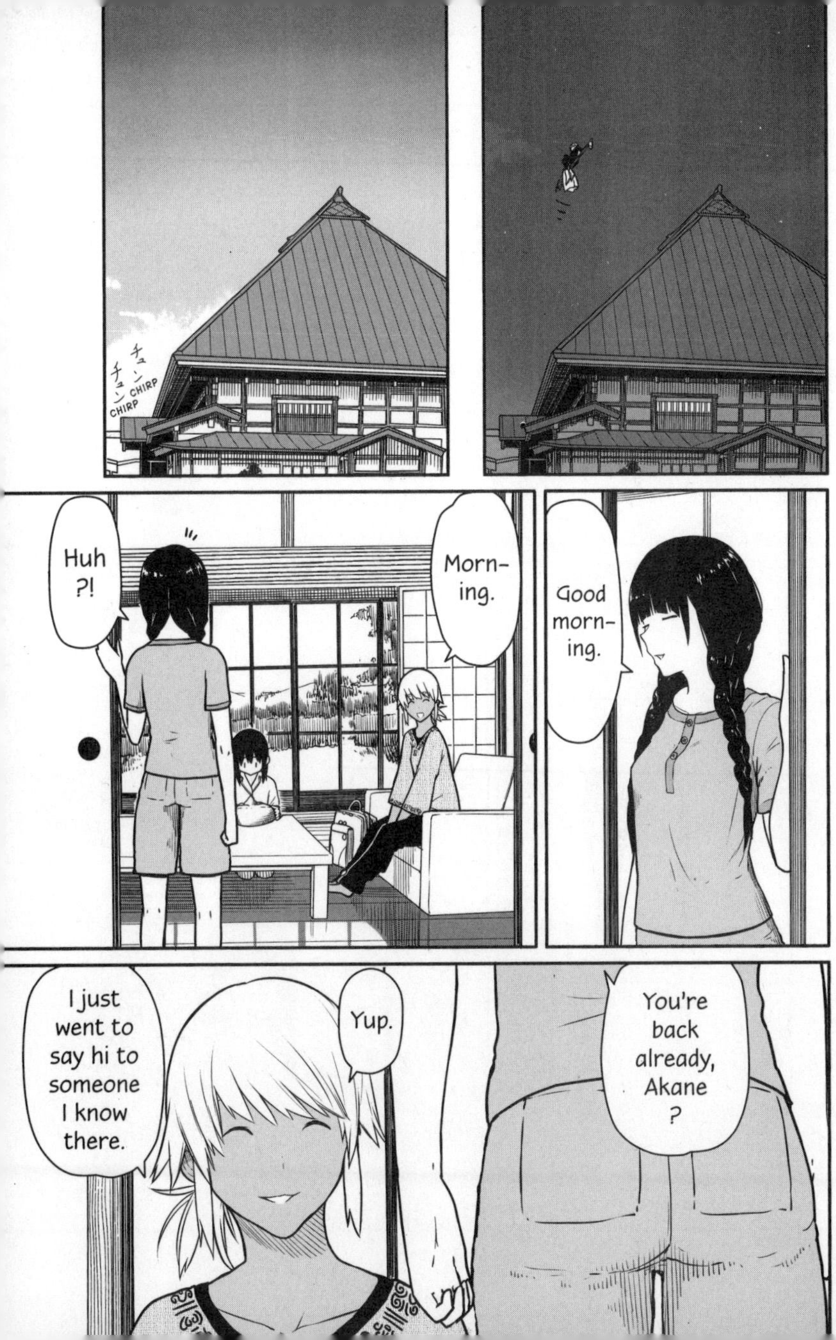
チュン チュン
CHIRP CHIRP
Good morning.
Morning.
Huh?!
You're back already, Akane?
Yup.
I just went to say hi to someone I know there.

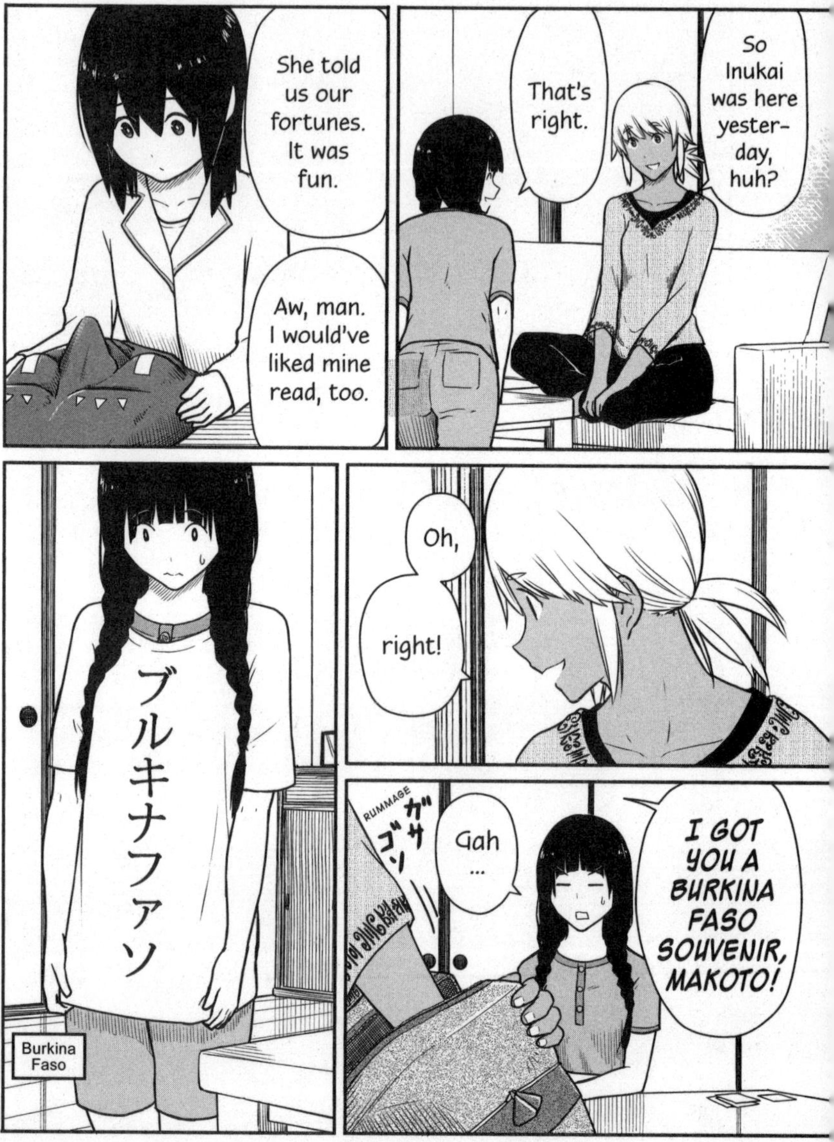
So Inukai was here yester-day, huh?
That's right.
She told us our fortunes. It was fun.
Aw, man. I would've liked mine read, too.
Oh,
right!
I GOT YOU A BURKINA FASO SOUVENIR, MAKOTO!
Gah ...
ガサゴソ
RUMMAGE
ブルキナファソ
Burkina Faso

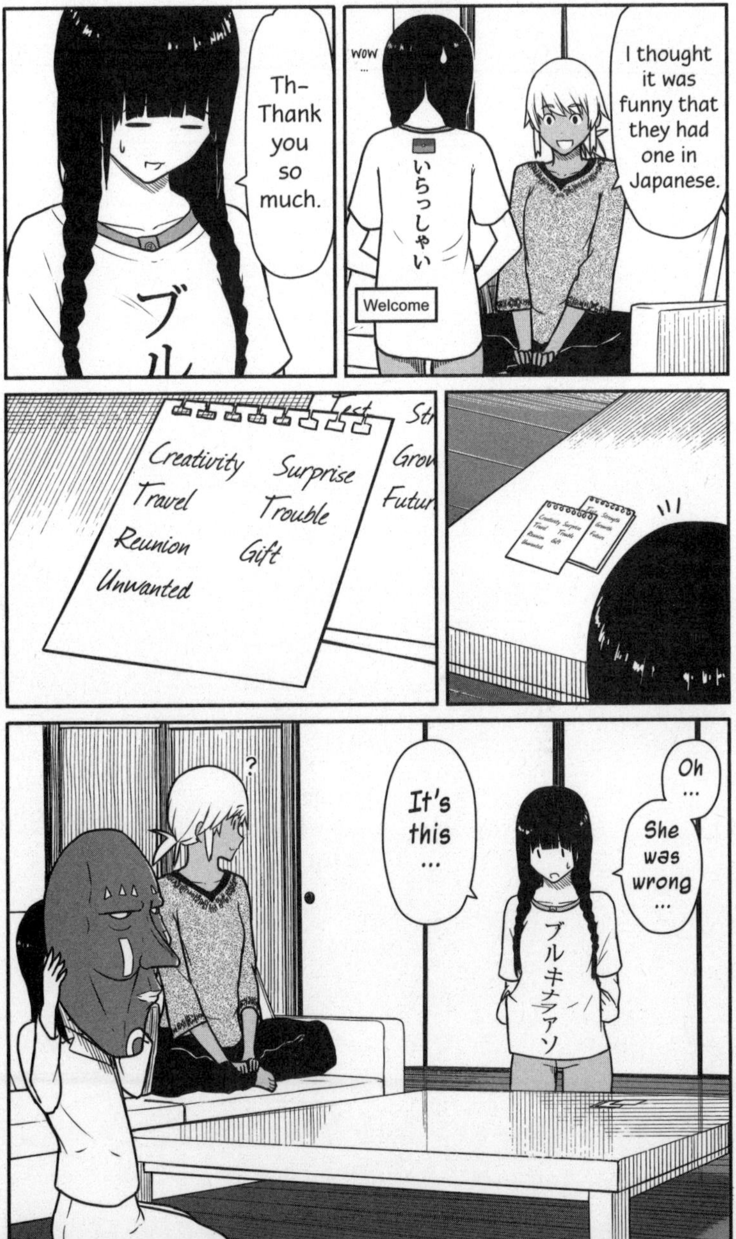
I thought it was funny that they had one in Japanese.
wow ...
いらっしゃい
Welcome
Th- Thank you so much.
ブル
Creativity
Surprise
Travel
Trouble
Reunion
Gift
Unwanted
Oh ... She was wrong ...
It's this ...
?
ブルキナファソ

You're wearing white today.
It's for flying in the daytime.

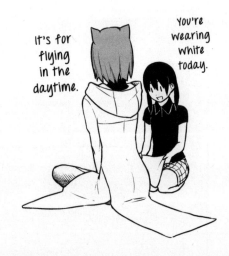

Chapter 16
The Medicine Goes Down Spicy

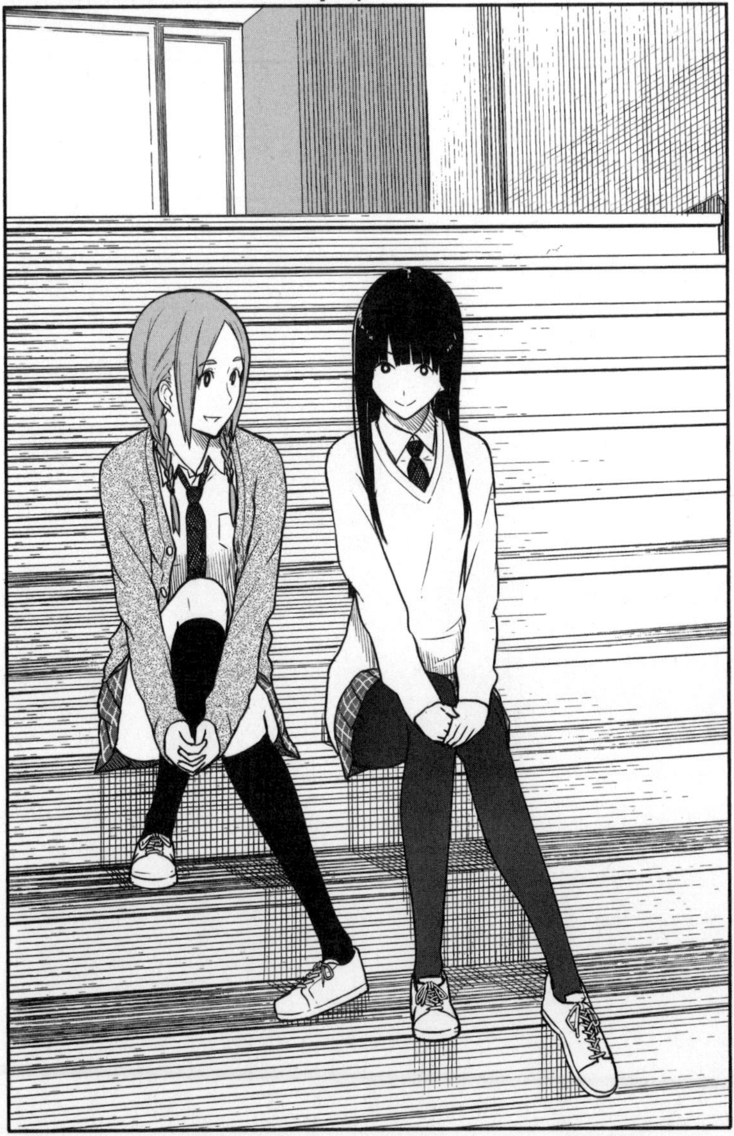

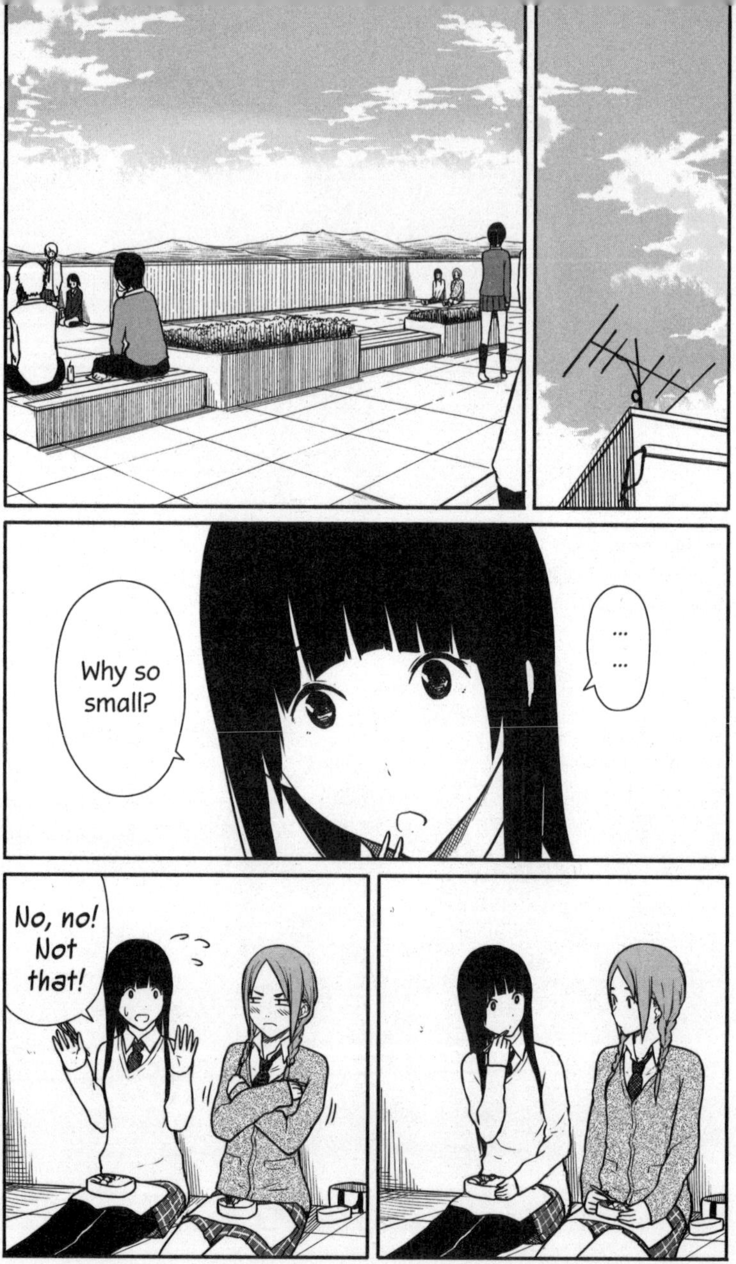
...
...
Why so small?
No, no! Not that!

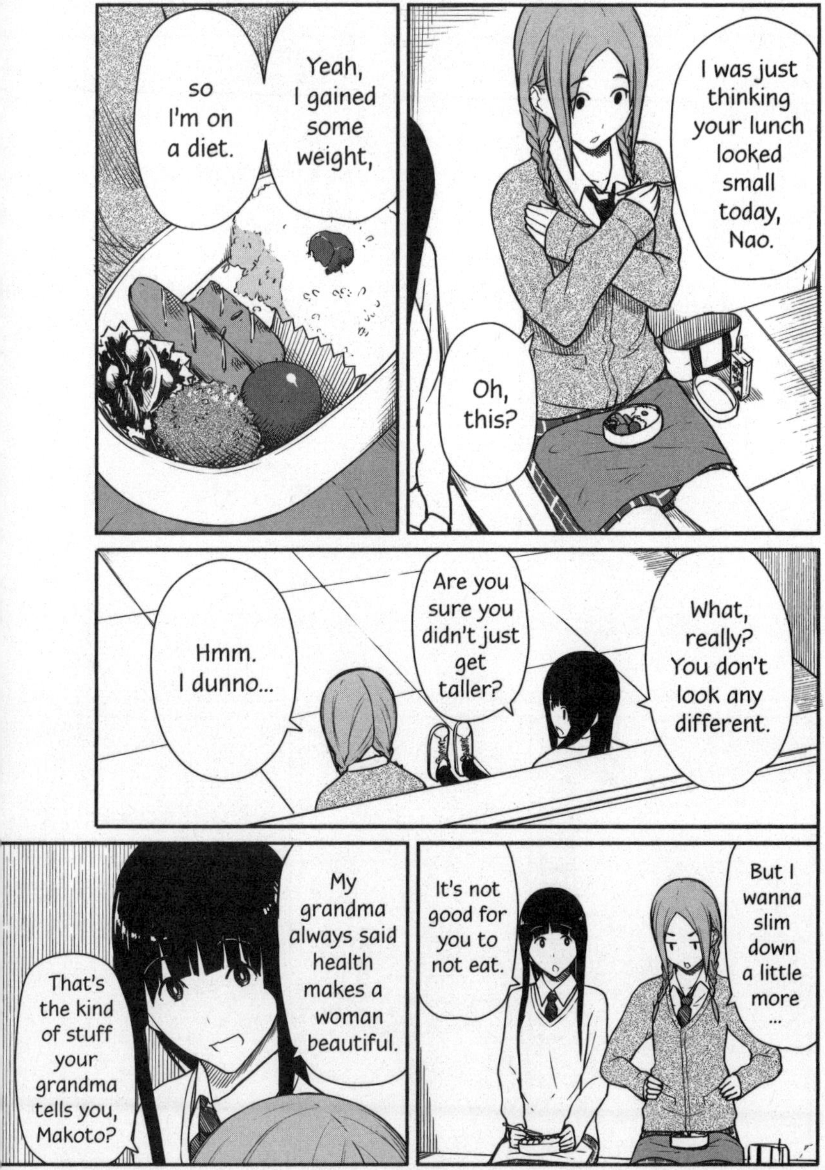
I was just thinking your lunch looked small today, Nao.
Oh, this?
Yeah, I gained some weight,
so I'm on a diet.
What, really? You don't look any different.
Are you sure you didn't just get taller?
Hmm. I dunno...
But I wanna slim down a little more ...
It's not good for you to not eat.
My grandma always said health makes a woman beautiful.
That's the kind of stuff your grandma tells you, Makoto?

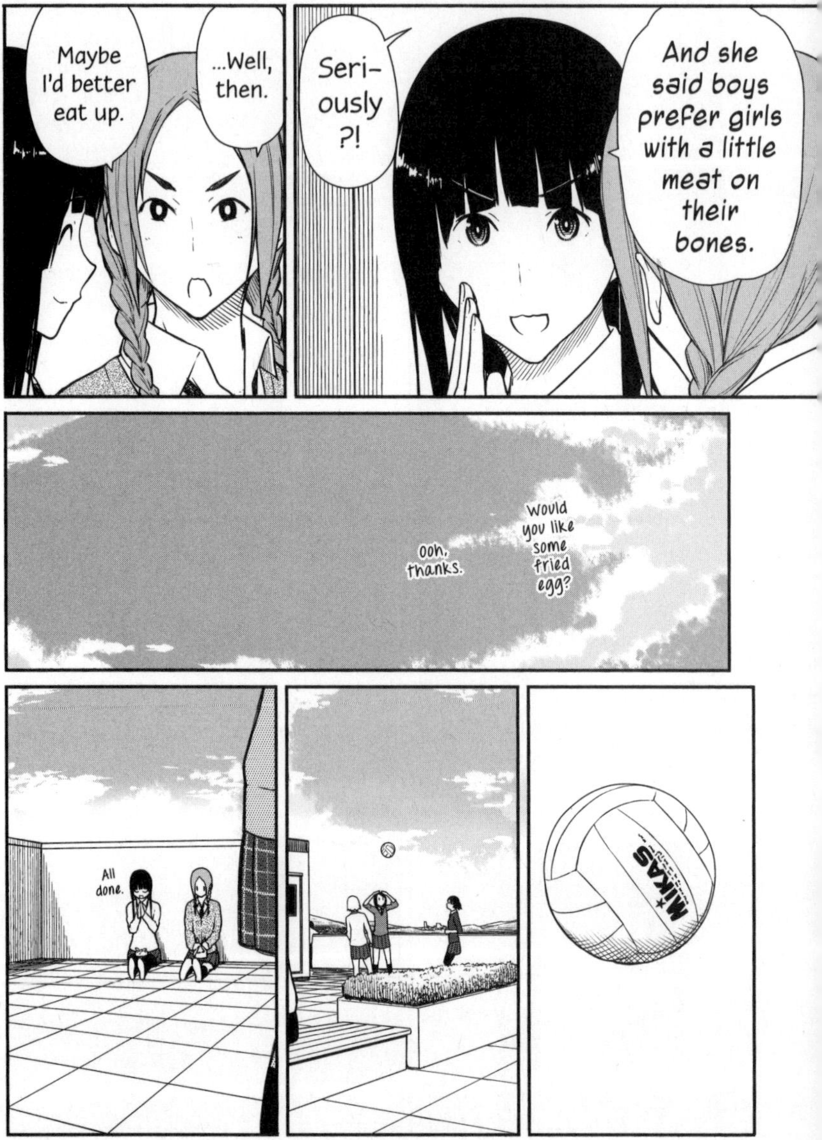
And she said boys prefer girls with a little meat on their bones.
Seri-ously?!
...Well, then.
Maybe I'd better eat up.
Would you like some fried egg?
Ooh, thanks.
MIKASA
All done.

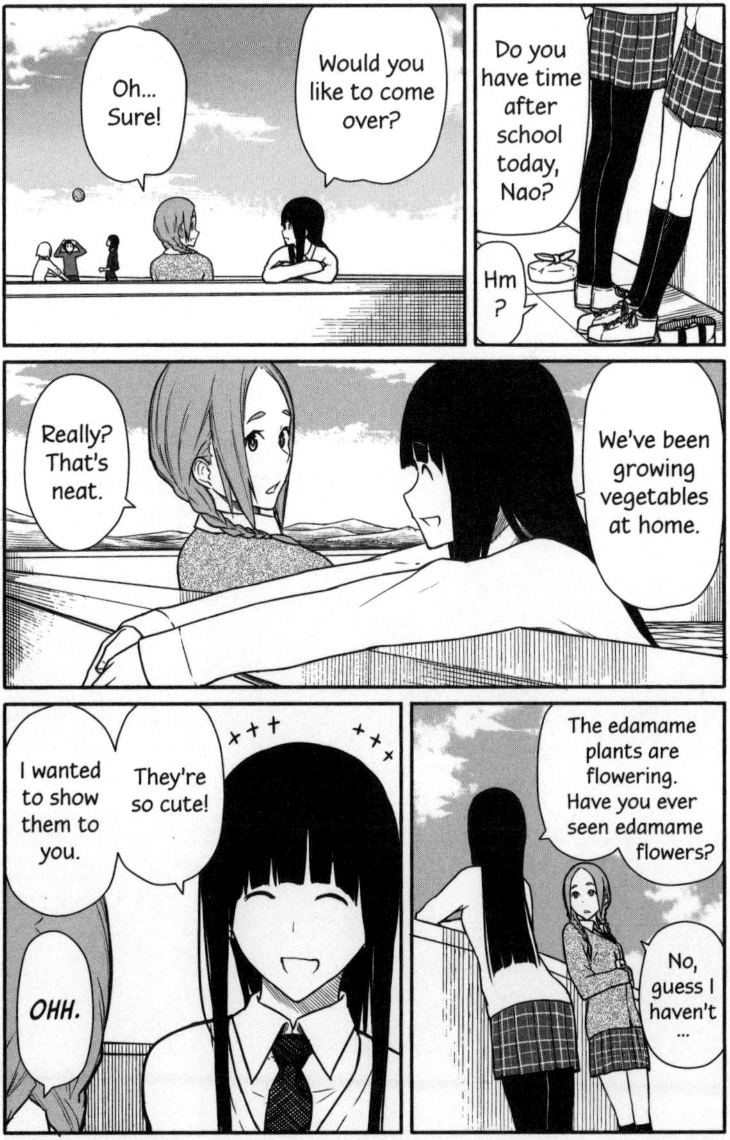
Do you have time after school today, Nao?
Hm?
Would you like to come over?
Oh... Sure!
We've been growing vegetables at home.
Really? That's neat.
The edamame plants are flowering. Have you ever seen edamame flowers?
No, guess I haven't ...
They're so cute!
I wanted to show them to you.
OHH.

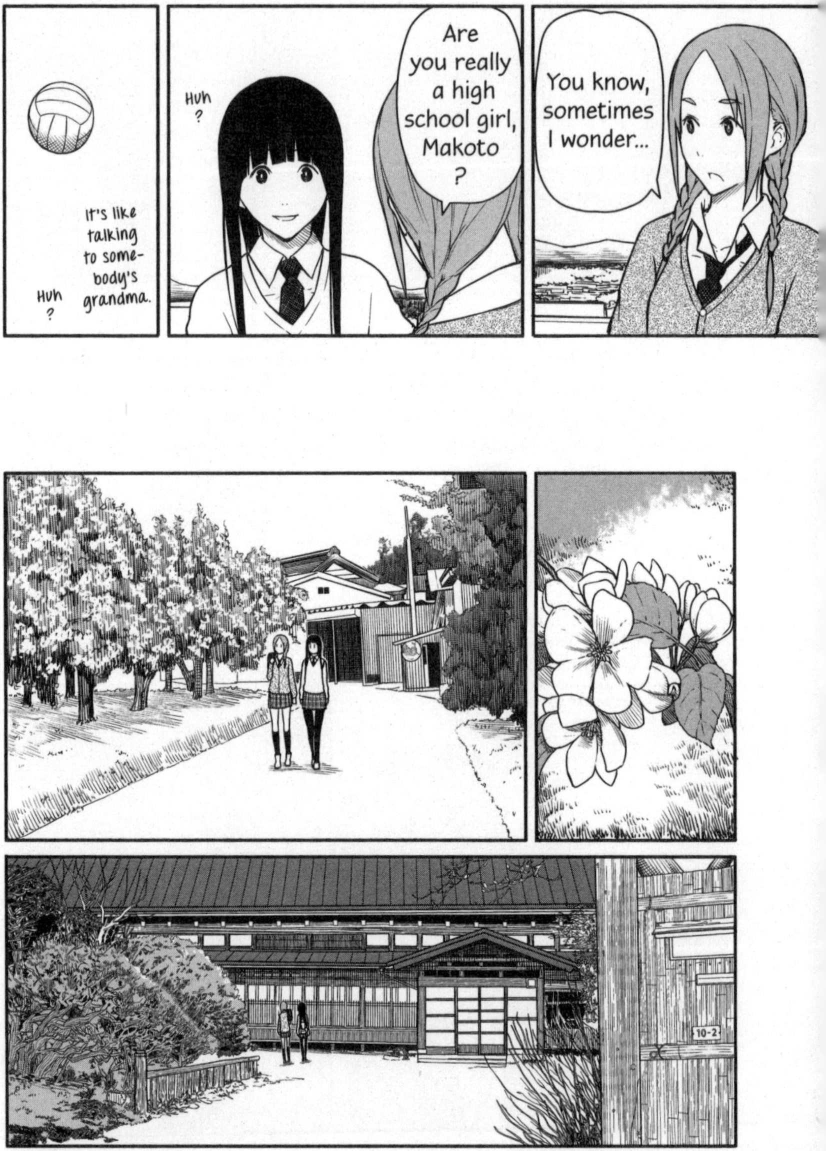
You know, sometimes I wonder...
Are you really a high school girl, Makoto?
Huh?
It's like talking to somebody's grandma.
Huh?
10-2

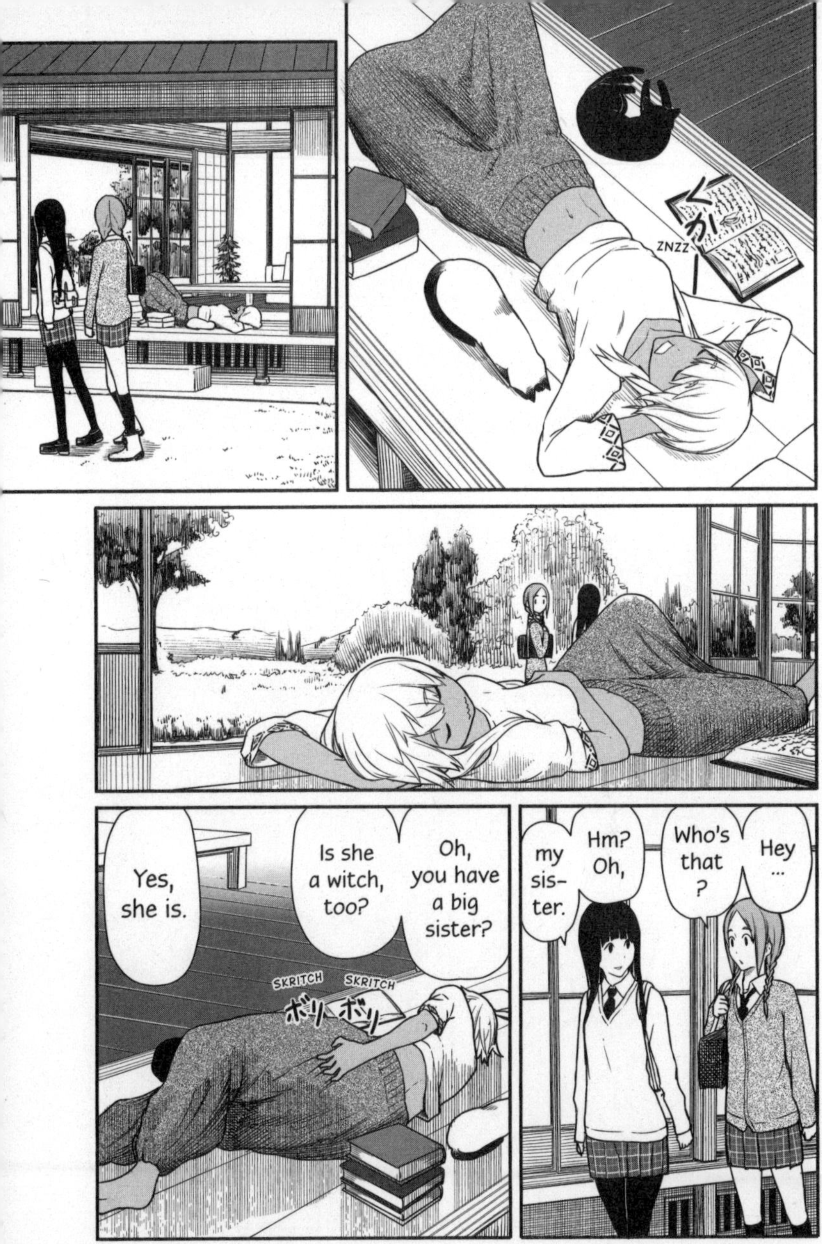

くか
ZNZZ
Hey ...
Who's that ?
Hm? Oh,
my sis-ter.
Oh, you have a big sister?
Is she a witch, too?
Yes, she is.
SKRITCH SKRITCH
ボリ ボリ

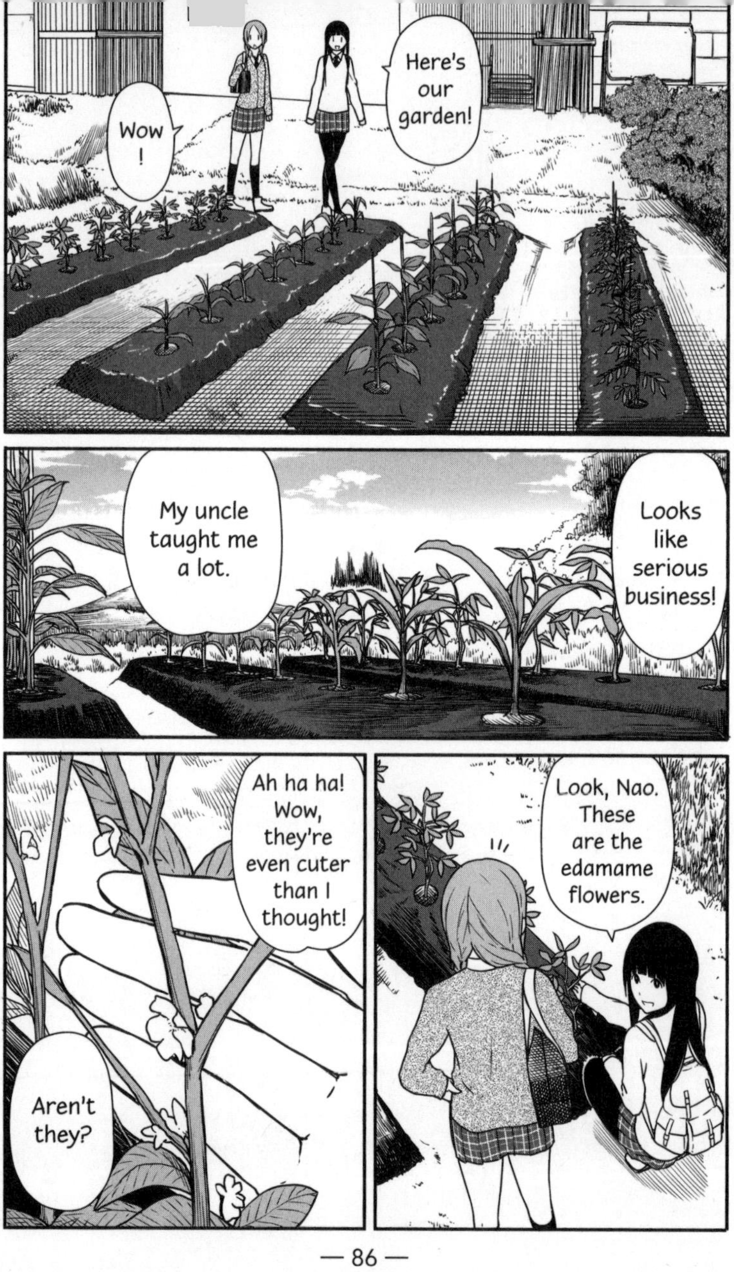
Here's our garden!
Wow!
Looks like serious business!
My uncle taught me a lot.
Look, Nao. These are the edamame flowers.
Ah ha ha! Wow, they're even cuter than I thought!
Aren't they?

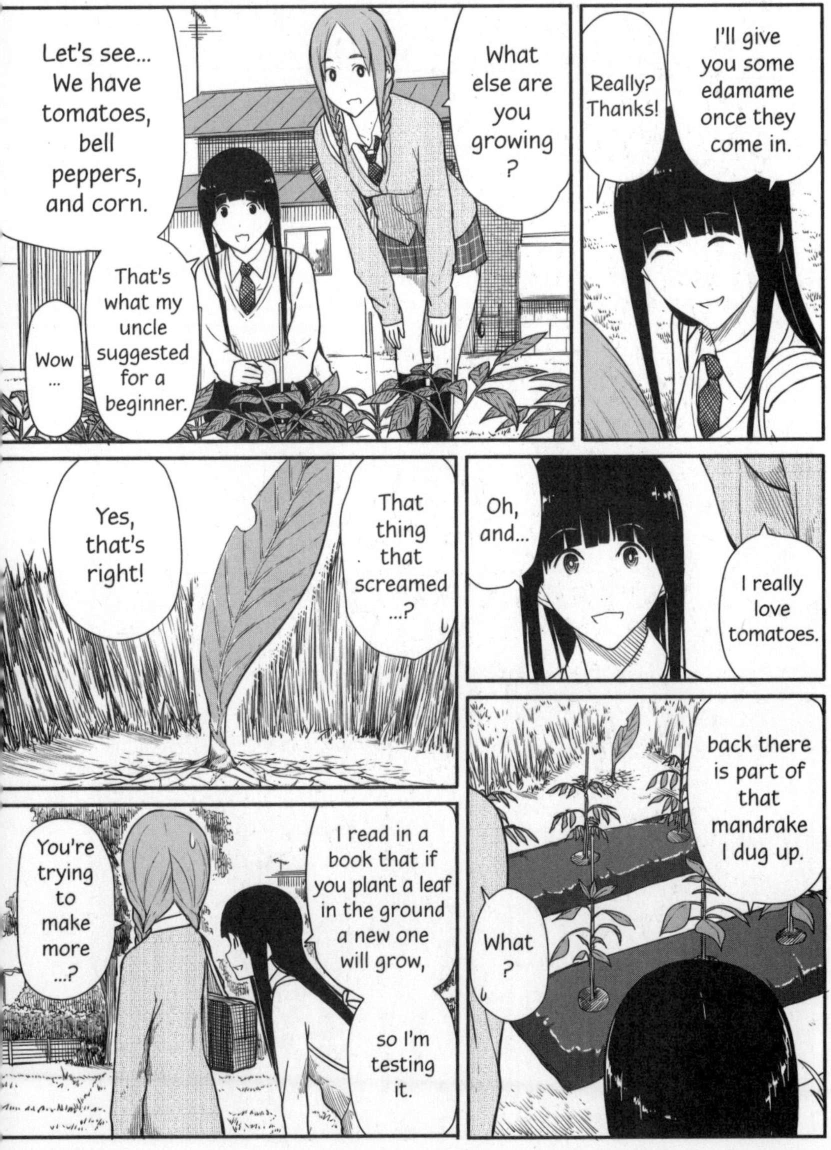
I'll give you some edamame once they come in.
Really? Thanks!
What else are you growing ?
Let's see... We have tomatoes, bell peppers, and corn.
That's what my uncle suggested for a beginner.
Wow ...
I really love tomatoes.
Oh, and...
back there is part of that mandrake I dug up.
What ?
That thing that screamed ...?
Yes, that's right!
I read in a book that if you plant a leaf in the ground a new one will grow,
so I'm testing it.
You're trying to make more ...?

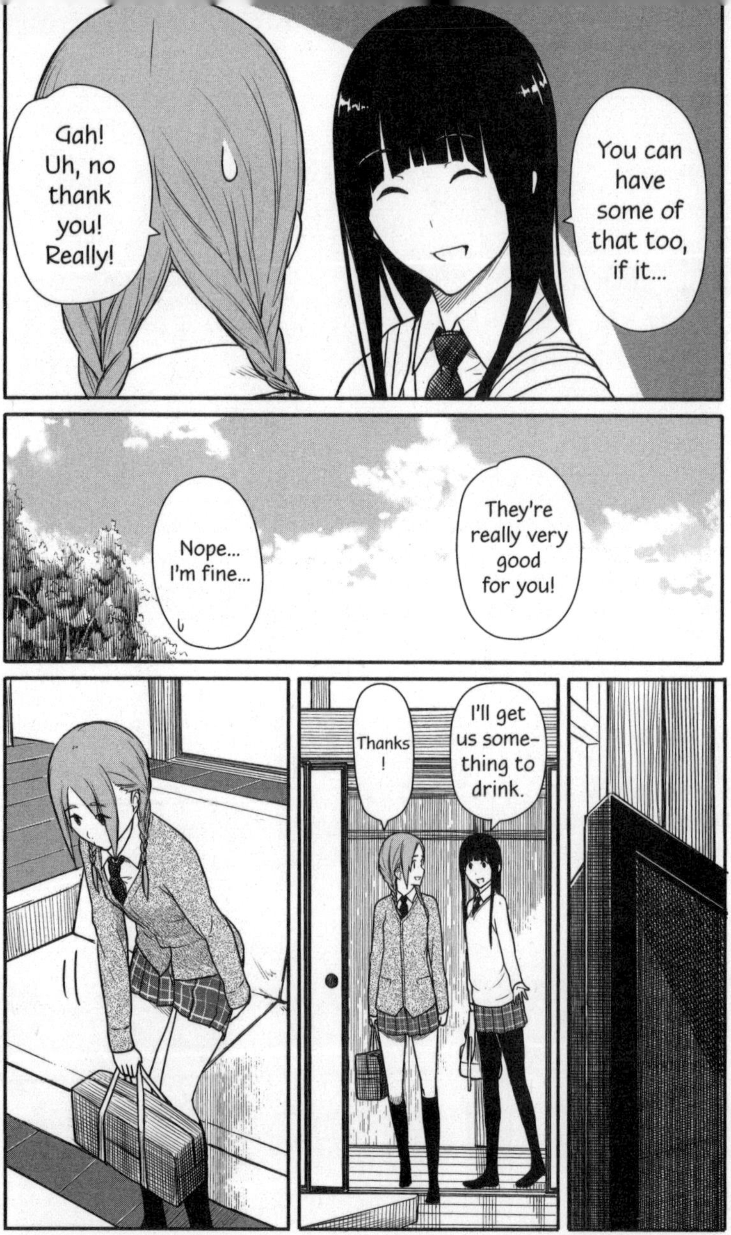
You can have some of that too, if it...
Gah! Uh, no thank you! Really!
They're really very good for you!
Nope... I'm fine...
I'll get us some-thing to drink.
Thanks!

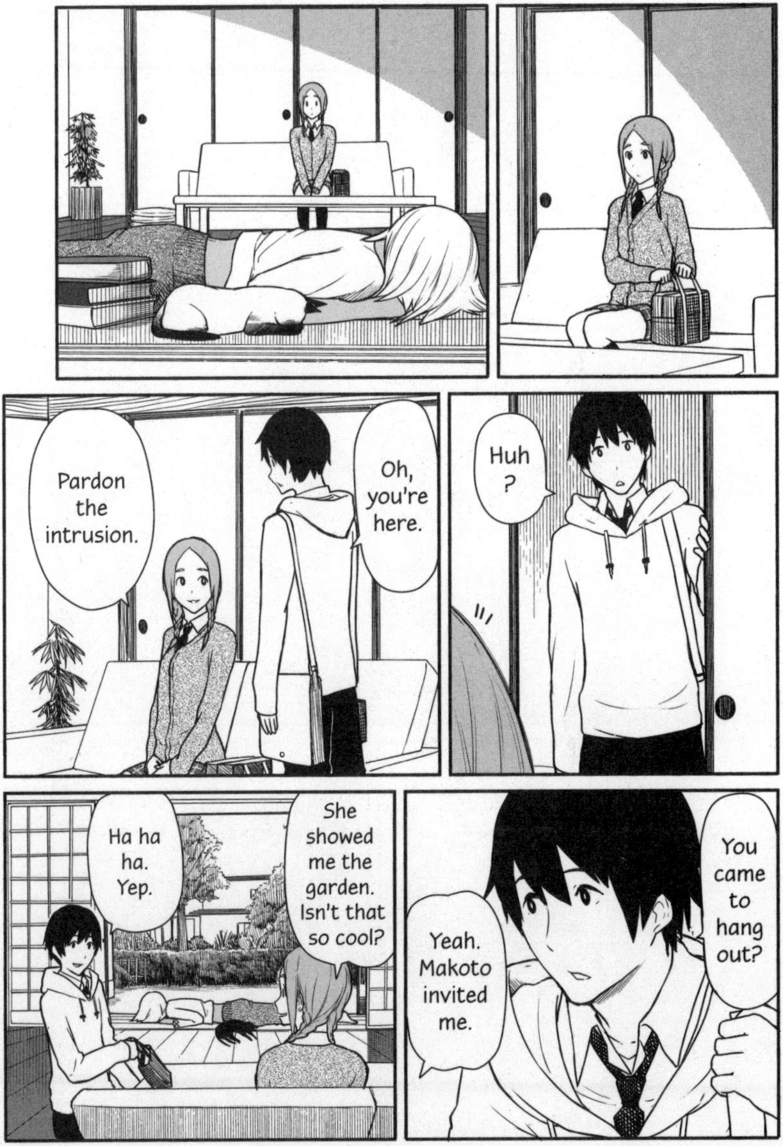
Huh?
Oh, you're here.
Pardon the intrusion.
You came to hang out?
Yeah. Makoto invited me.
She showed me the garden. Isn't that so cool?
Ha ha ha. Yep.

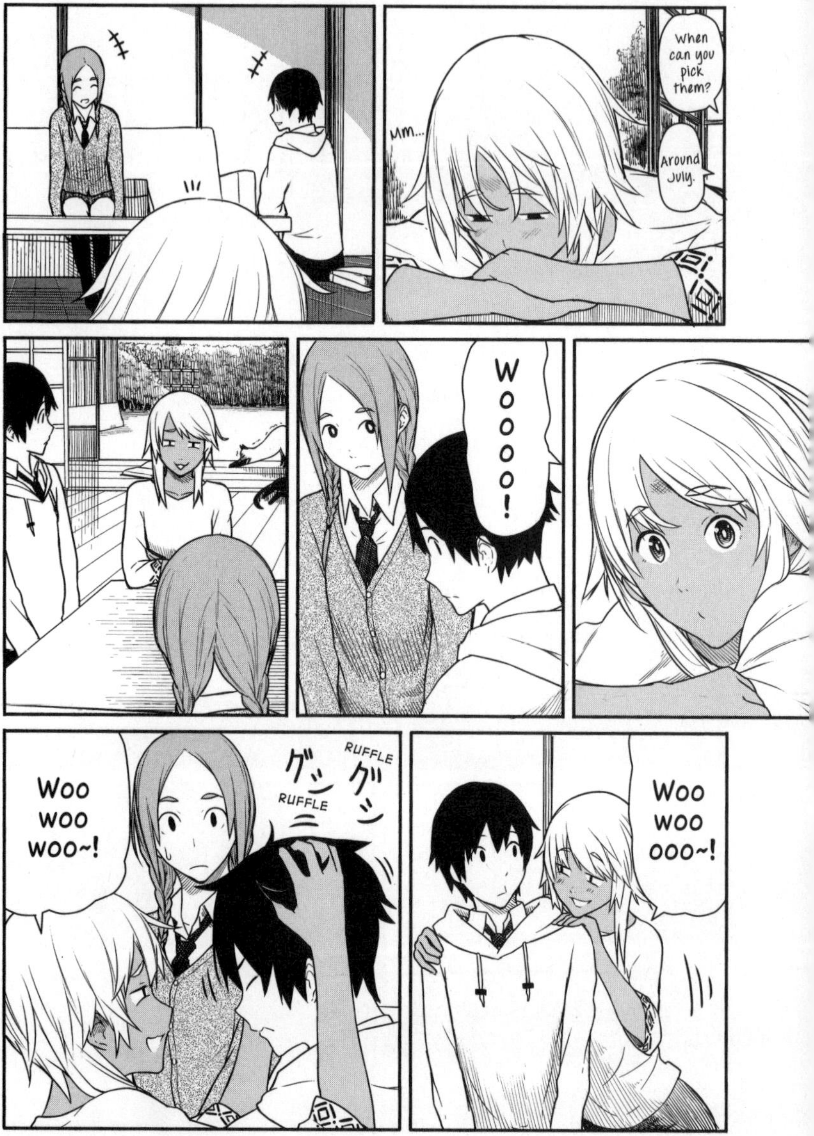
When can you pick them?
Around July.
Mm...
WOOOOO!
Woo woo ooo~!
Woo woo woo~!
RUFFLE
グシ
グッ
RUFFLE

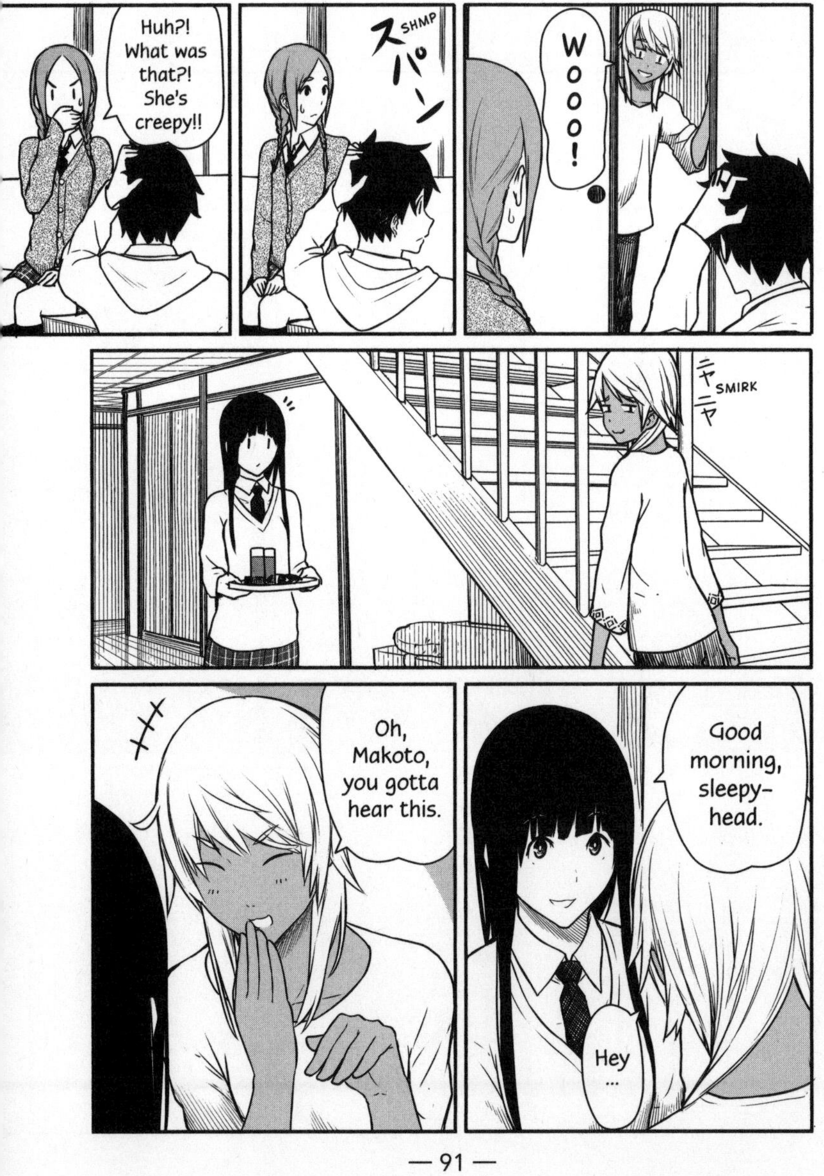
WOOOO!
スパン
SHMP
Huh?! What was that?! She's creepy!!
ニヤニヤ
SMIRK
Good morning, sleepy-head.
Hey ...
Oh, Makoto, you gotta hear this.

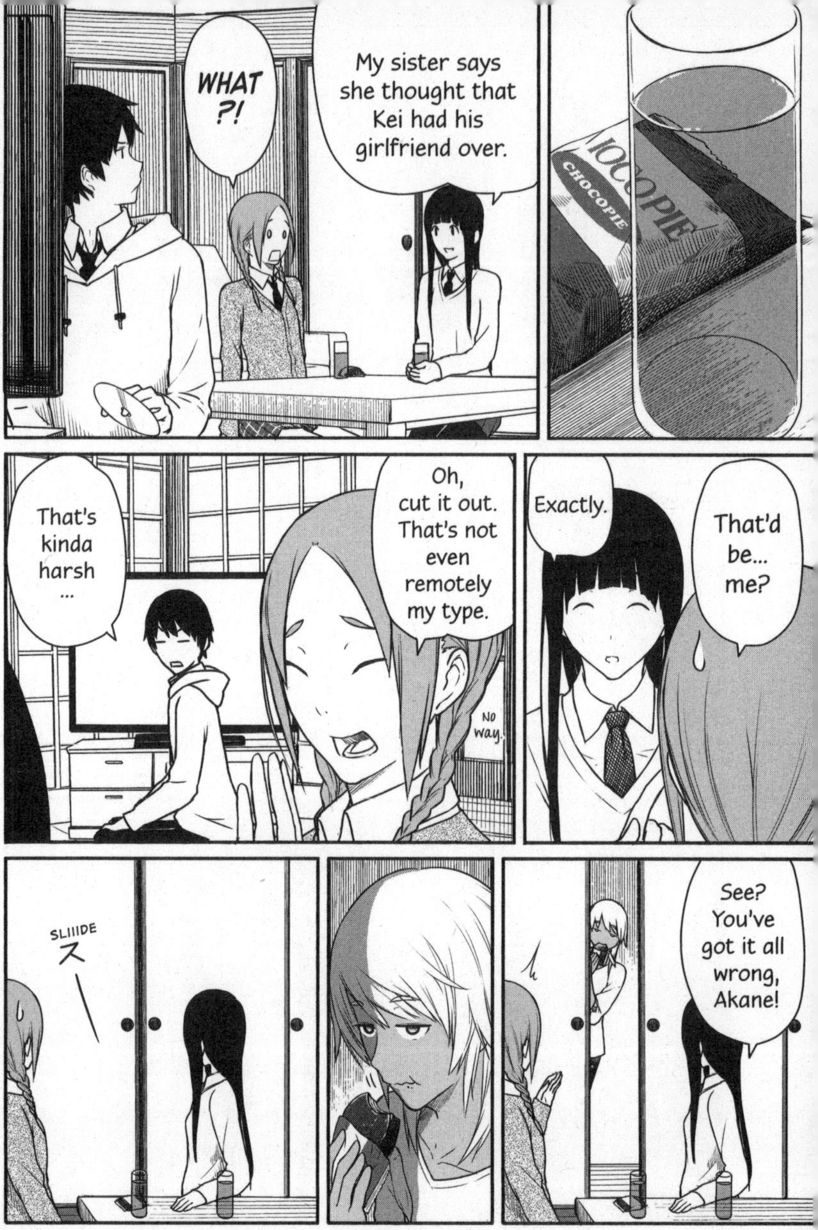

CHOCOPIE
CHOCOPIE
My sister says she thought that Kei had his girlfriend over.
WHAT ?!
That'd be... me?
Exactly.
Oh, cut it out. That's not even remotely my type.
No way.
That's kinda harsh ...
See? You've got it all wrong, Akane!
SLIIIDE
ス

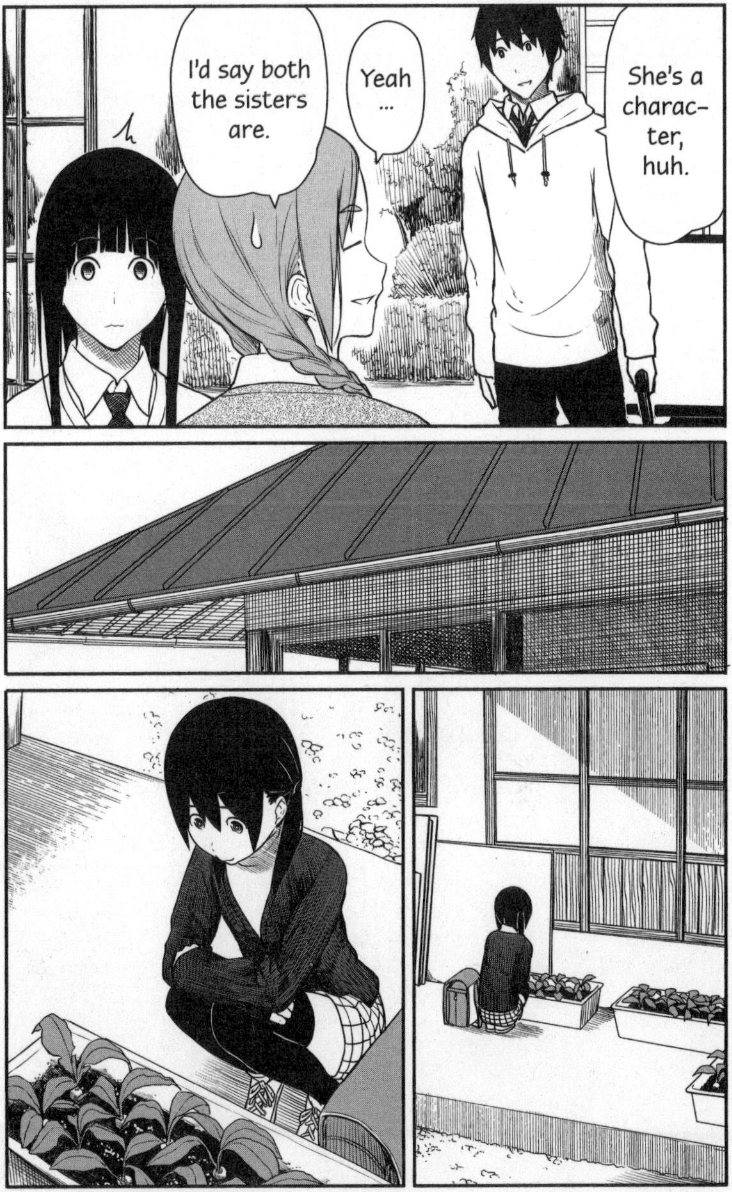
She's a charac-ter, huh.
Yeah ...
I'd say both the sisters are.

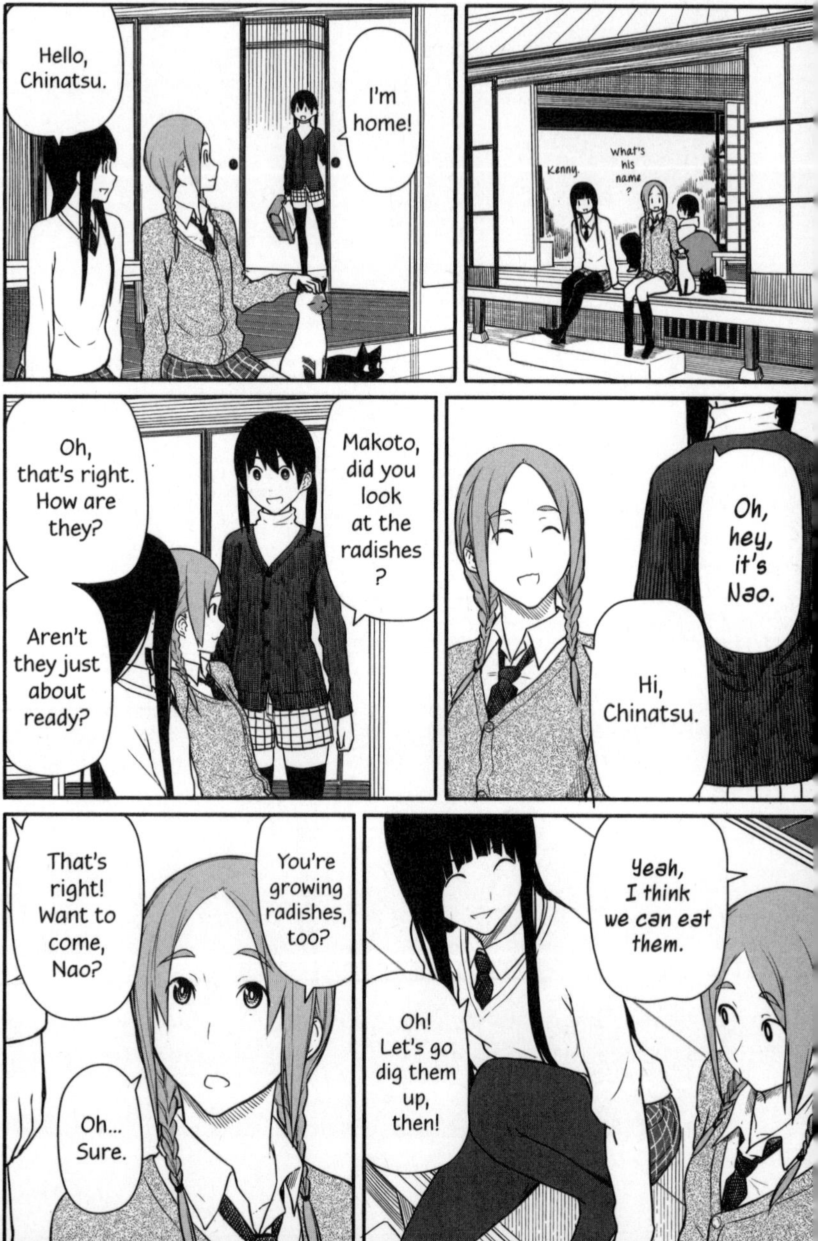
What's his name?
Kenny.
I'm home!
Hello, Chinatsu.
Oh, hey, it's Nao.
Hi, Chinatsu.
Makoto, did you look at the radishes?
Oh, that's right. How are they?
Aren't they just about ready?
Yeah, I think we can eat them.
Oh! Let's go dig them up, then!
You're growing radishes, too?
That's right! Want to come, Nao?
Oh... Sure.

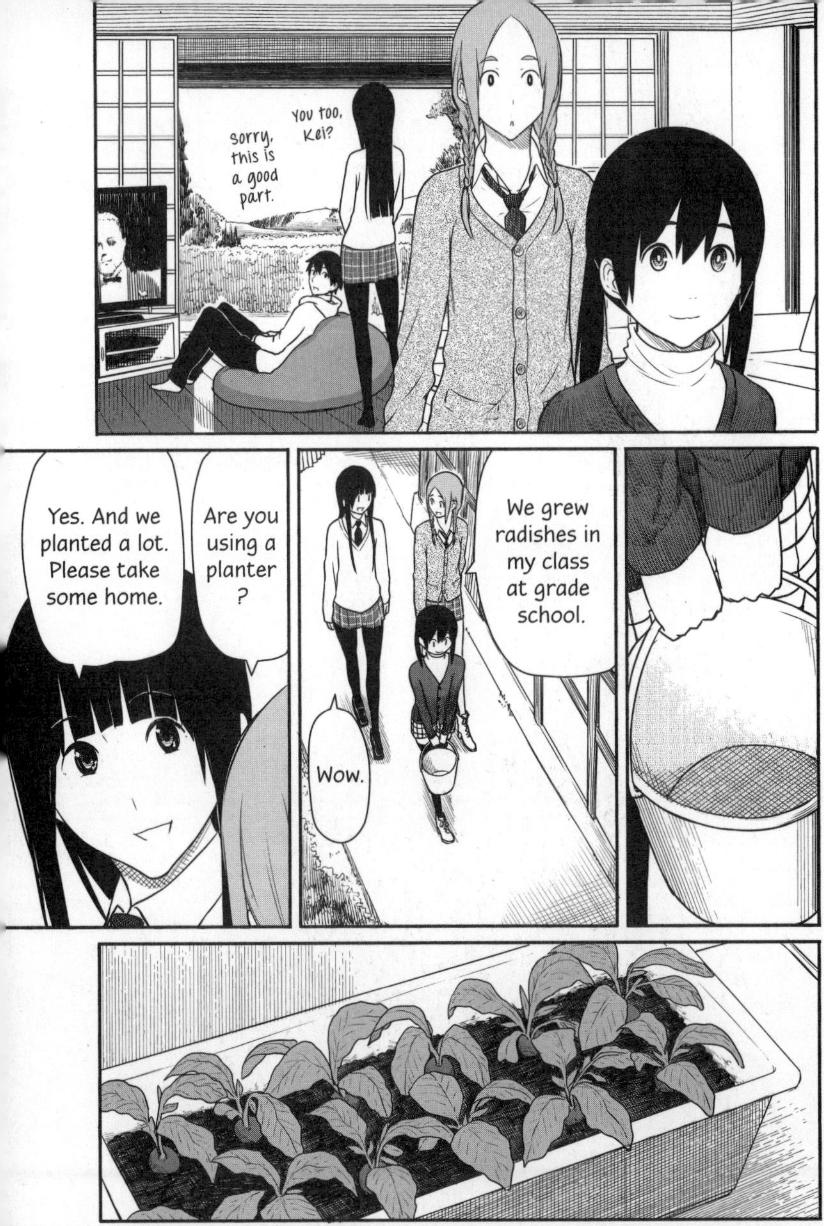
You too, Kei?
sorry, this is a good part.
We grew radishes in my class at grade school.
Wow.
Are you using a planter?
Yes. And we planted a lot. Please take some home.

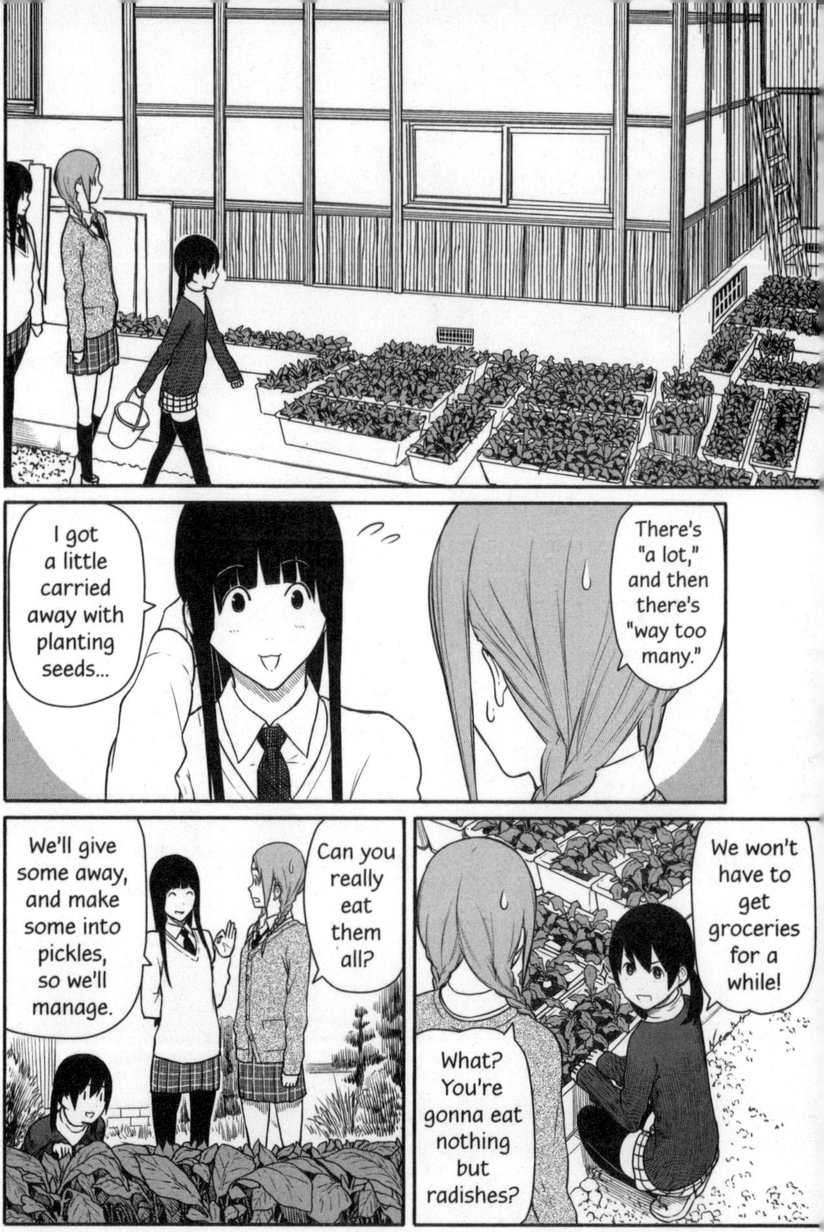
There's "a lot," and then there's "way too many."
I got a little carried away with planting seeds...
We won't have to get groceries for a while!
What? You're gonna eat nothing but radishes?
Can you really eat them all?
We'll give some away, and make some into pickles, so we'll manage.

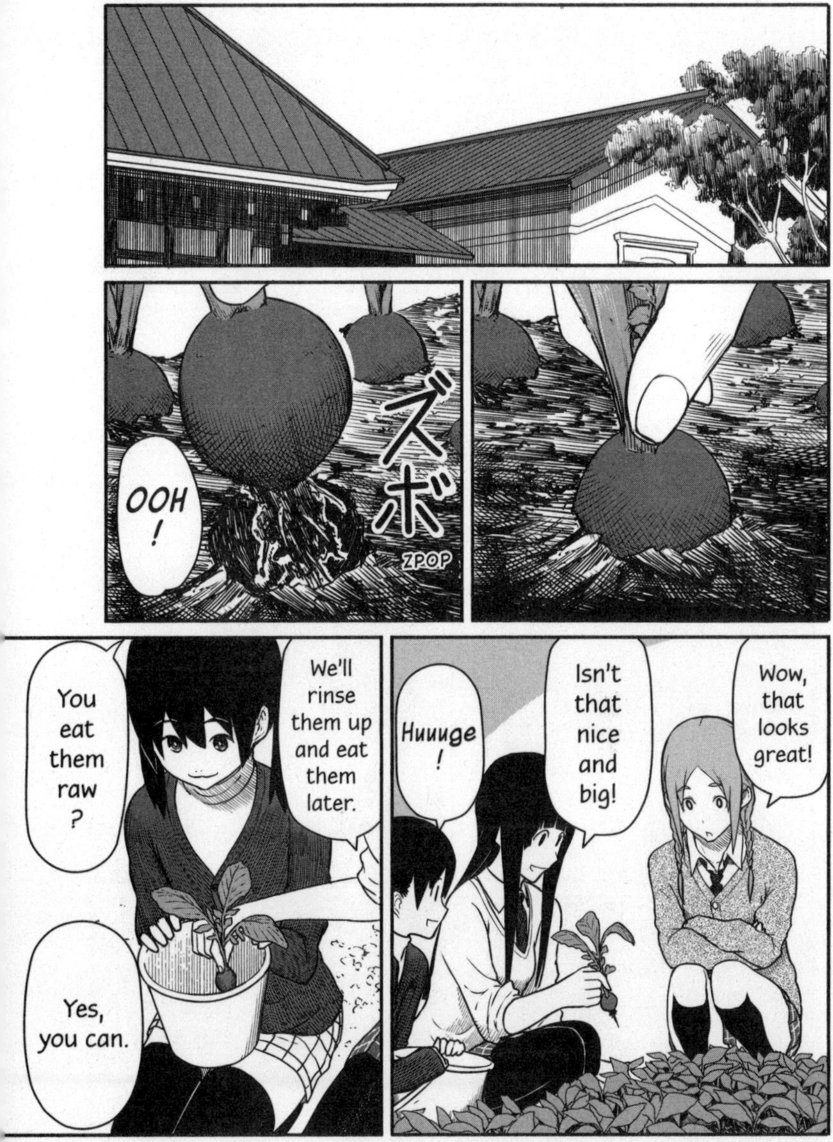
ズボ
ZPOP
OOH!
Wow, that looks great!
Isn't that nice and big!
Huuuge!
We'll rinse them up and eat them later.
You eat them raw?
Yes, you can.

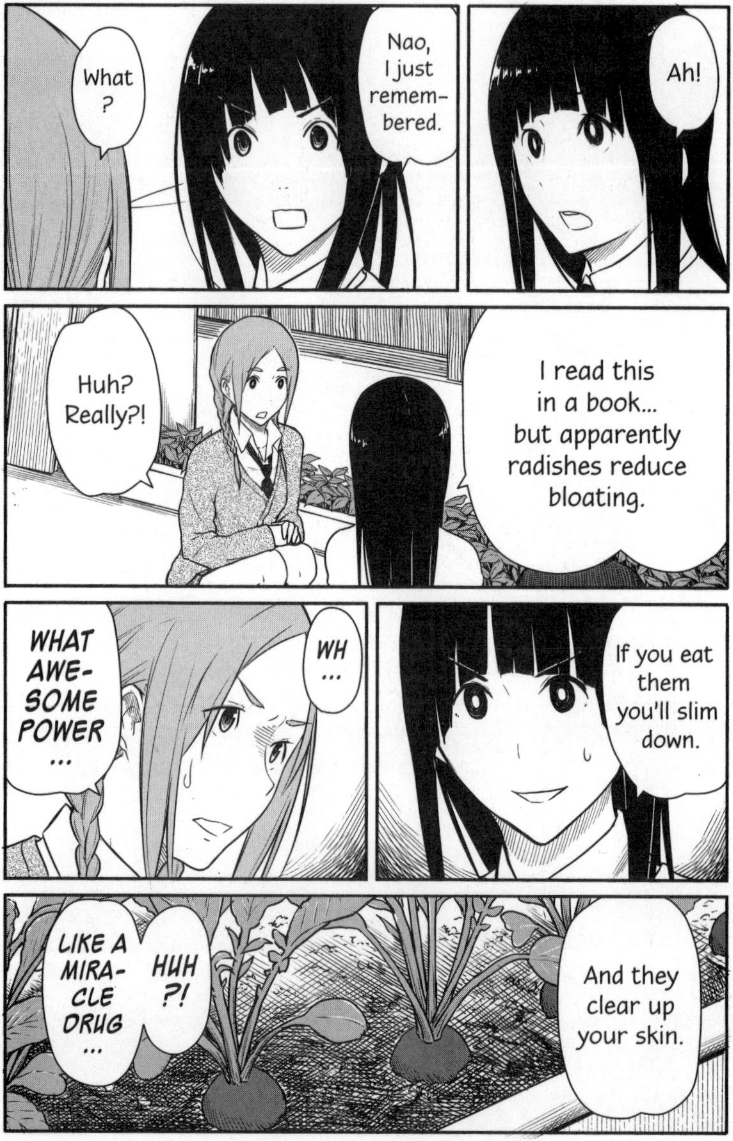
Ah!
Nao, I just remembered.
What?
I read this in a book... but apparently radishes reduce bloating.
Huh? Really?!
If you eat them you'll slim down.
WH...
WHAT AWESOME POWER...
And they clear up your skin.
HUH?!
LIKE A MIRACLE DRUG...

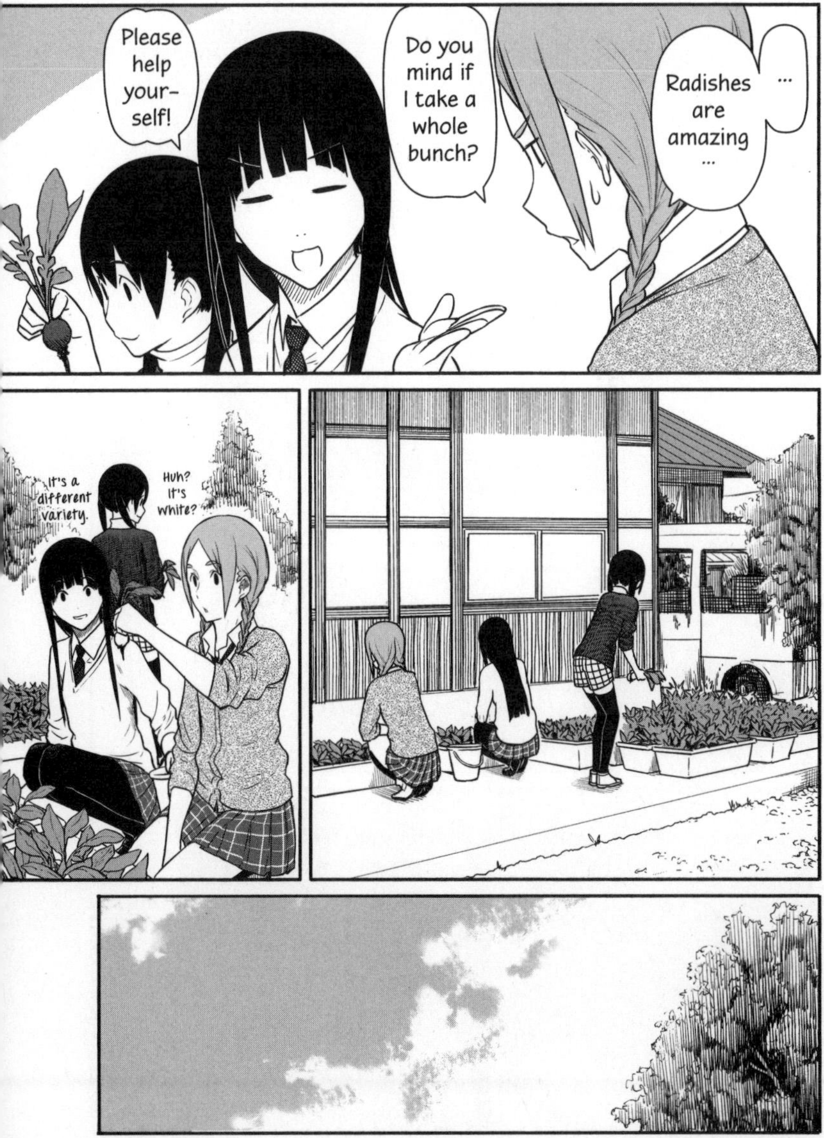
...
Radishes are amazing ...
Do you mind if I take a whole bunch?
Please help your-self!
Huh? It's white?
It's a different variety.

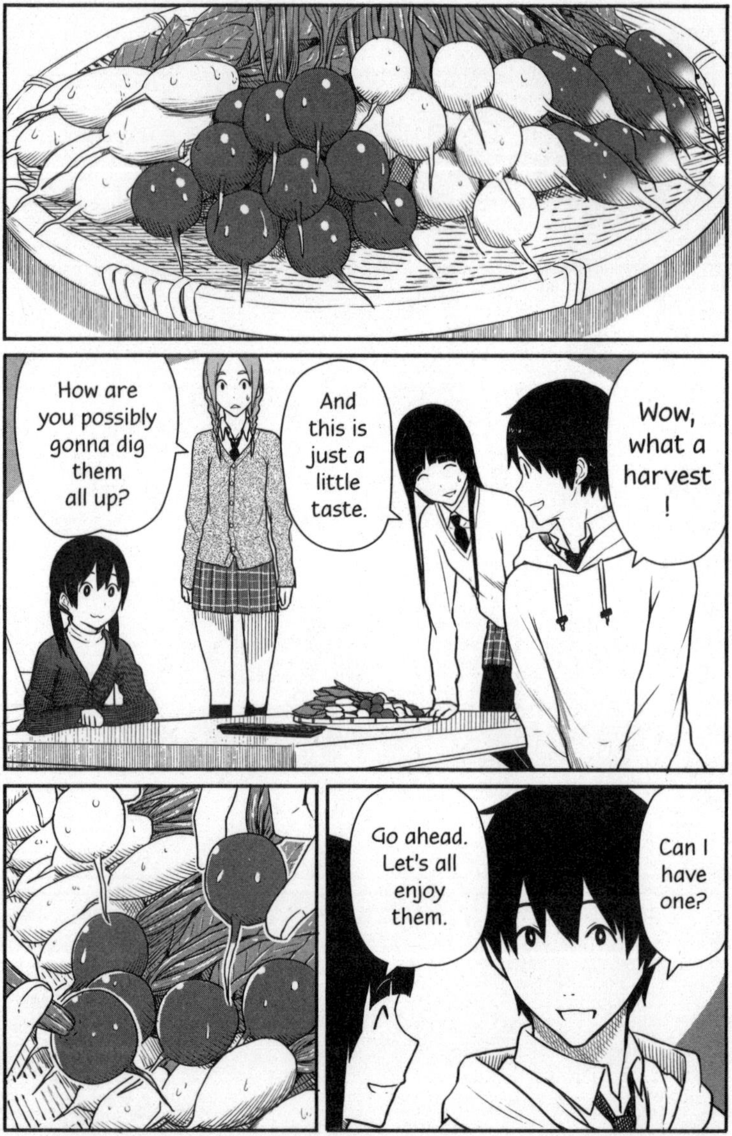
Wow, what a harvest!
And this is just a little taste.
How are you possibly gonna dig them all up?
Can I have one?
Go ahead. Let's all enjoy them.

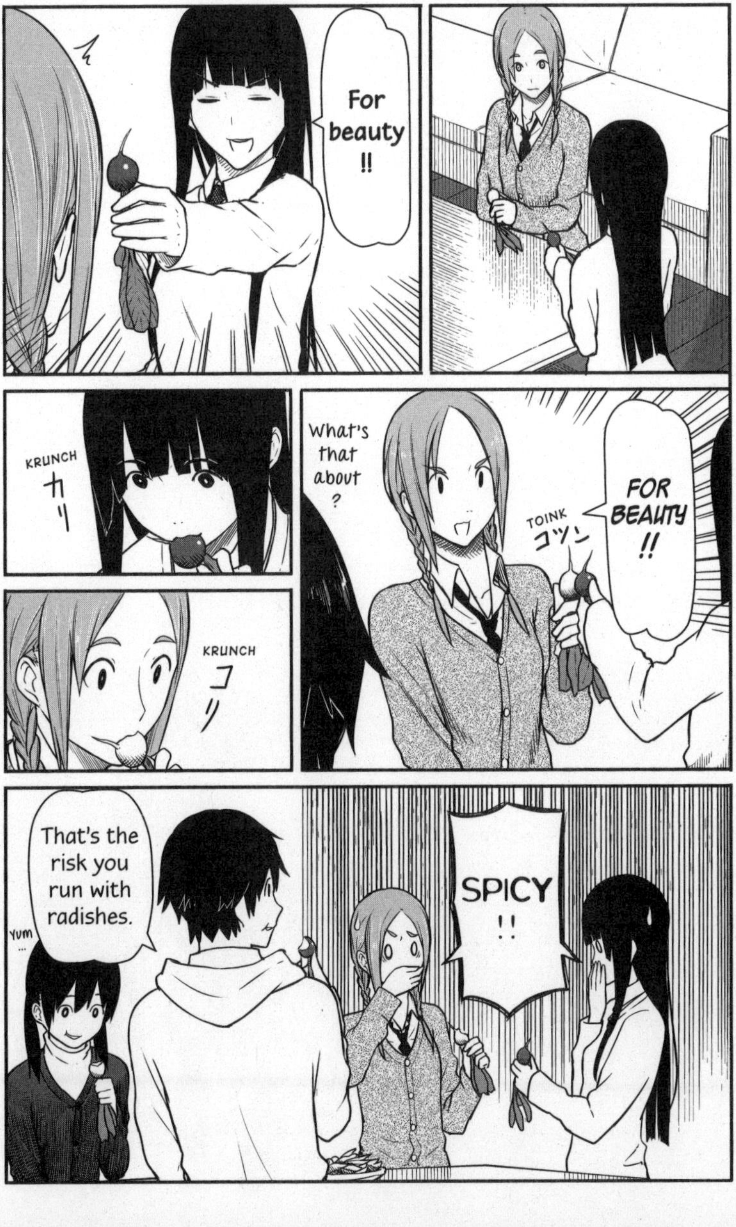
For beauty!!
FOR BEAUTY!!
TOINK
コツン
What's that about?
KRUNCH
カリ
KRUNCH
コリ
SPICY!!
That's the risk you run with radishes.
Yum...

For
beauty...

Chapter 17
The Paperboy and the Whale

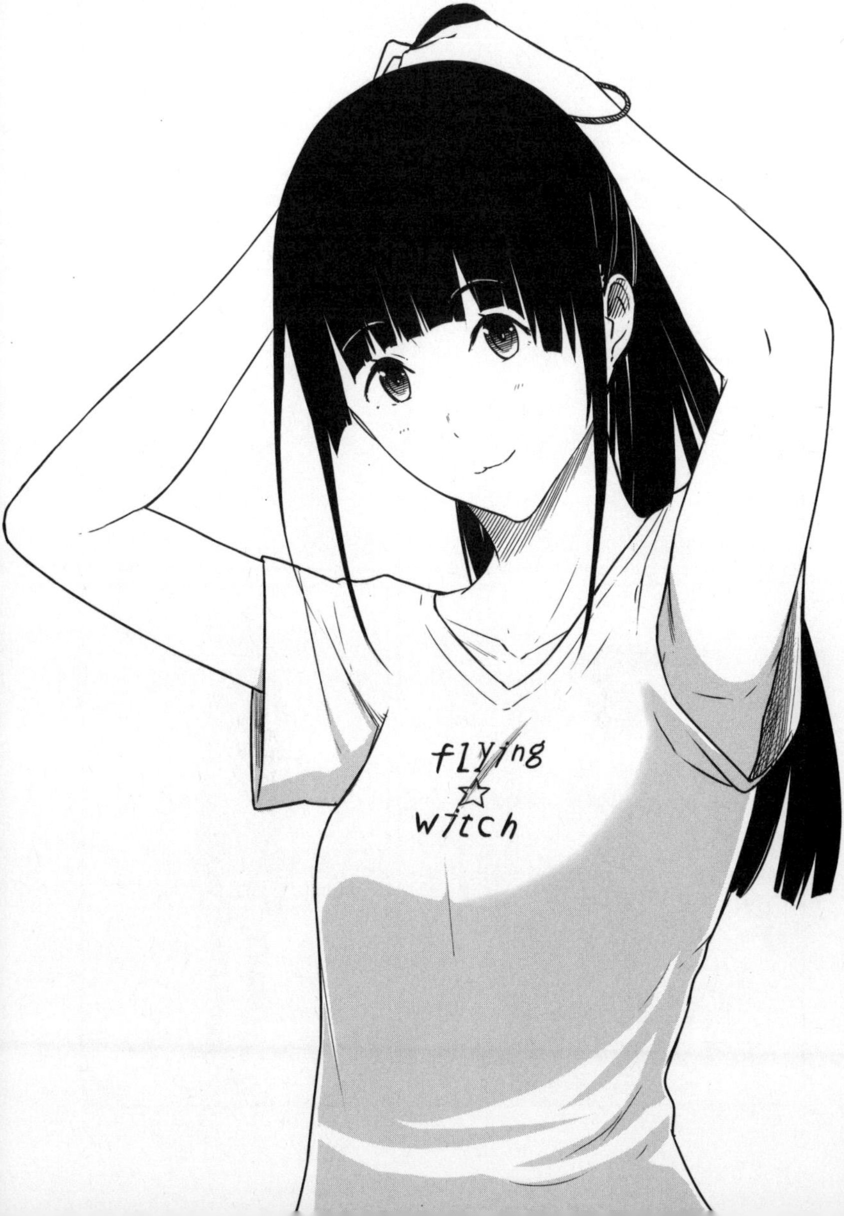
flying
witch

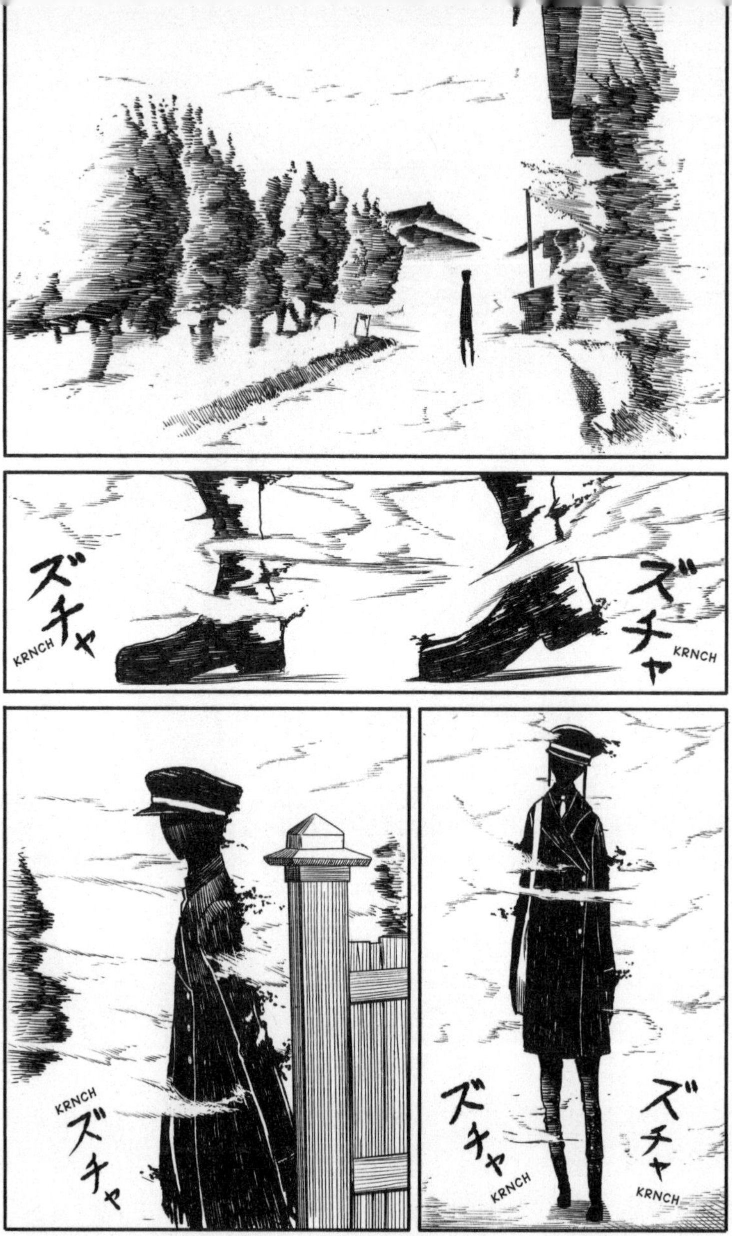
ズチャ
KRNCH
ズチャ
KRNCH
ズチャ
KRNCH
ズチャ
KRNCH
KRNCH
ズチャ

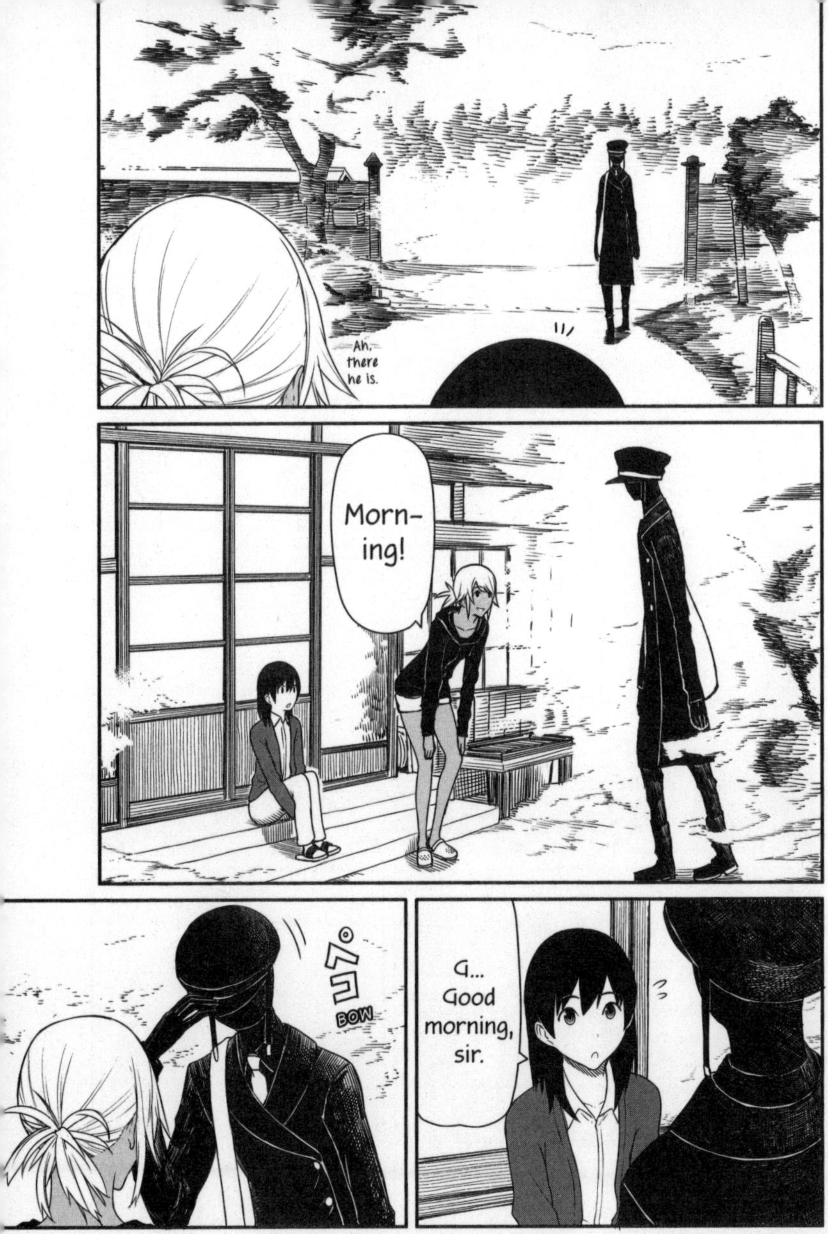
Ah, there he is.
Morn-ing!
G... Good morning, sir.
ペコ
BOW

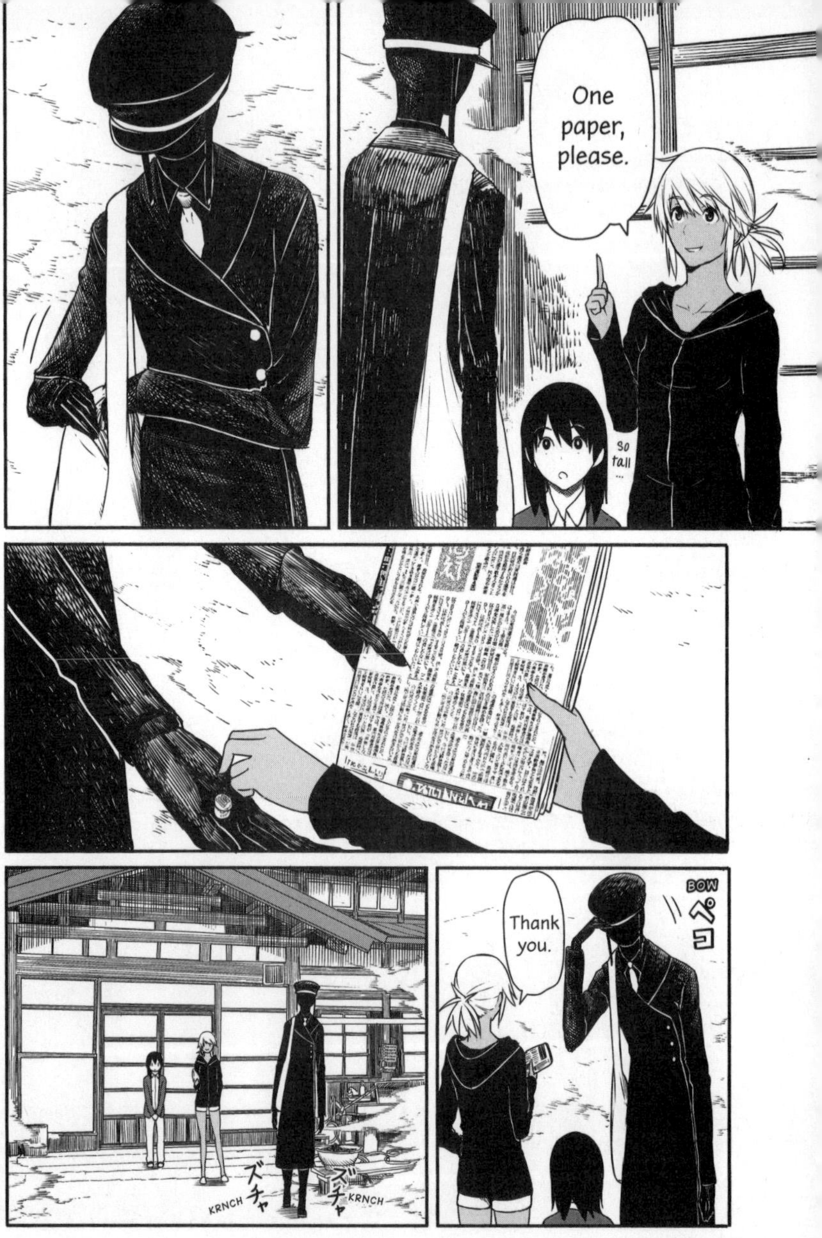
One paper, please.
So tall...
Thank you.
ペコ
BOW
ズチャ
KRNCH
ズチャ
KRNCH

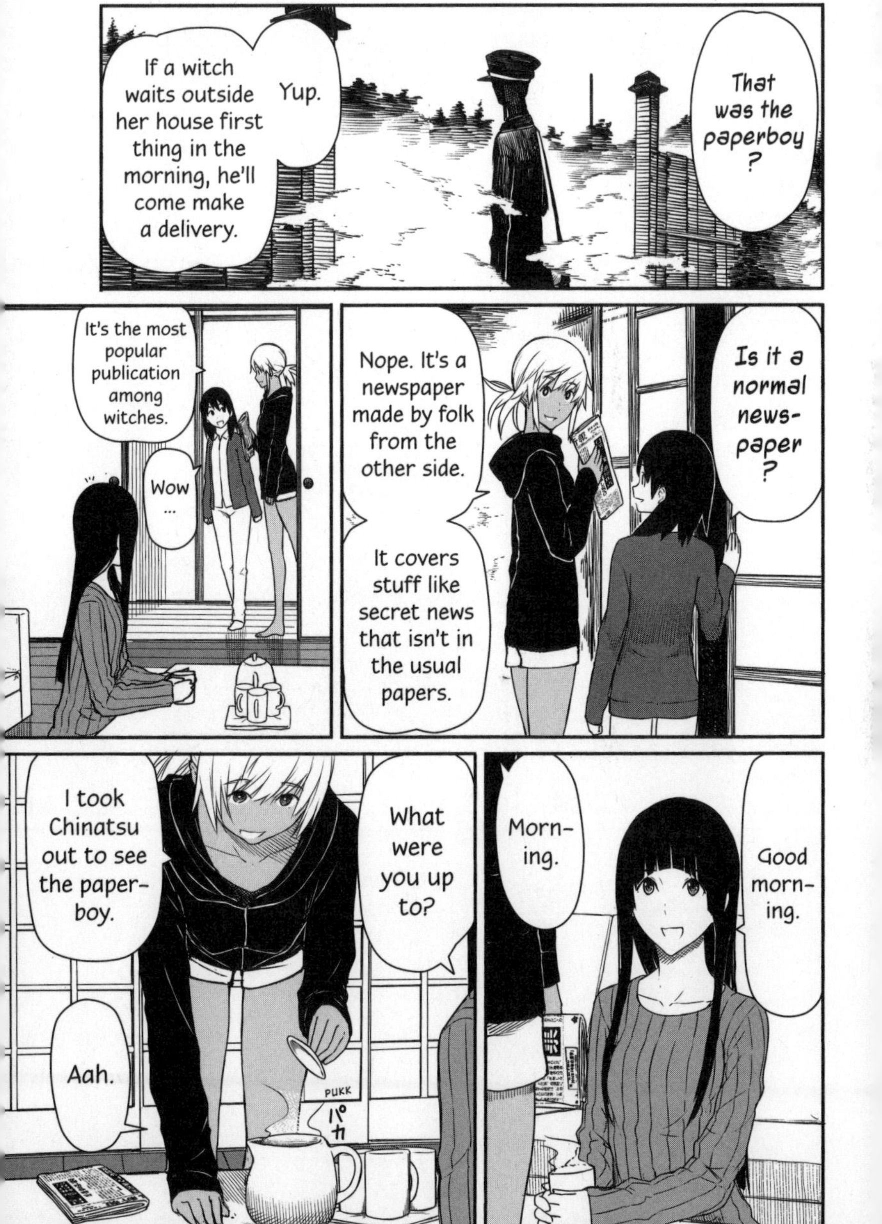
That was the paperboy?
Yup.
If a witch waits outside her house first thing in the morning, he'll come make a delivery.
Is it a normal news-paper?
Nope. It's a newspaper made by folk from the other side.
It covers stuff like secret news that isn't in the usual papers.
It's the most popular publication among witches.
Wow ...
Good morn-ing.
Morn-ing.
What were you up to?
I took Chinatsu out to see the paper-boy.
Aah.
PUKK
パカ

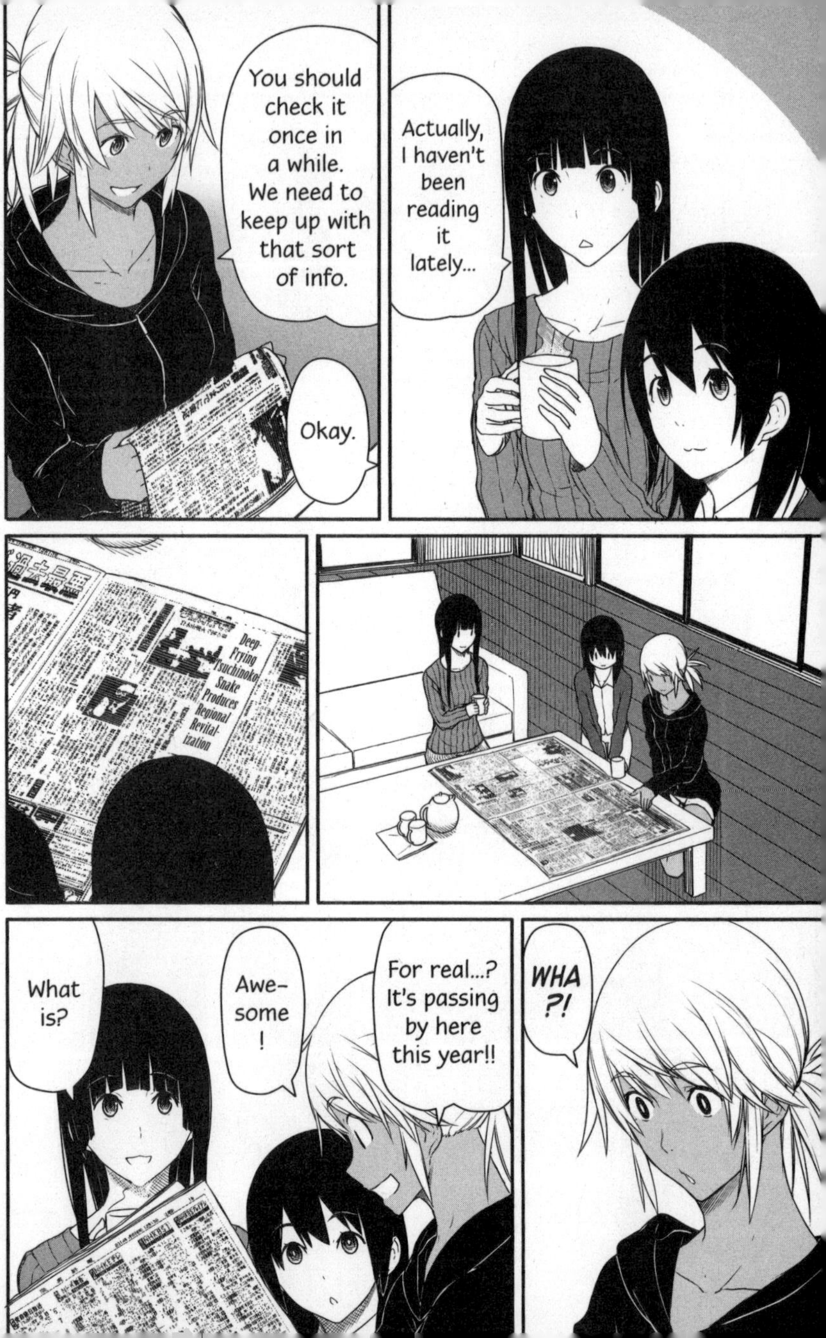
Actually, I haven't been reading it lately...
You should check it once in a while. We need to keep up with that sort of info.
Okay.
Deep-Frying Tsuchinoko Snake Produces Regional Revital-ization
WHA ?!
For real...? It's passing by here this year!!
Awe-some !
What is?

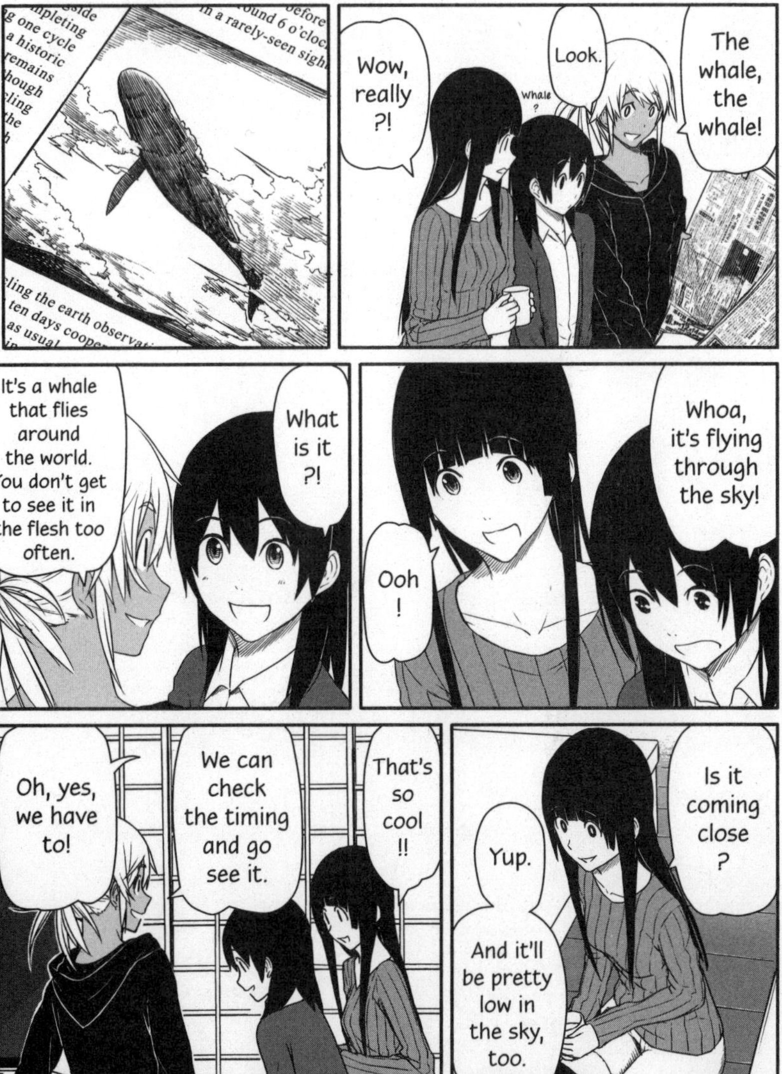
The whale, the whale!
Look.
Whale?
Wow, really?!
Whoa, it's flying through the sky!
Ooh!
What is it?!
It's a whale that flies around the world. You don't get to see it in the flesh too often.
Is it coming close?
Yup.
And it'll be pretty low in the sky, too.
That's so cool!!
We can check the timing and go see it.
Oh, yes, we have to!

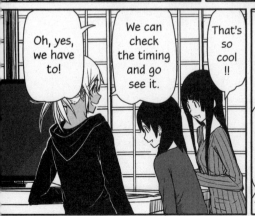

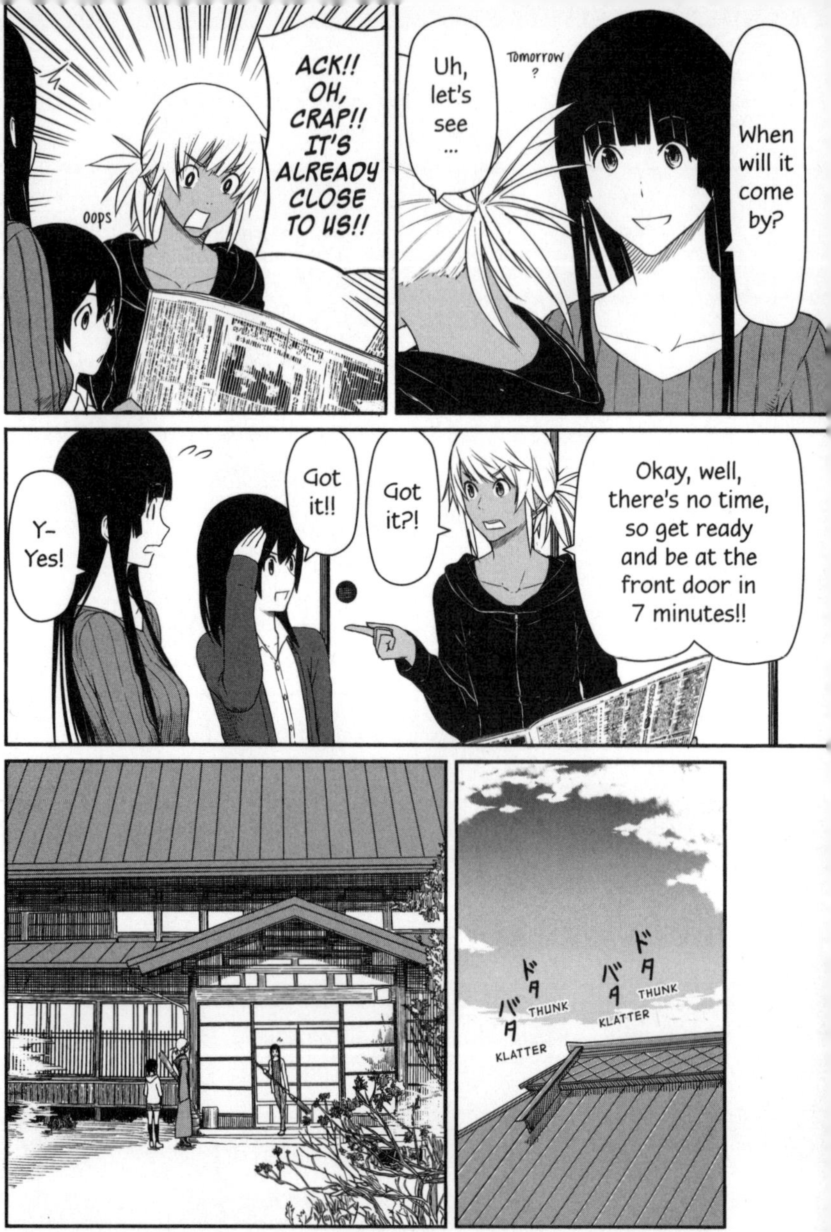
When will it come by?
Tomorrow ?
Uh, let's see ...
ACK!! OH, CRAP!! IT'S ALREADY CLOSE TO US!!
oops
Okay, well, there's no time, so get ready and be at the front door in 7 minutes!!
Got it?!
Got it!!
Y- Yes!
ドタ THUNK
バタ KLATTER
ドタ THUNK
バタ KLATTER

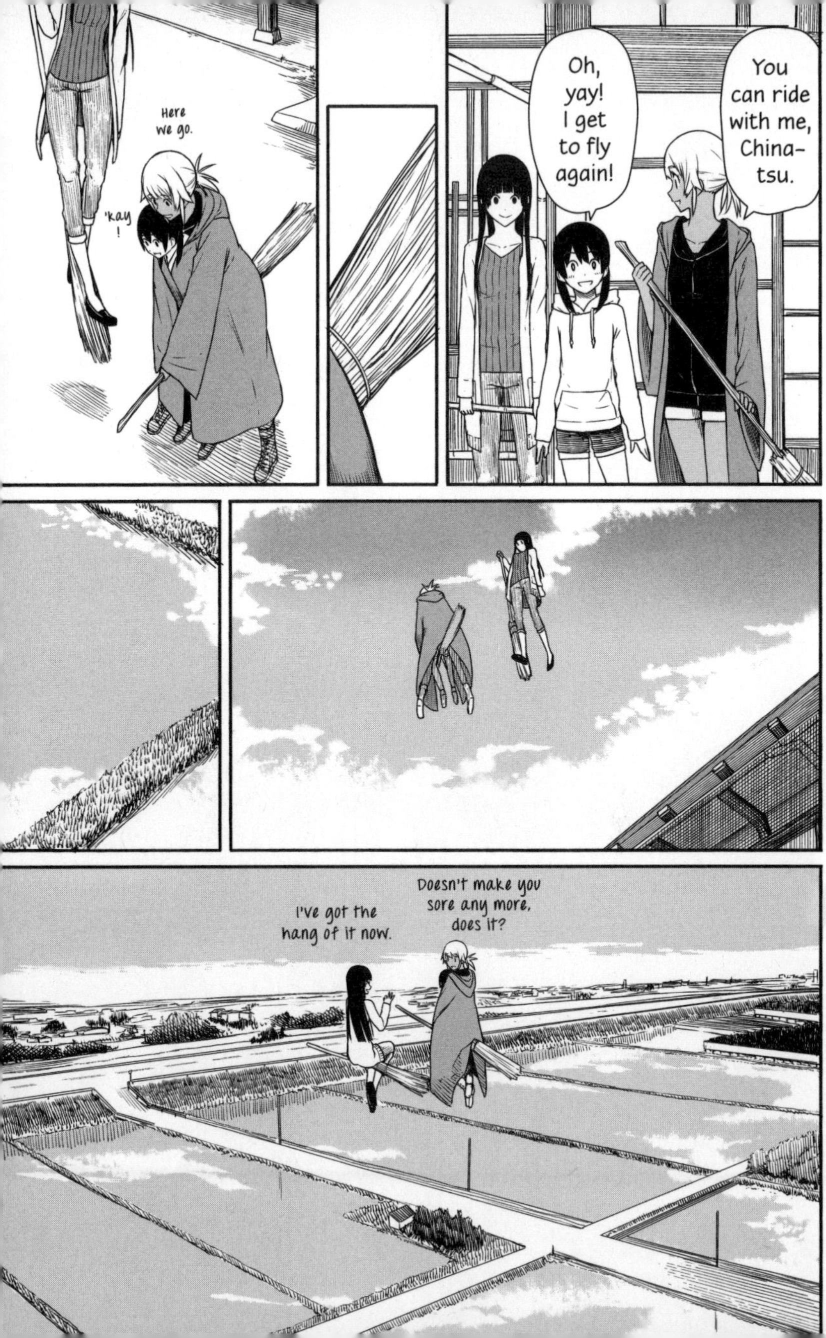
You can ride with me, China-tsu.
Oh, yay! I get to fly again!
Here we go.
'kay!
Doesn't make you sore any more, does it?
I've got the hang of it now.

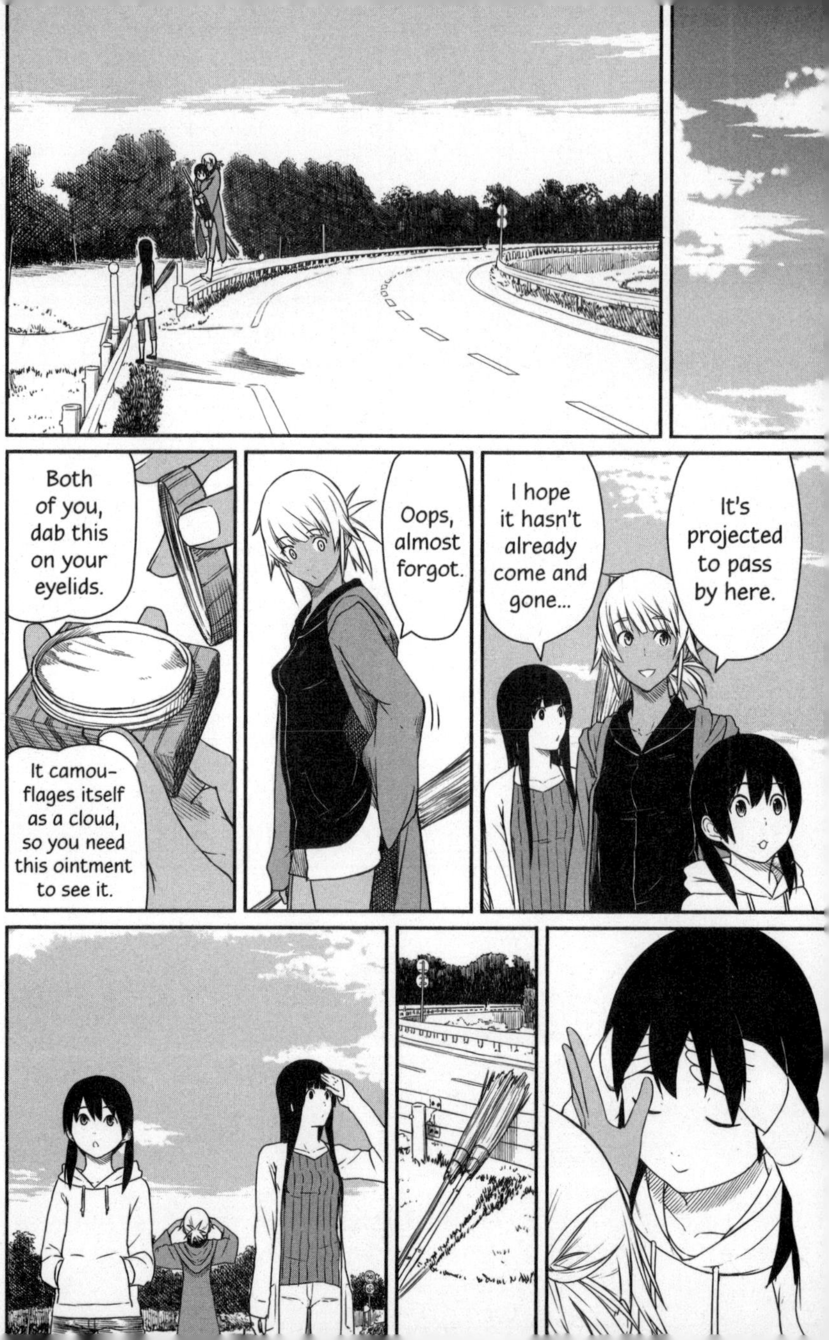
It's projected to pass by here.
I hope it hasn't already come and gone...
Oops, almost forgot.
Both of you, dab this on your eyelids.
It camou-flages itself as a cloud, so you need this ointment to see it.

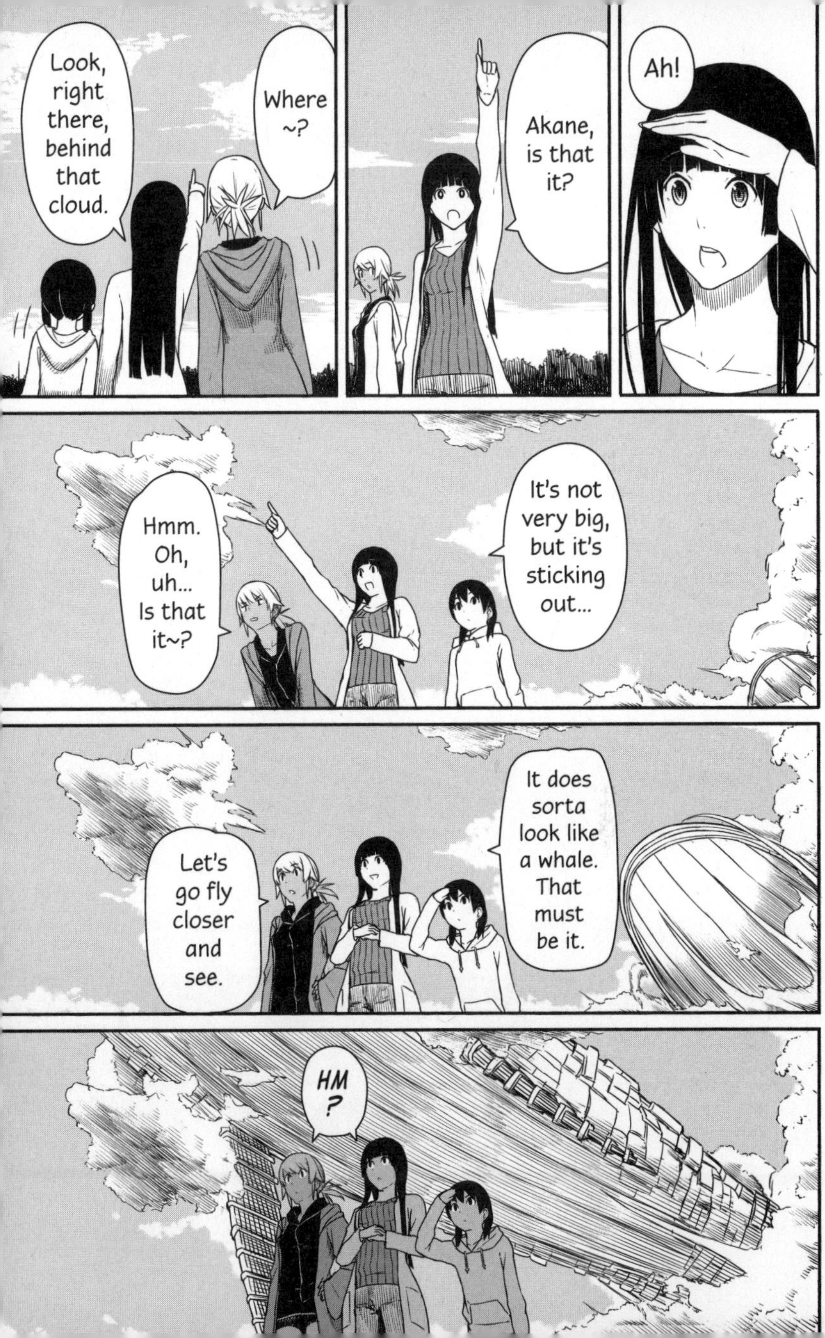

Ah!
Akane, is that it?
Where ~?
Look, right there, behind that cloud.
It's not very big, but it's sticking out...
Hmm. Oh, uh... Is that it~?
It does sorta look like a whale. That must be it.
Let's go fly closer and see.
HM?

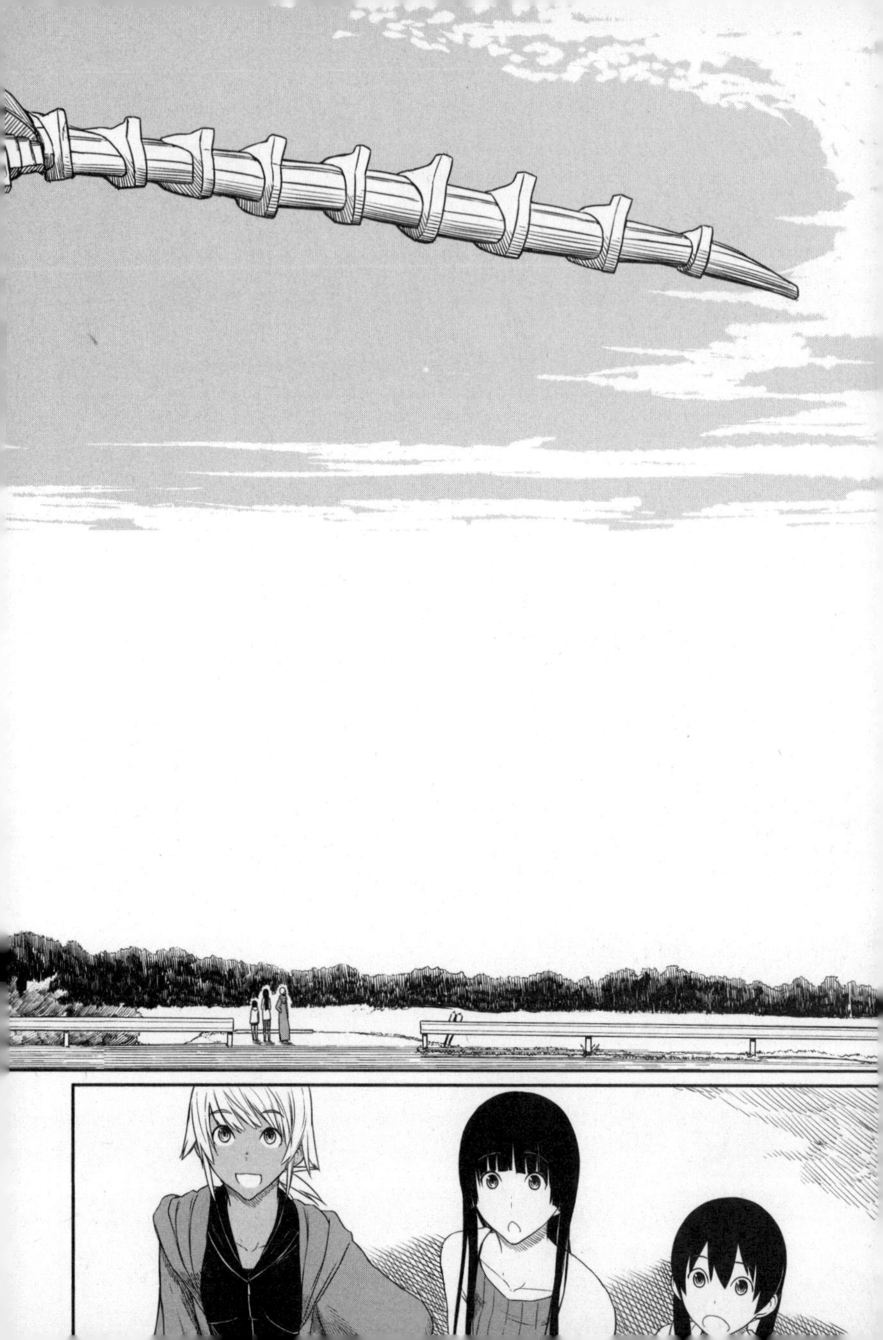

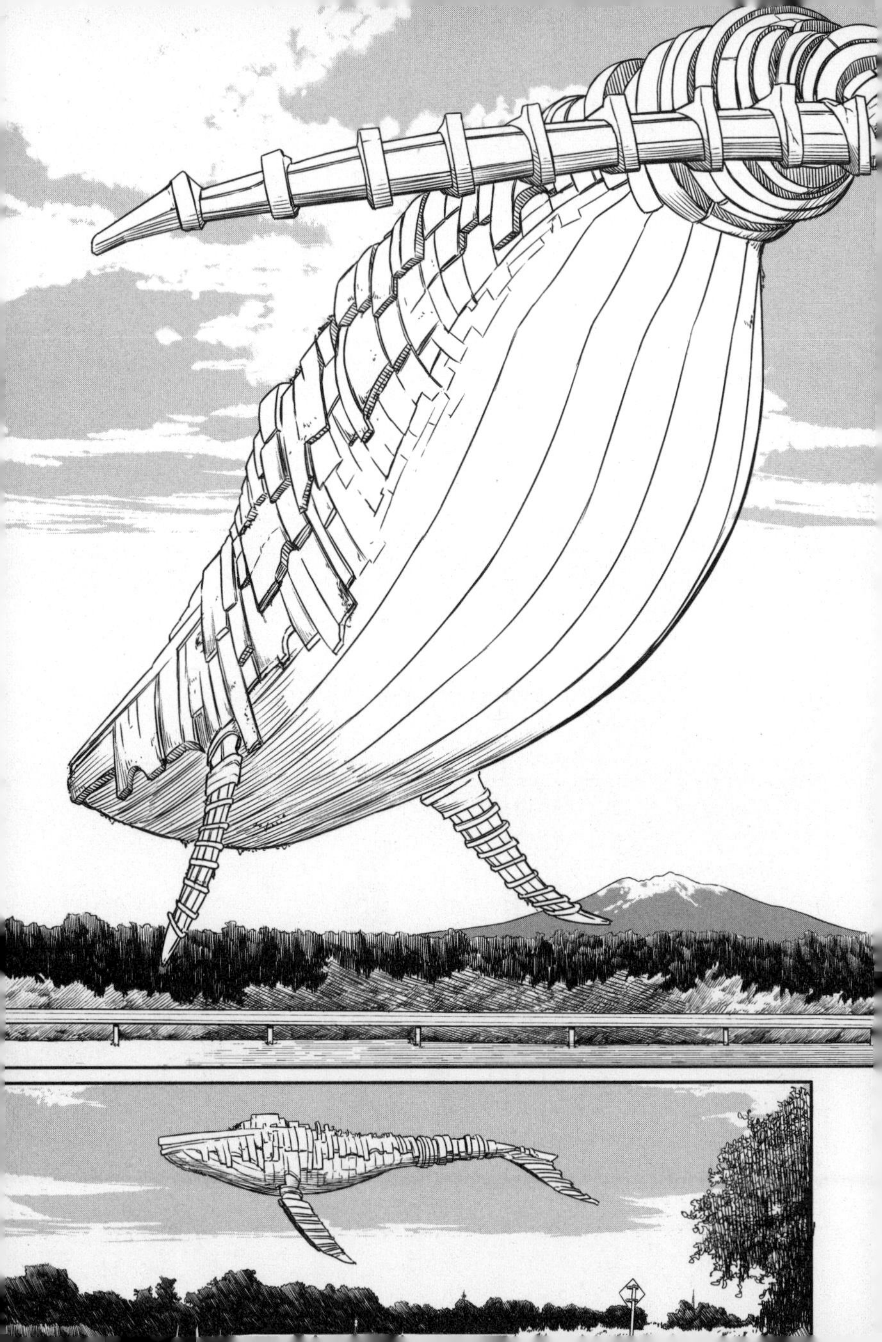

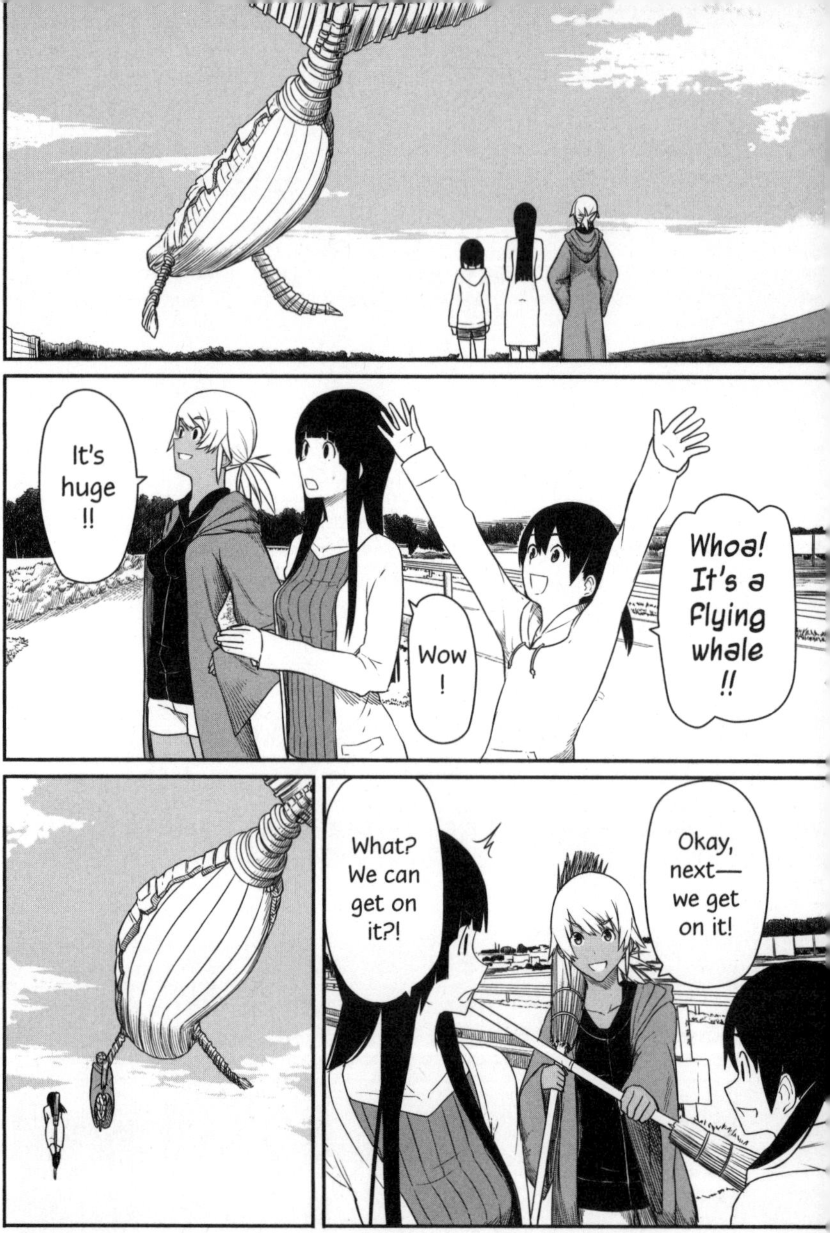
Whoa! It's a flying whale!!
Wow!
It's huge!!
Okay, next— we get on it!
What? We can get on it?!

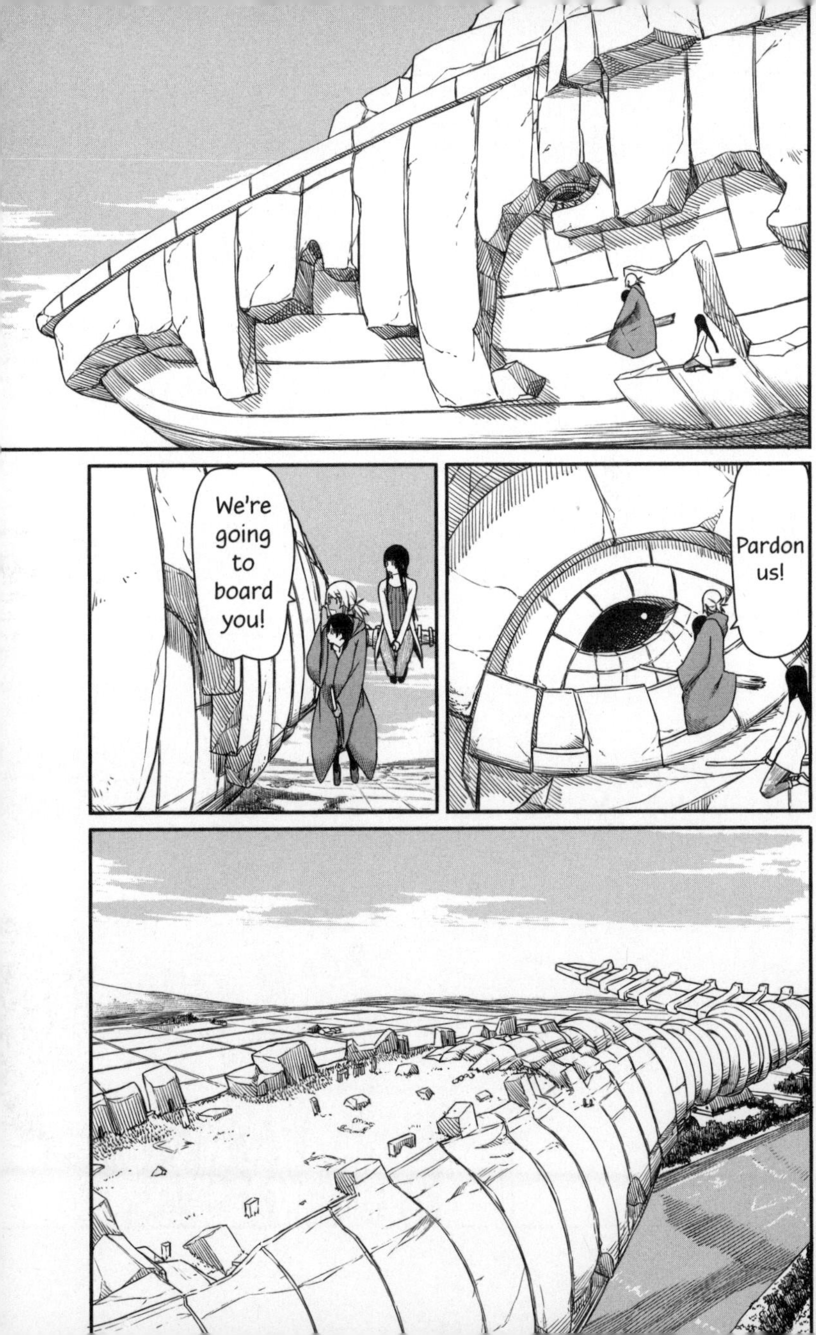
Pardon us!
We're going to board you!

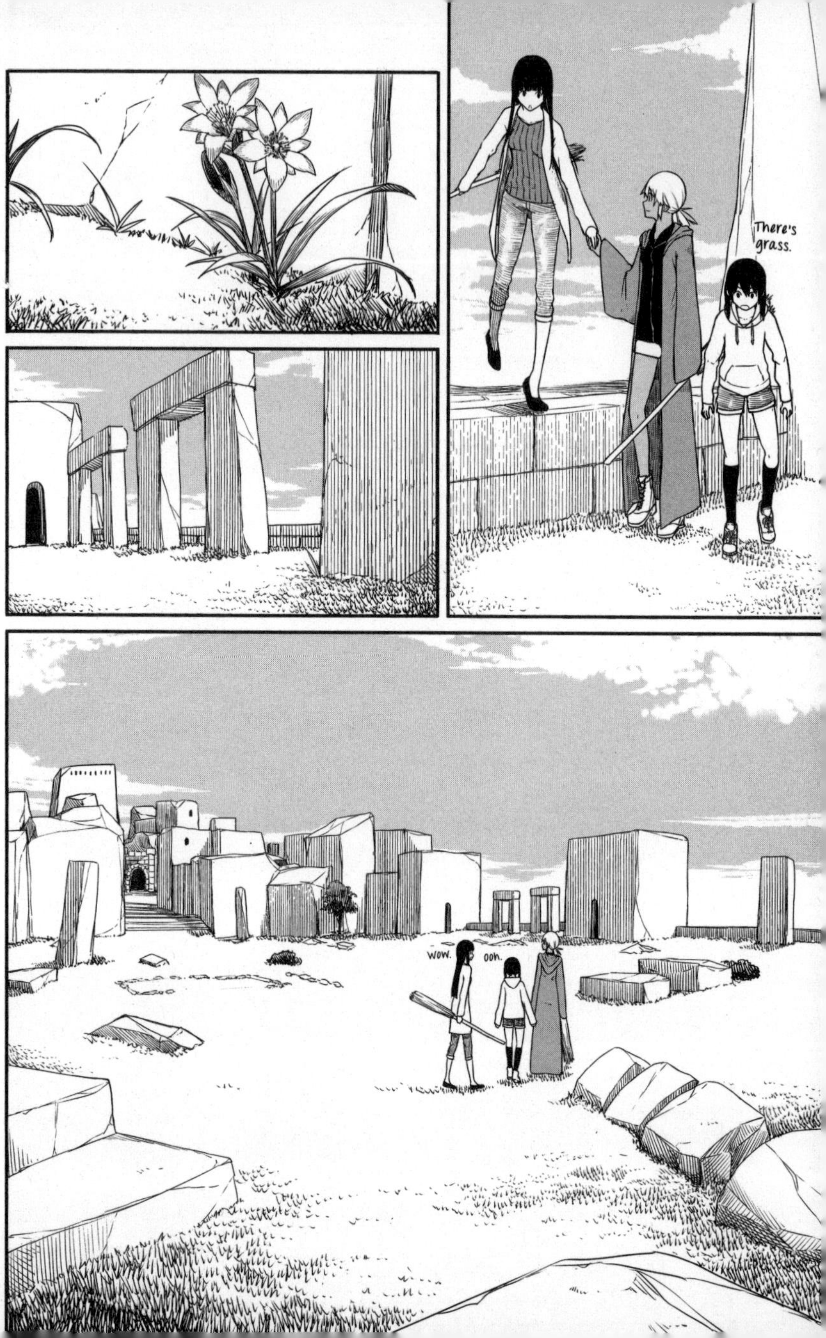
There's grass.
ooh.
wow.

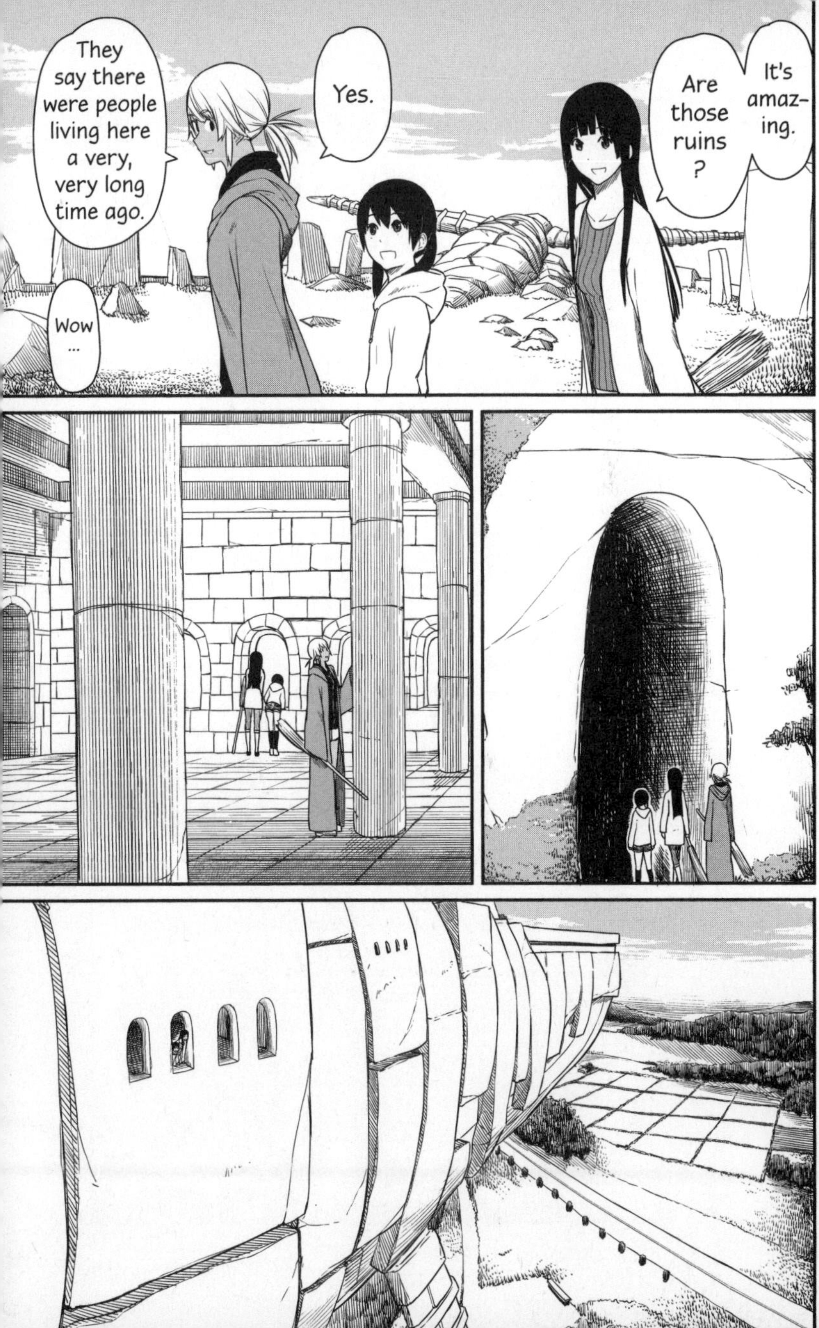
It's amazing.
Are those ruins?
Yes.
They say there were people living here a very, very long time ago.
Wow ...

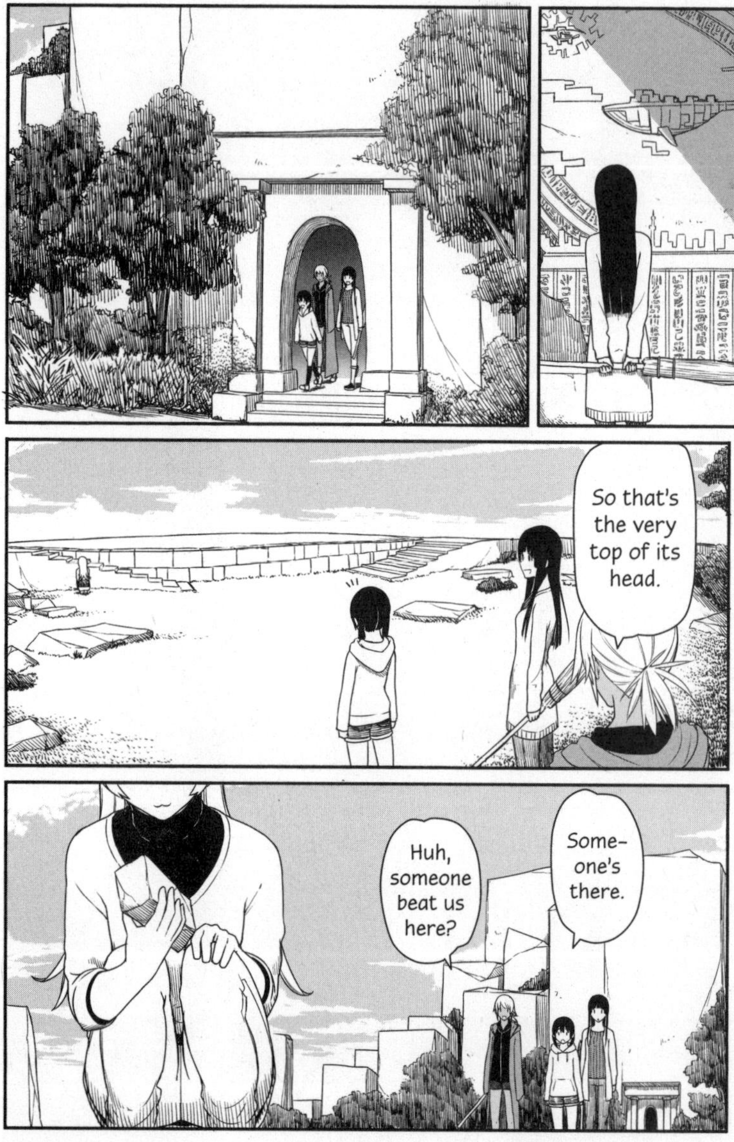
So that's the very top of its head.
Some-one's there.
Huh, someone beat us here?

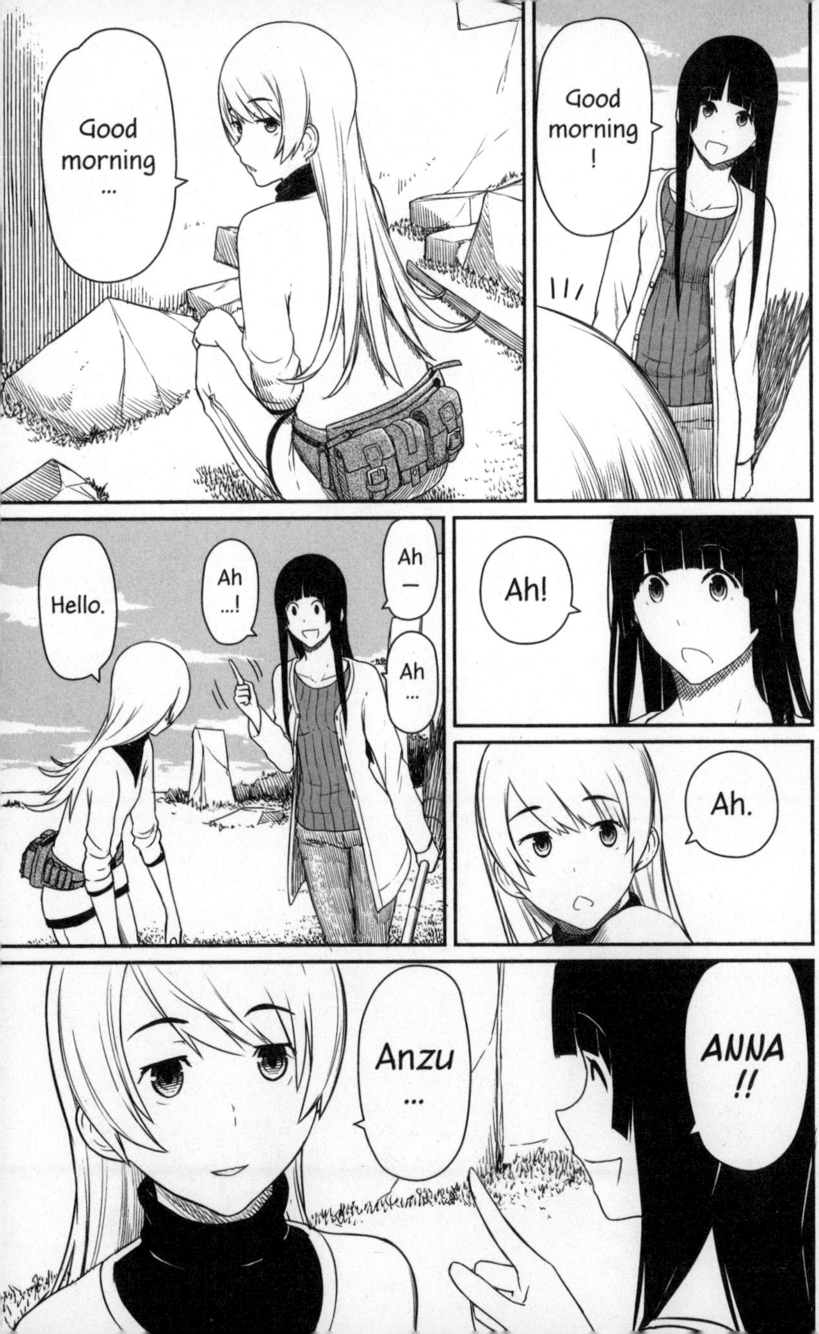
Good morning !
Good morning ...
Ah!
Ah.
Ah —
Ah ...
Ah ...!
Hello.
ANNA !!
Anzu ...

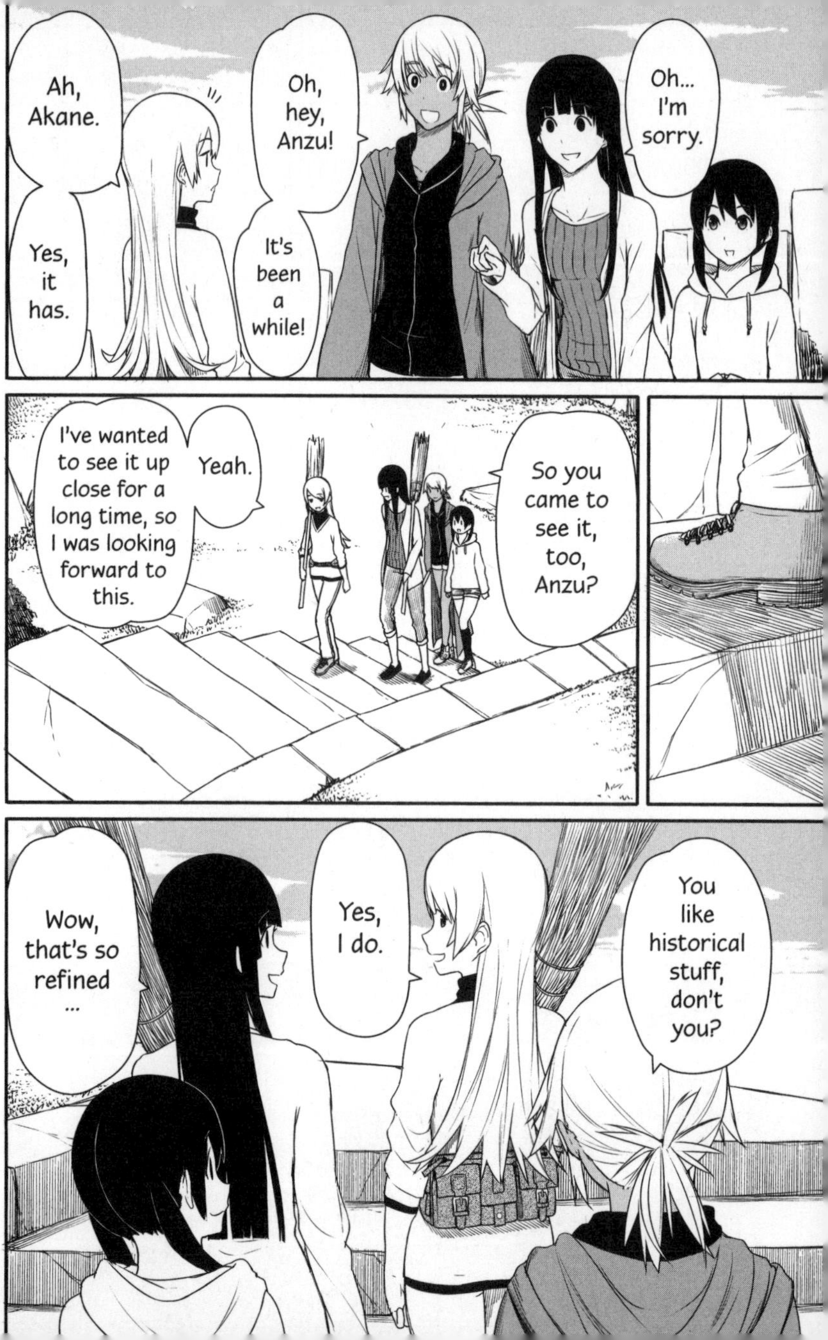
Oh... I'm sorry.
Oh, hey, Anzu!
It's been a while!
Ah, Akane.
Yes, it has.
So you came to see it, too, Anzu?
Yeah.
I've wanted to see it up close for a long time, so I was looking forward to this.
You like historical stuff, don't you?
Yes, I do.
Wow, that's so refined ...

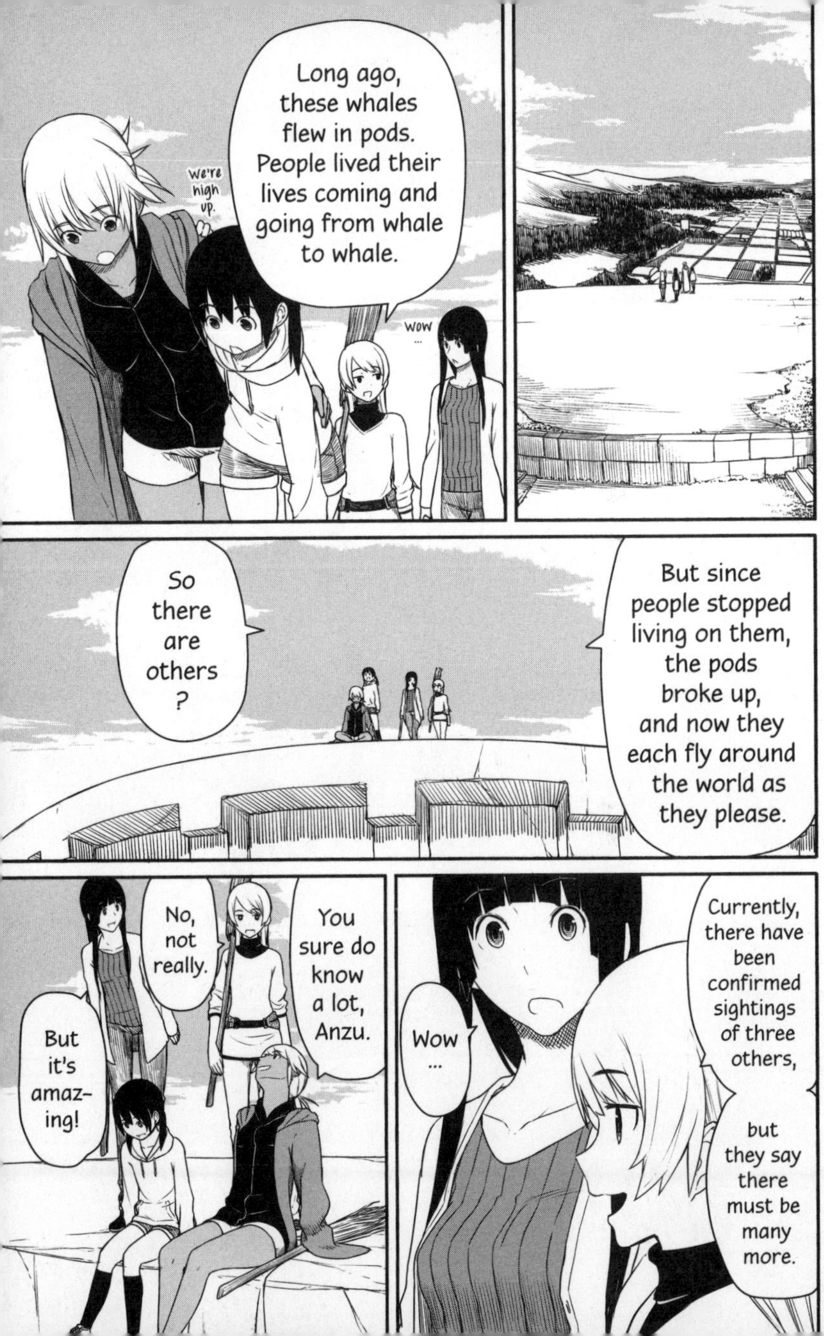

Long ago, these whales flew in pods. People lived their lives coming and going from whale to whale.
Wow ...
We're high up.
But since people stopped living on them, the pods broke up, and now they each fly around the world as they please.
So there are others ?
Currently, there have been confirmed sightings of three others,
but they say there must be many more.
Wow ...
You sure do know a lot, Anzu.
No, not really.
But it's amaz-ing!

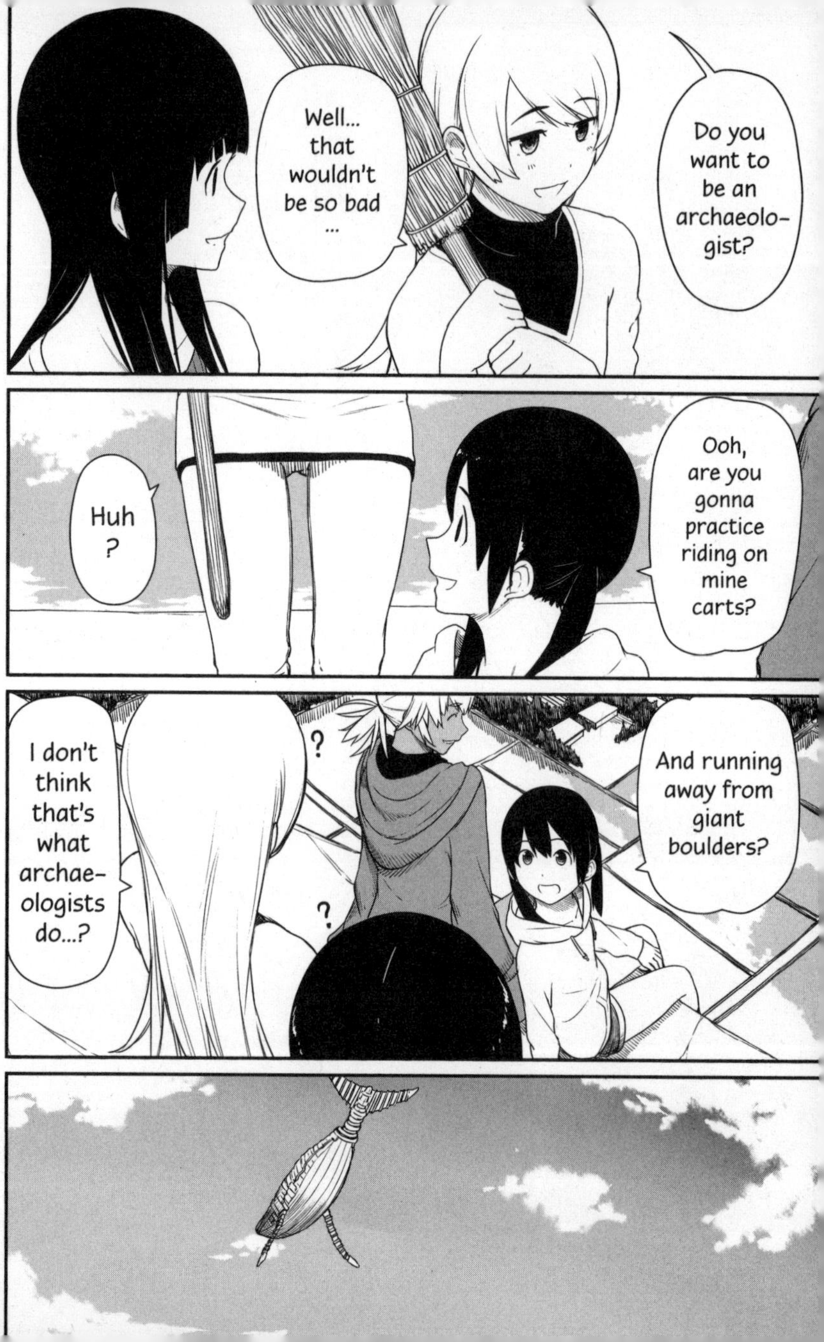
Do you want to be an archaeologist?
Well... that wouldn't be so bad ...
Ooh, are you gonna practice riding on mine carts?
Huh ?
And running away from giant boulders?
?
?
I don't think that's what archaeologists do...?

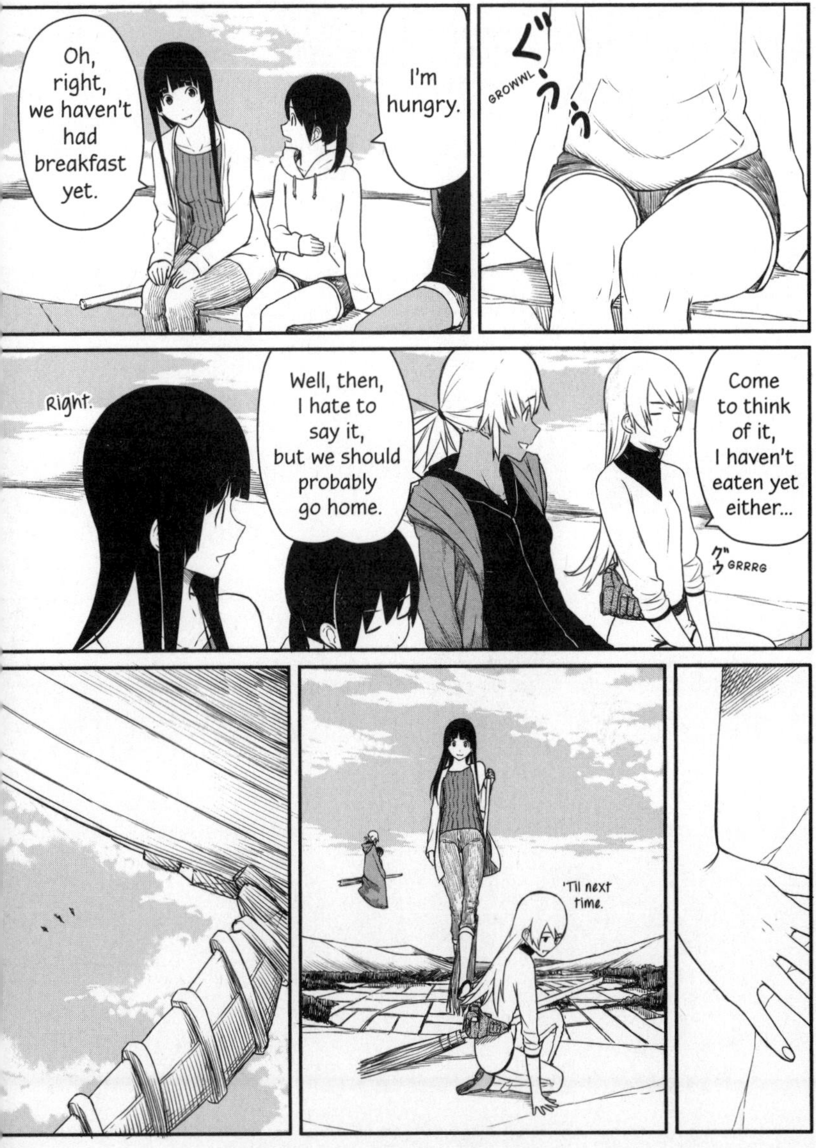
ぐうう
GROWWL
I'm hungry.
Oh, right, we haven't had breakfast yet.
Come to think of it, I haven't eaten yet either...
グゥ
GRRRG
Well, then, I hate to say it, but we should probably go home.
Right.
'Til next time.

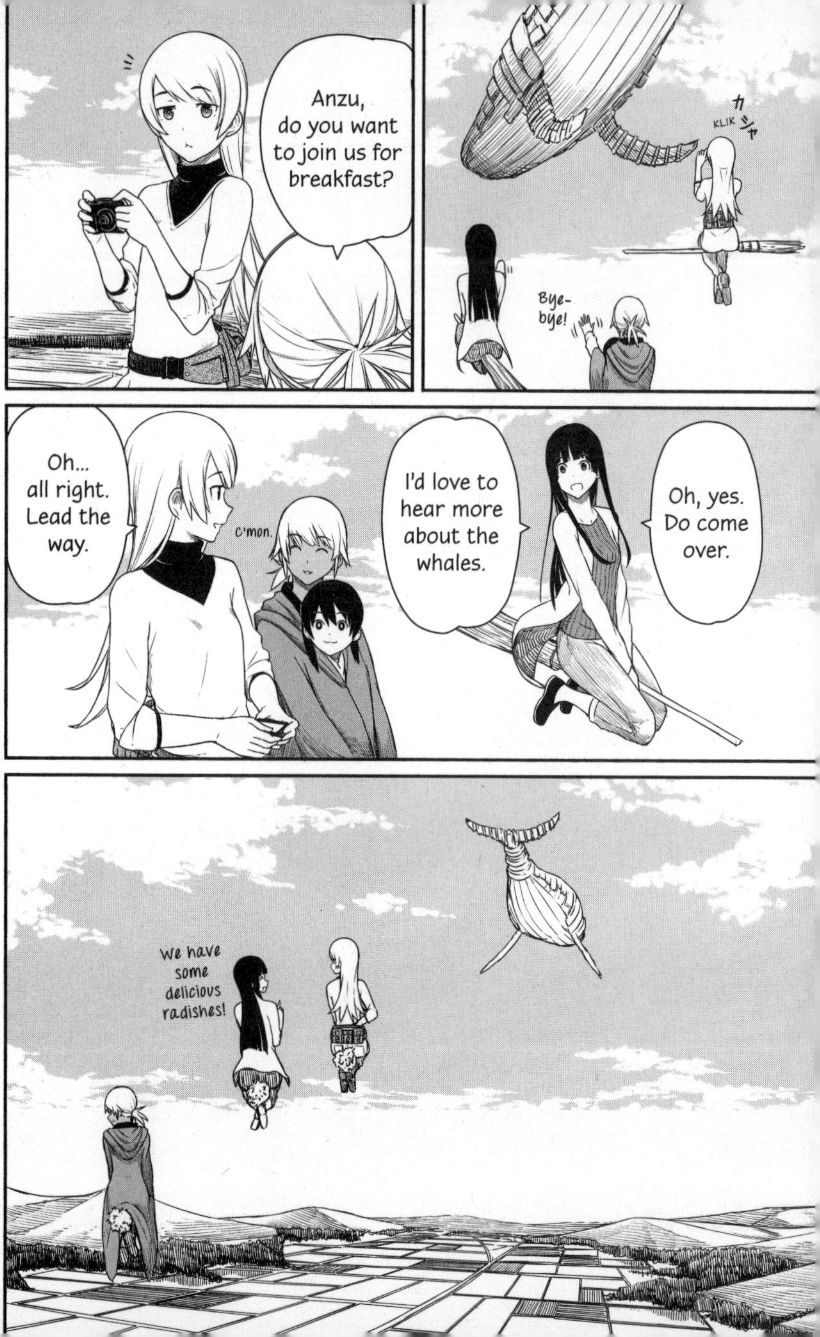
KLIK カシャ
Bye-bye!
Anzu, do you want to join us for breakfast?
Oh, yes. Do come over.
I'd love to hear more about the whales.
C'mon.
Oh... all right. Lead the way.
We have some delicious radishes!

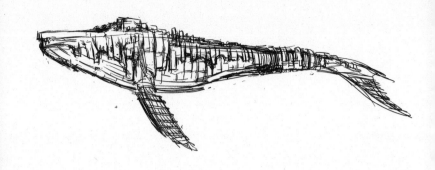

Flying
Witch

Chapter 18
The Connection Between the Frying Pan and Hotcakes

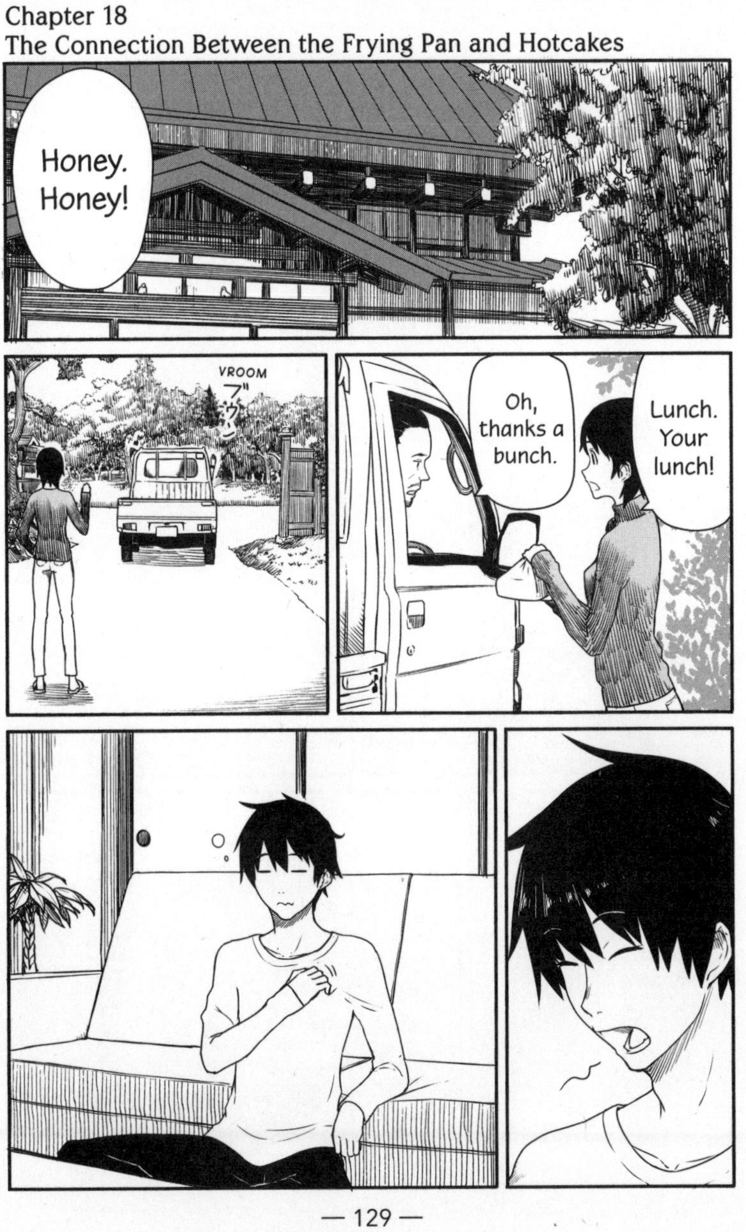
Honey. Honey!
Lunch. Your lunch!
Oh, thanks a bunch.
VROOM

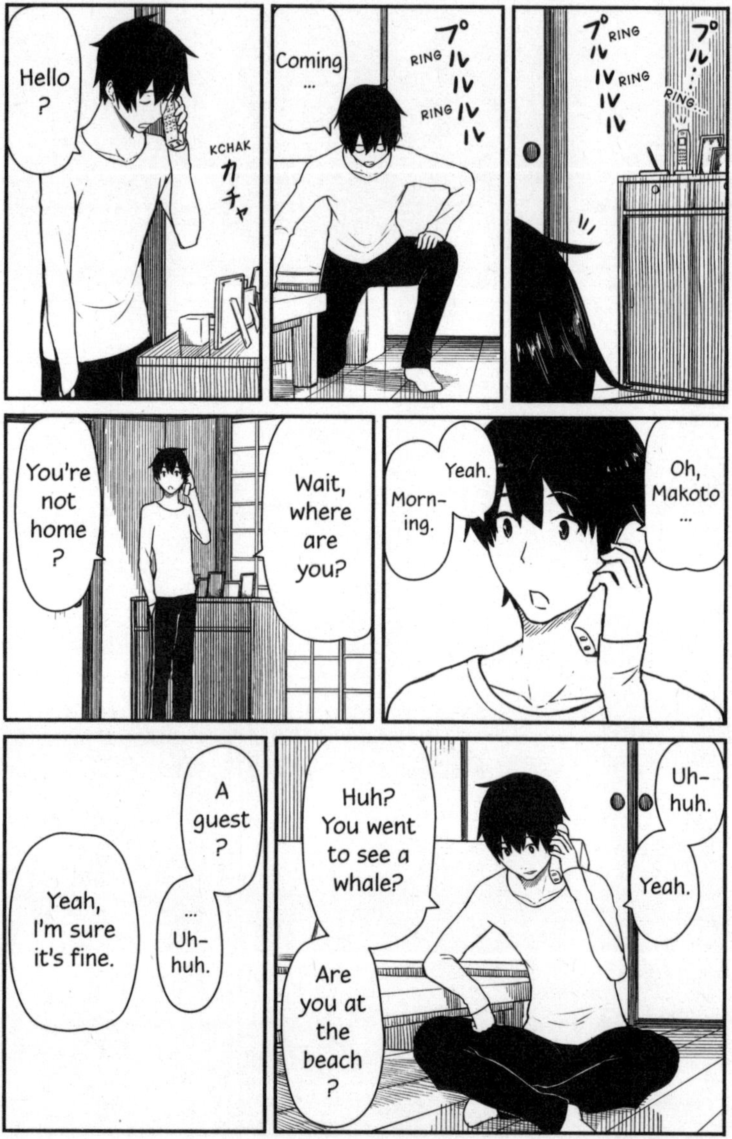
プルルルル RING RING
プル… RING…
Coming …
RING プルルルル RING
Hello ?
KCHAK カチャ
Oh, Makoto …
Yeah. Morn- ing.
Wait, where are you?
You're not home ?
Uh- huh.
Yeah.
Huh? You went to see a whale?
Are you at the beach ?
A guest ?
… Uh- huh.
Yeah, I'm sure it's fine.

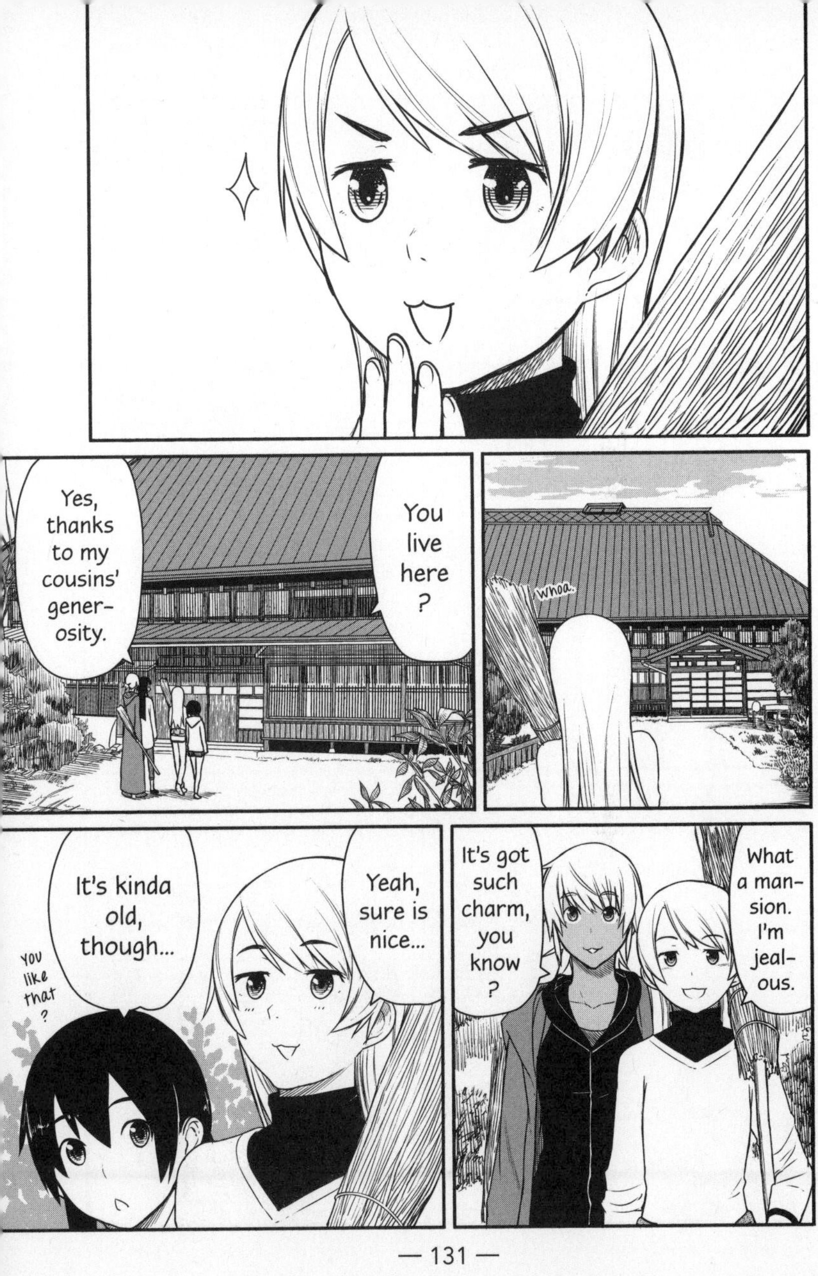
Whoa.
You live here?
Yes, thanks to my cousins' gener-osity.
What a man-sion. I'm jeal-ous.
It's got such charm, you know?
Yeah, sure is nice...
It's kinda old, though...
You like that?

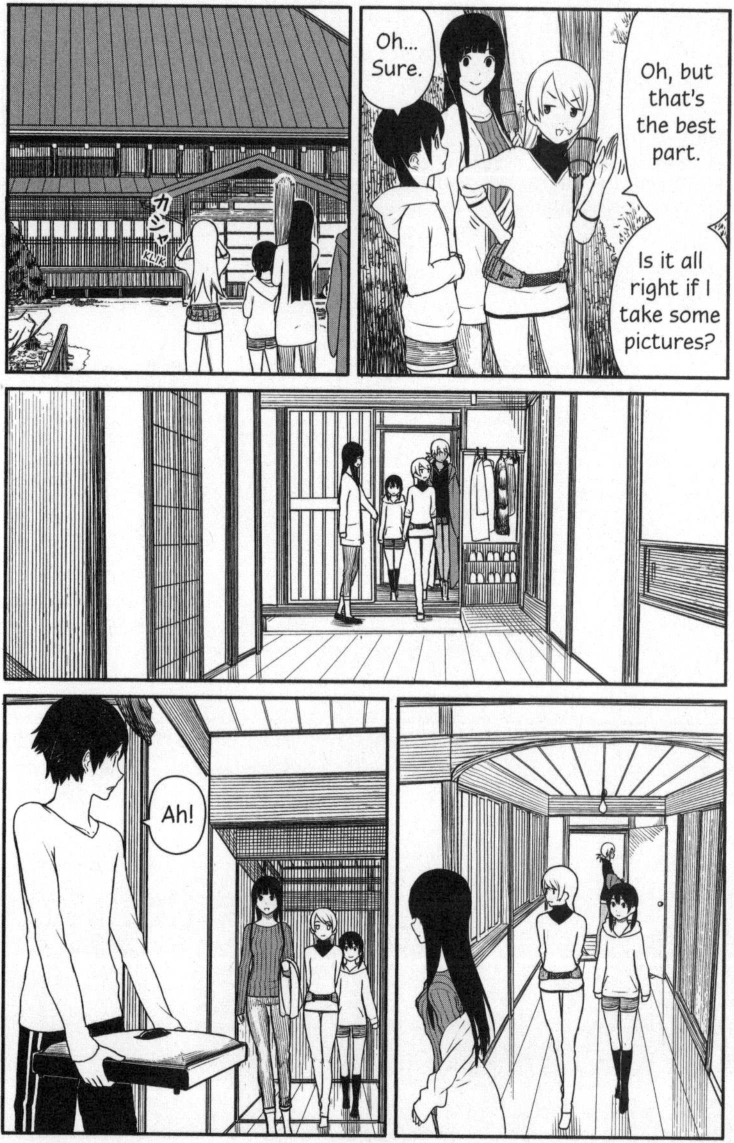
Oh, but that's the best part.
Is it all right if I take some pictures?
Oh... Sure.
カシャ
KLIK
Ah!

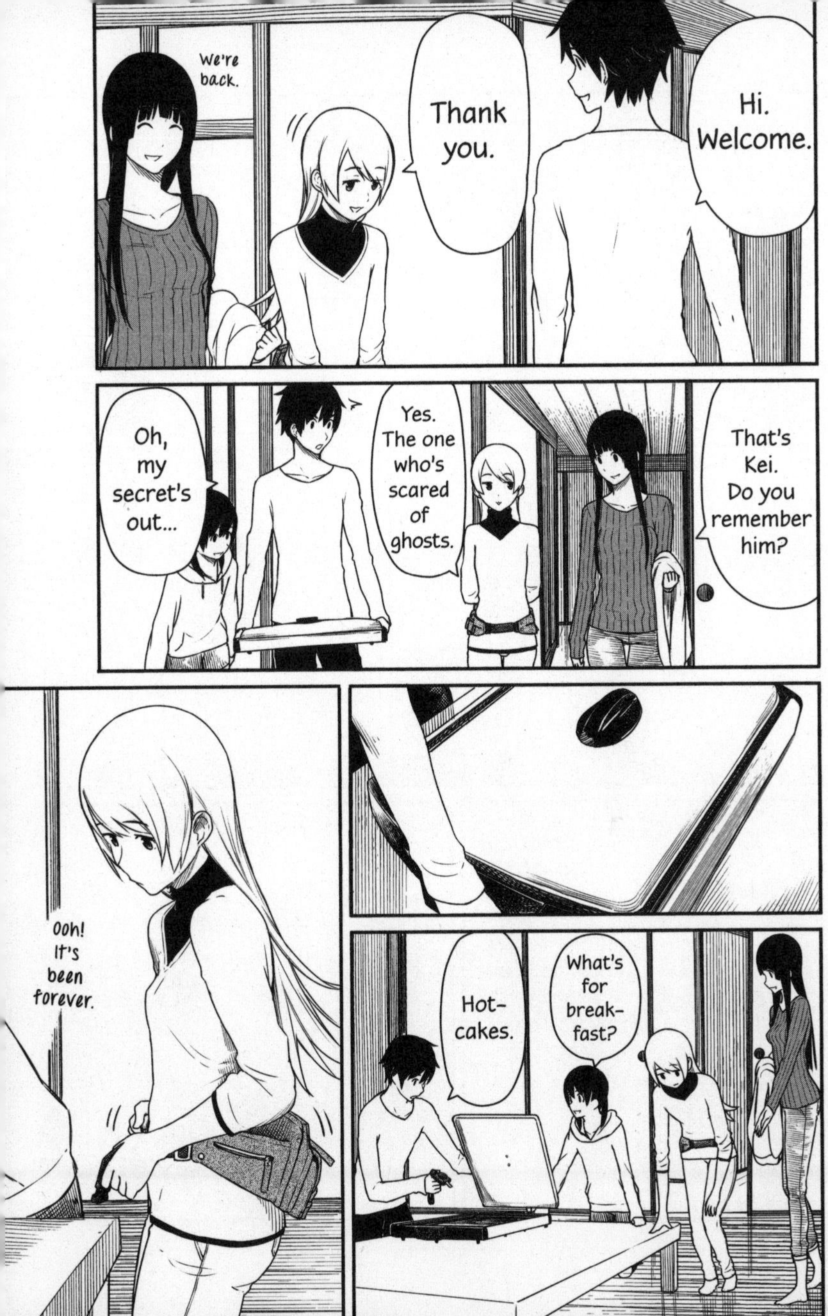
Hi. Welcome.
Thank you.
We're back.
That's Kei. Do you remember him?
Yes. The one who's scared of ghosts.
Oh, my secret's out...
What's for break-fast?
Hot-cakes.
Ooh! It's been forever.

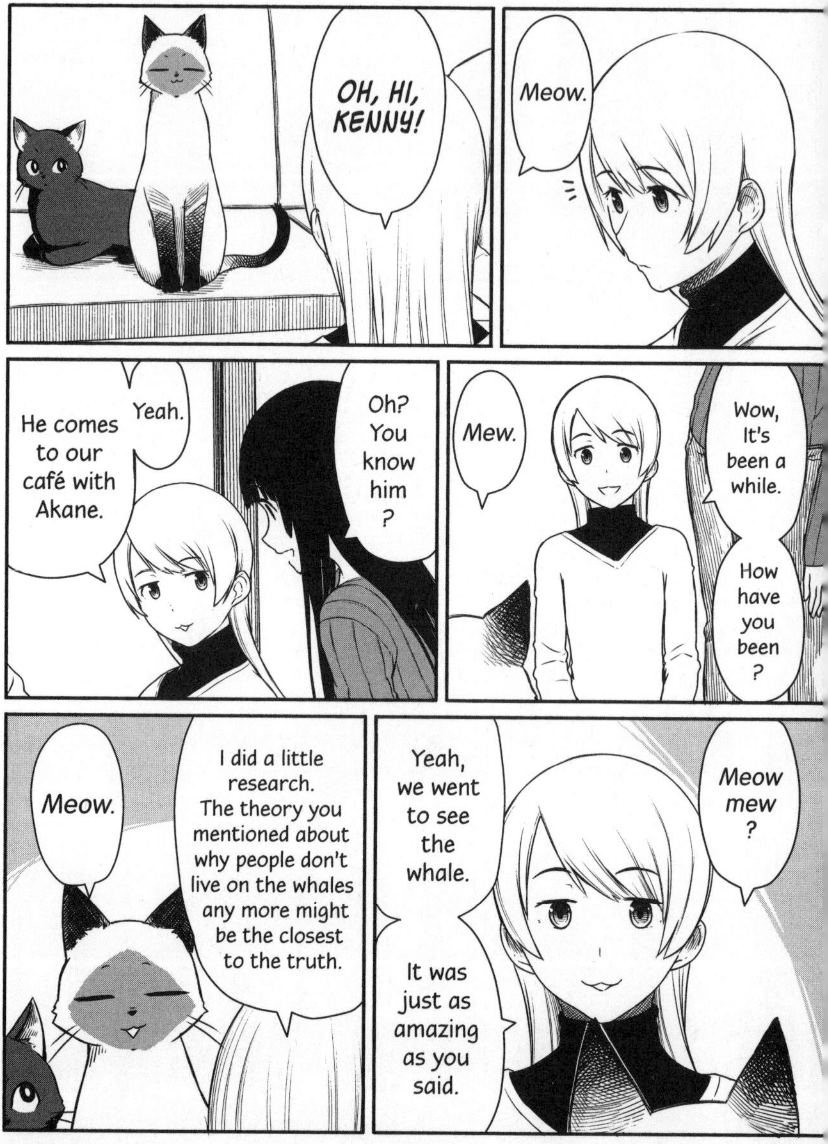
Meow.
OH, HI, KENNY!
Wow, It's been a while.
How have you been?
Mew.
Oh? You know him?
Yeah.
He comes to our café with Akane.
Meow mew?
Yeah, we went to see the whale.
It was just as amazing as you said.
I did a little research. The theory you mentioned about why people don't live on the whales any more might be the closest to the truth.
Meow.

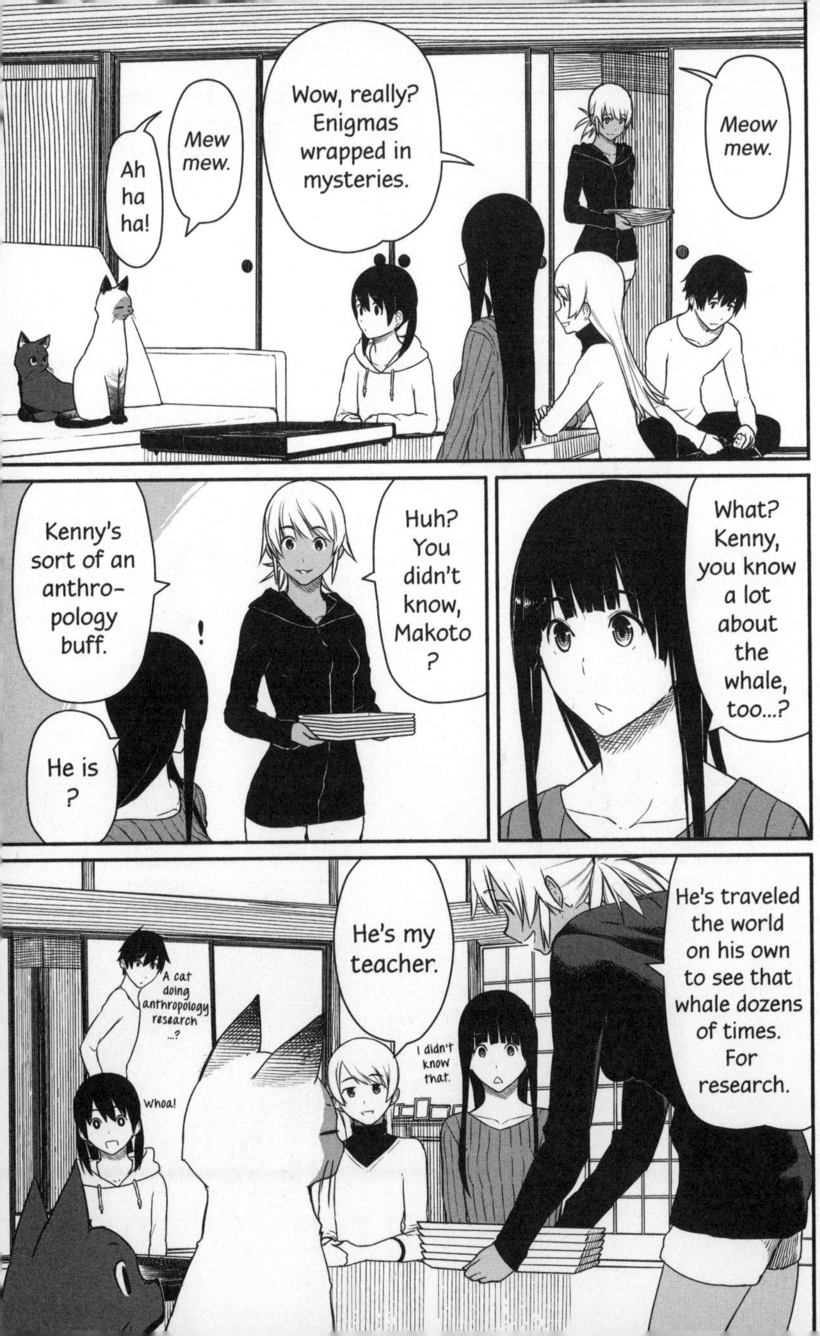
Meow mew.
Wow, really? Enigmas wrapped in mysteries.
Mew mew.
Ah ha ha!
What? Kenny, you know a lot about the whale, too...?
Huh? You didn't know, Makoto?
Kenny's sort of an anthropology buff.
!
He is ?
He's traveled the world on his own to see that whale dozens of times. For research.
I didn't know that.
He's my teacher.
A cat doing anthropology research ...?
Whoa!

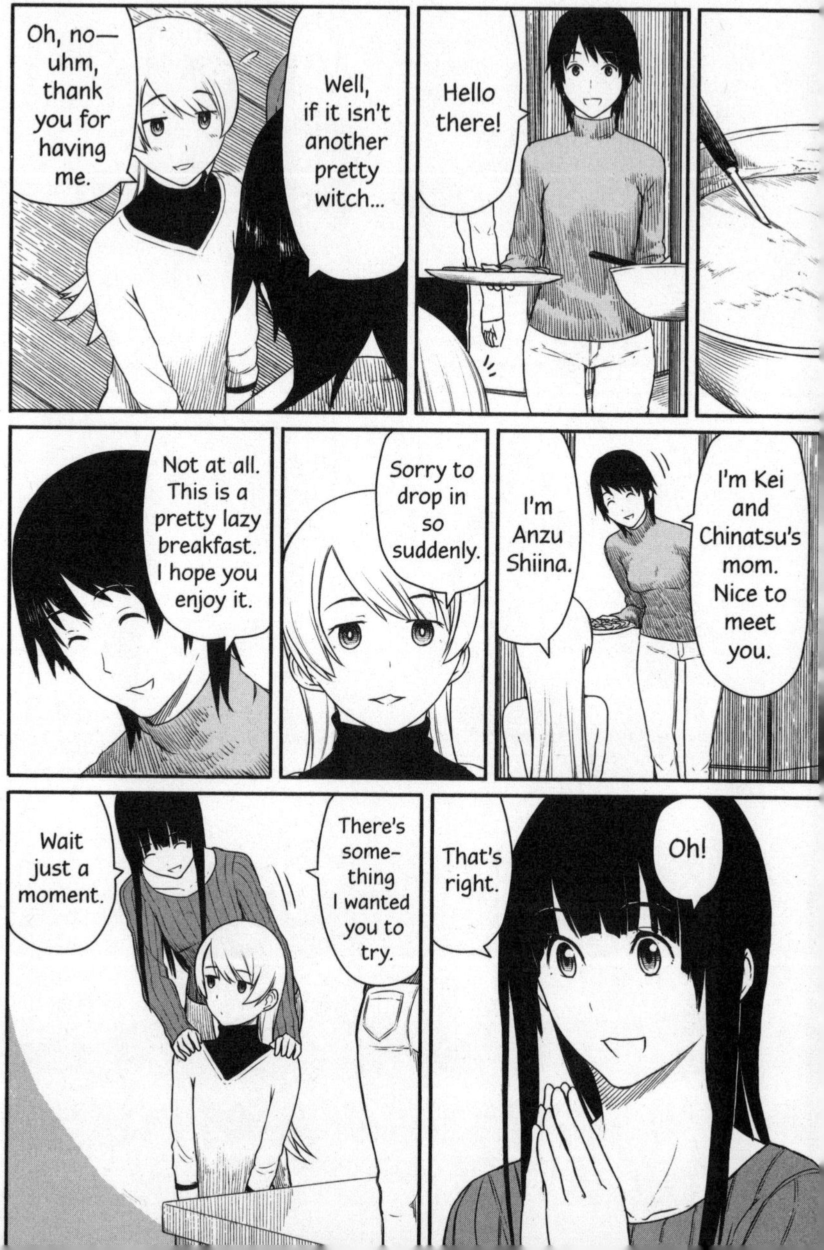
Hello there!
Well, if it isn't another pretty witch...
Oh, no— uhm, thank you for having me.
I'm Kei and Chinatsu's mom. Nice to meet you.
I'm Anzu Shiina.
Sorry to drop in so suddenly.
Not at all. This is a pretty lazy breakfast. I hope you enjoy it.
Oh!
That's right.
There's some-thing I wanted you to try.
Wait just a moment.

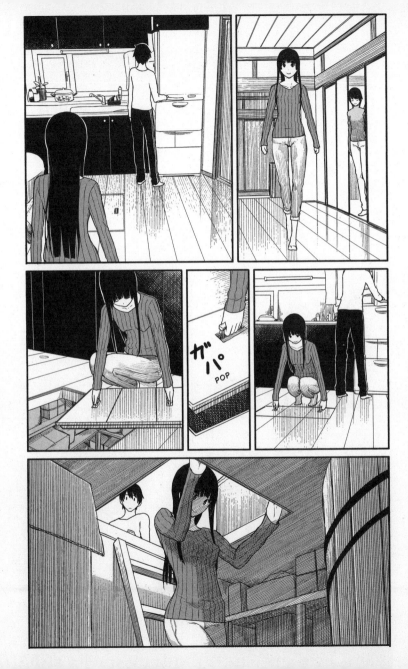

ガ
パ
POP

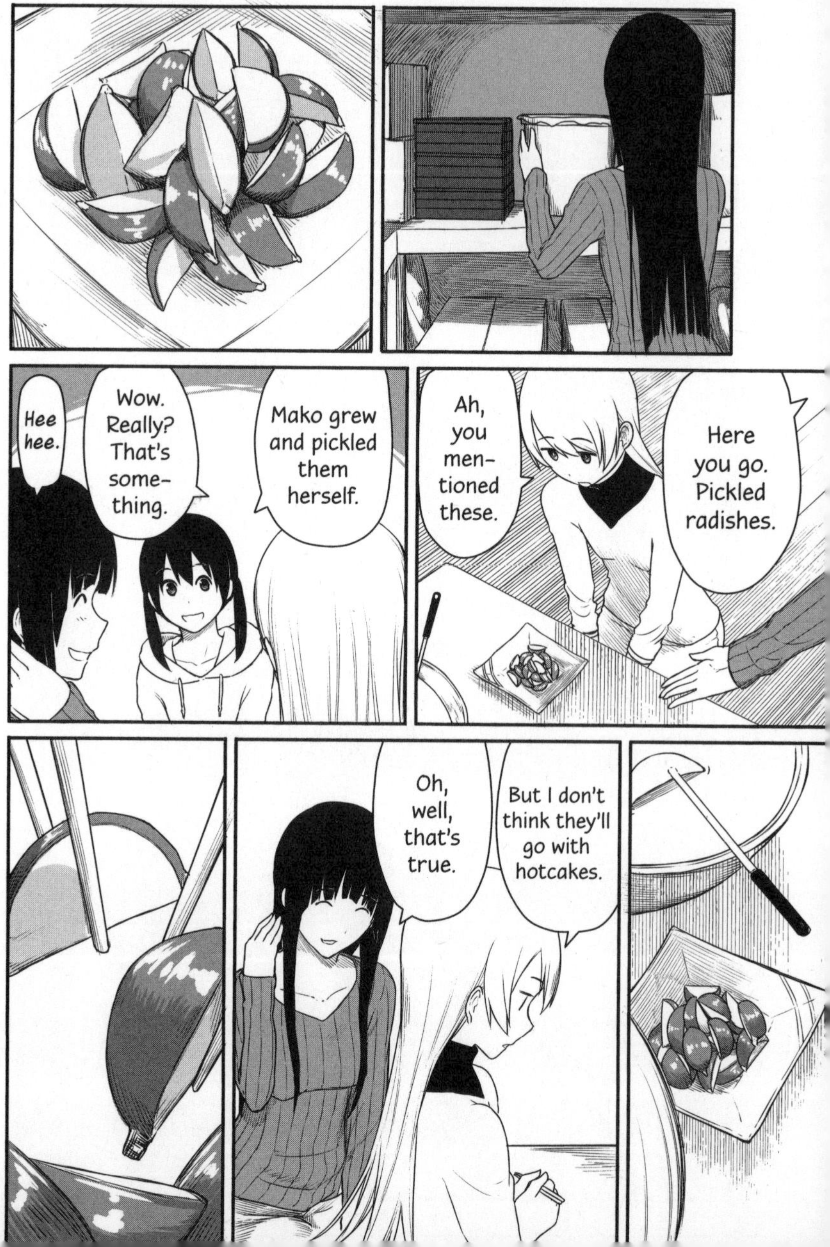
Here you go. Pickled radishes.
Ah, you mentioned these.
Mako grew and pickled them herself.
Wow. Really? That's something.
Hee hee.
But I don't think they'll go with hotcakes.
Oh, well, that's true.

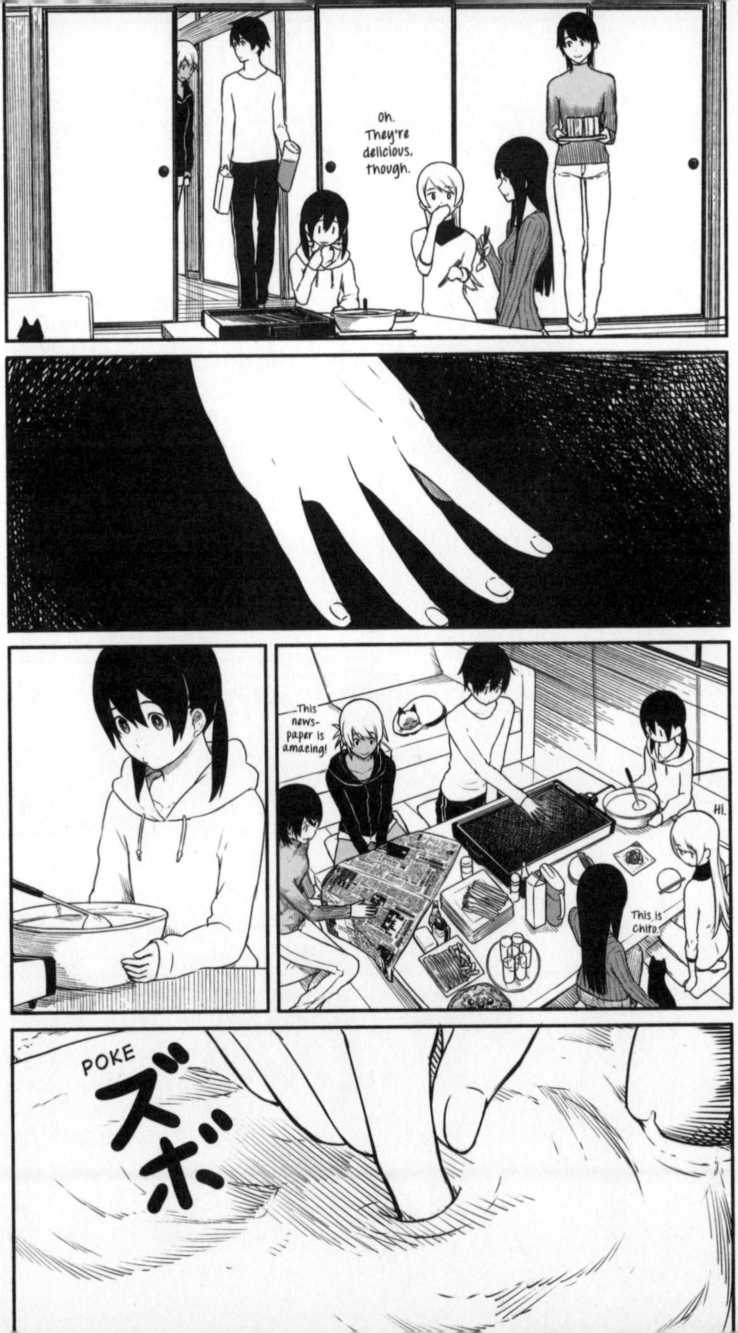
Oh. They're delicious, though.
Hi.
This is Chito.
This news-paper is amazing!
POKE
ズボ

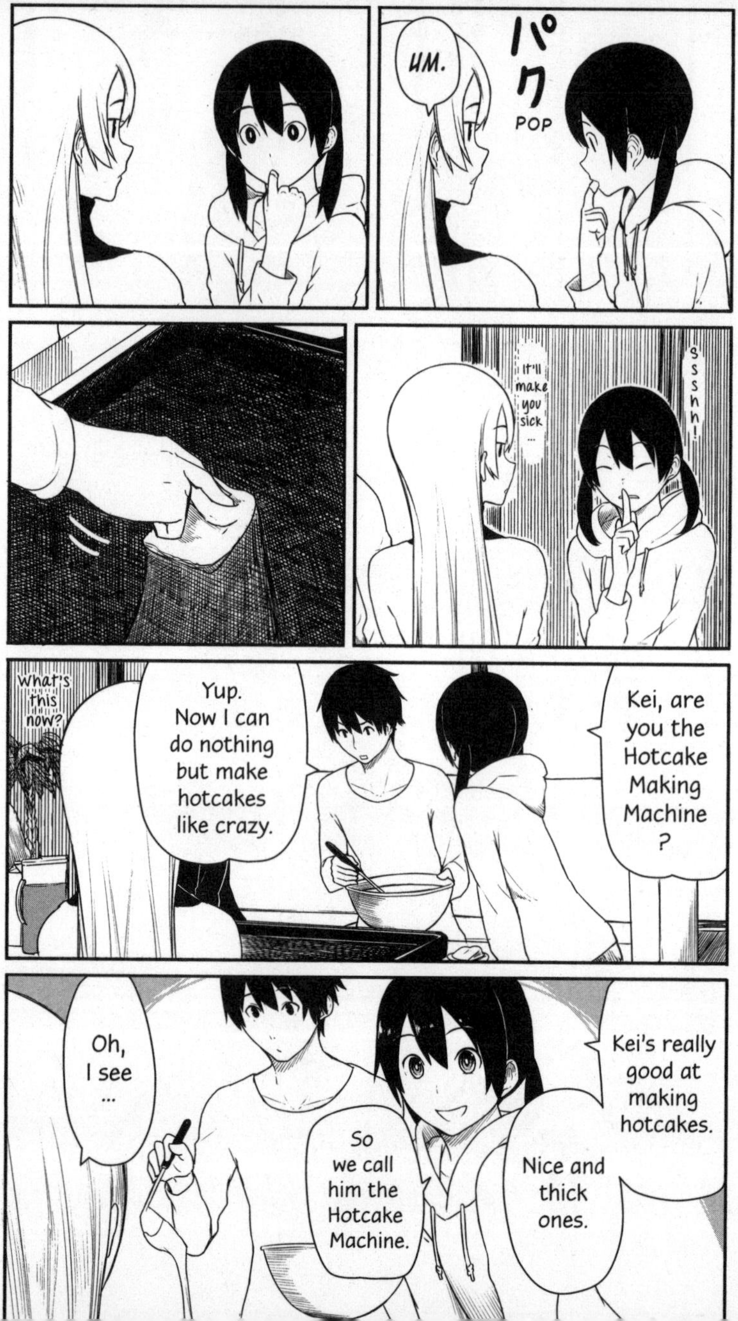
UM.
パク
POP
Ssshh!
It'll make you sick ...
Kei, are you the Hotcake Making Machine ?
Yup. Now I can do nothing but make hotcakes like crazy.
What's this now?
Kei's really good at making hotcakes.
Nice and thick ones.
So we call him the Hotcake Machine.
Oh, I see ...

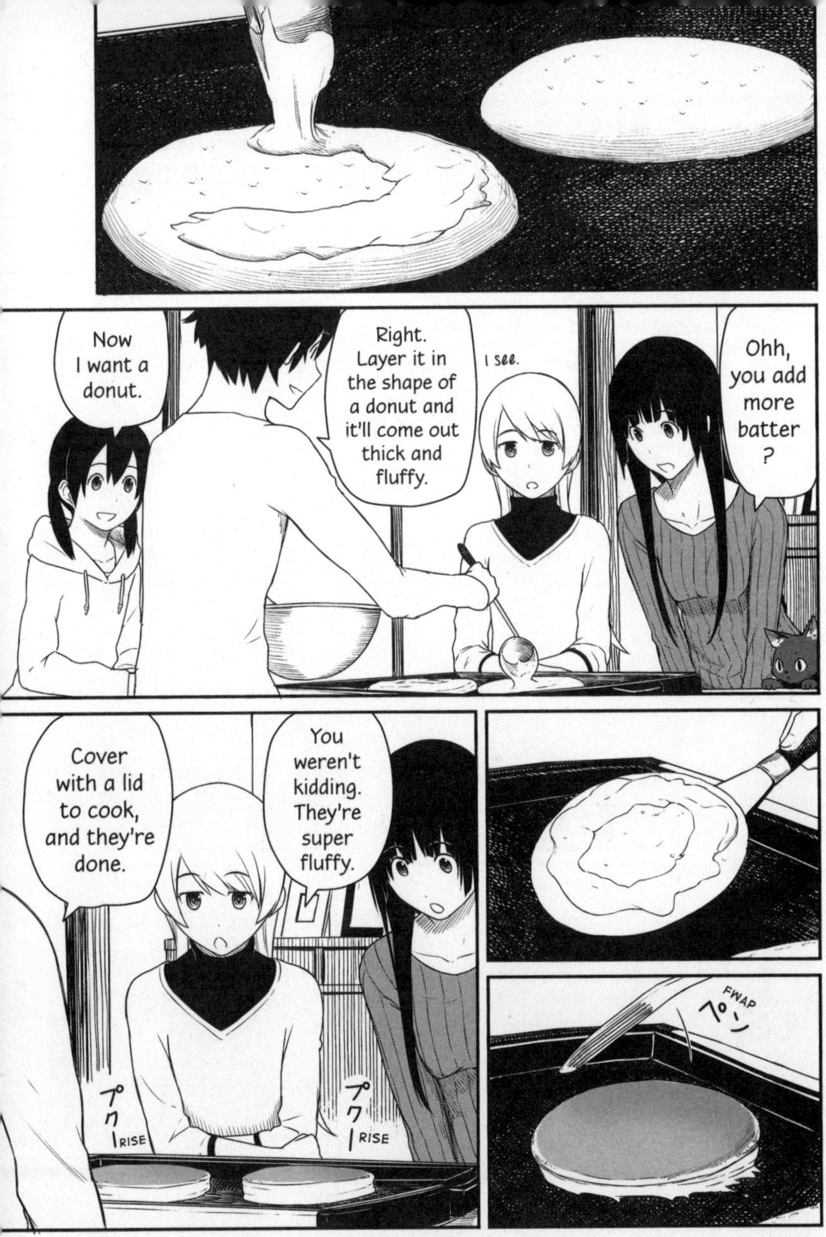
Ohh, you add more batter?
I see.
Right. Layer it in the shape of a donut and it'll come out thick and fluffy.
Now I want a donut.
ペン
FWAP
You weren't kidding. They're super fluffy.
Cover with a lid to cook, and they're done.
プクー
RISE
プクー
RISE

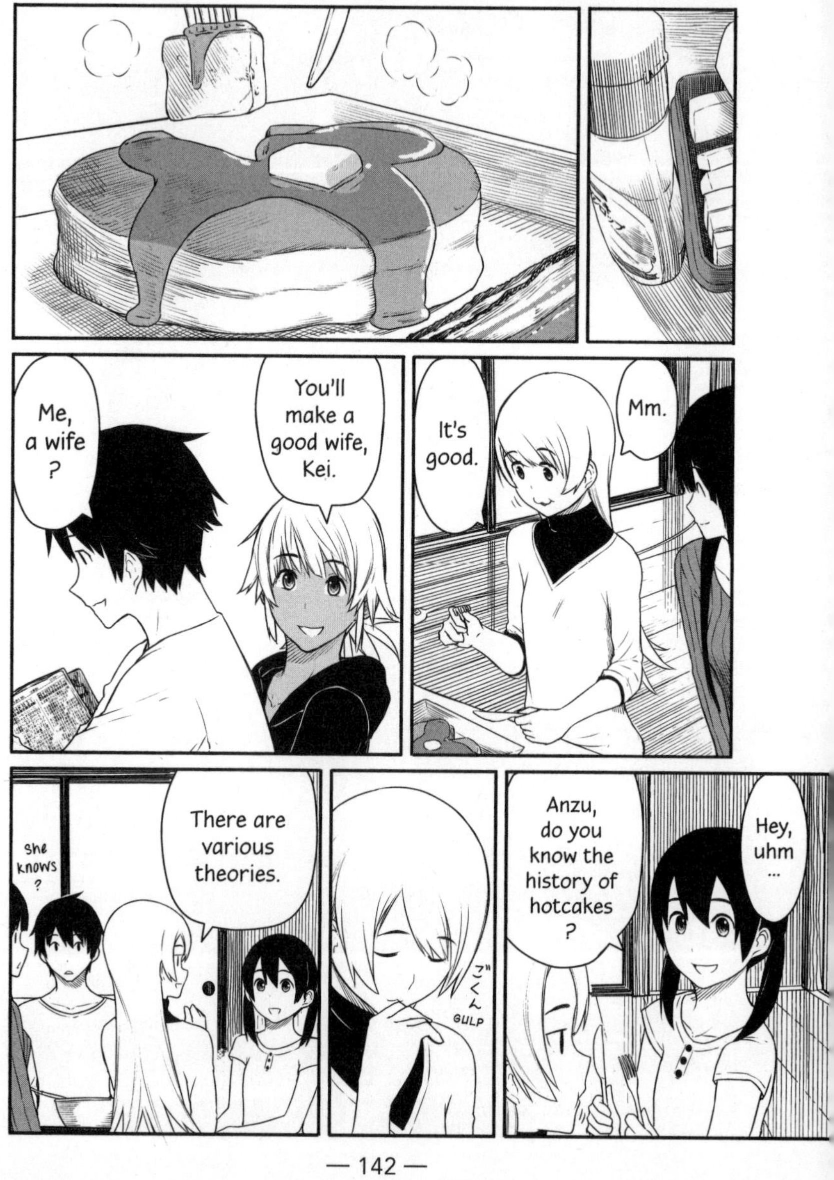
Mm.
It's good.
You'll make a good wife, Kei.
Me, a wife ?
Hey, uhm ...
Anzu, do you know the history of hotcakes ?
ごくん
GULP
There are various theories.
She knows ?

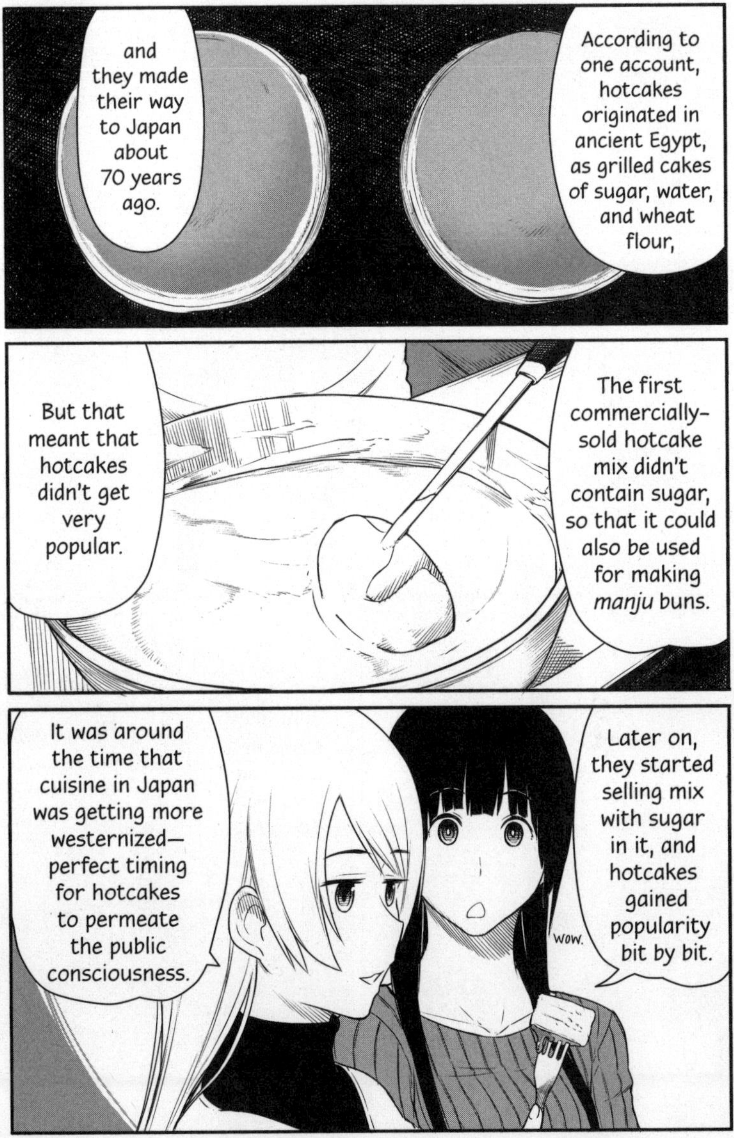
According to one account, hotcakes originated in ancient Egypt, as grilled cakes of sugar, water, and wheat flour,
and they made their way to Japan about 70 years ago.
The first commercially-sold hotcake mix didn't contain sugar, so that it could also be used for making *manju* buns.
But that meant that hotcakes didn't get very popular.
Later on, they started selling mix with sugar in it, and hotcakes gained popularity bit by bit.
wow.
It was around the time that cuisine in Japan was getting more westernized—perfect timing for hotcakes to permeate the public consciousness.

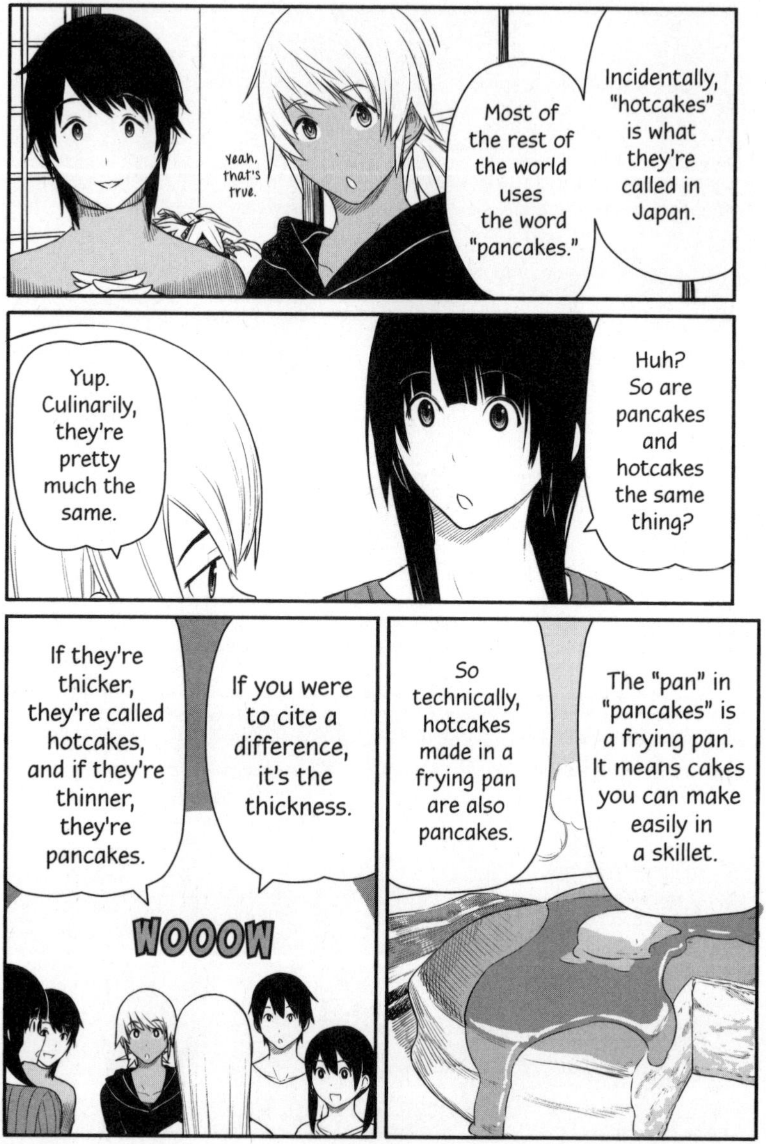

Incidentally, "hotcakes" is what they're called in Japan.
Most of the rest of the world uses the word "pancakes."
Yeah, that's true.
Huh? So are pancakes and hotcakes the same thing?
Yup. Culinarily, they're pretty much the same.
The "pan" in "pancakes" is a frying pan. It means cakes you can make easily in a skillet.
So technically, hotcakes made in a frying pan are also pancakes.
If you were to cite a difference, it's the thickness.
If they're thicker, they're called hotcakes, and if they're thinner, they're pancakes.
WOOOW

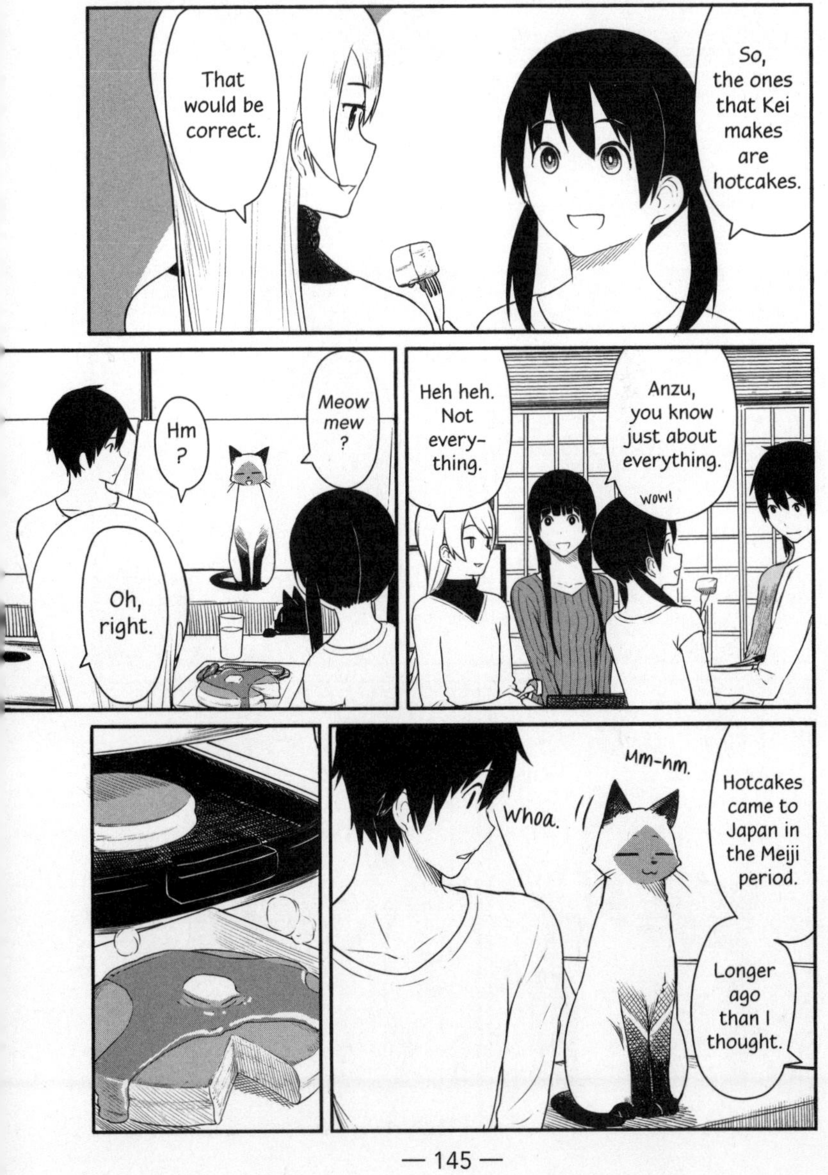
So, the ones that Kei makes are hotcakes.
That would be correct.
Anzu, you know just about everything.
WOW!
Heh heh. Not every-thing.
Meow mew?
Hm?
Oh, right.
Hotcakes came to Japan in the Meiji period.
Mm-hm.
Whoa.
Longer ago than I thought.

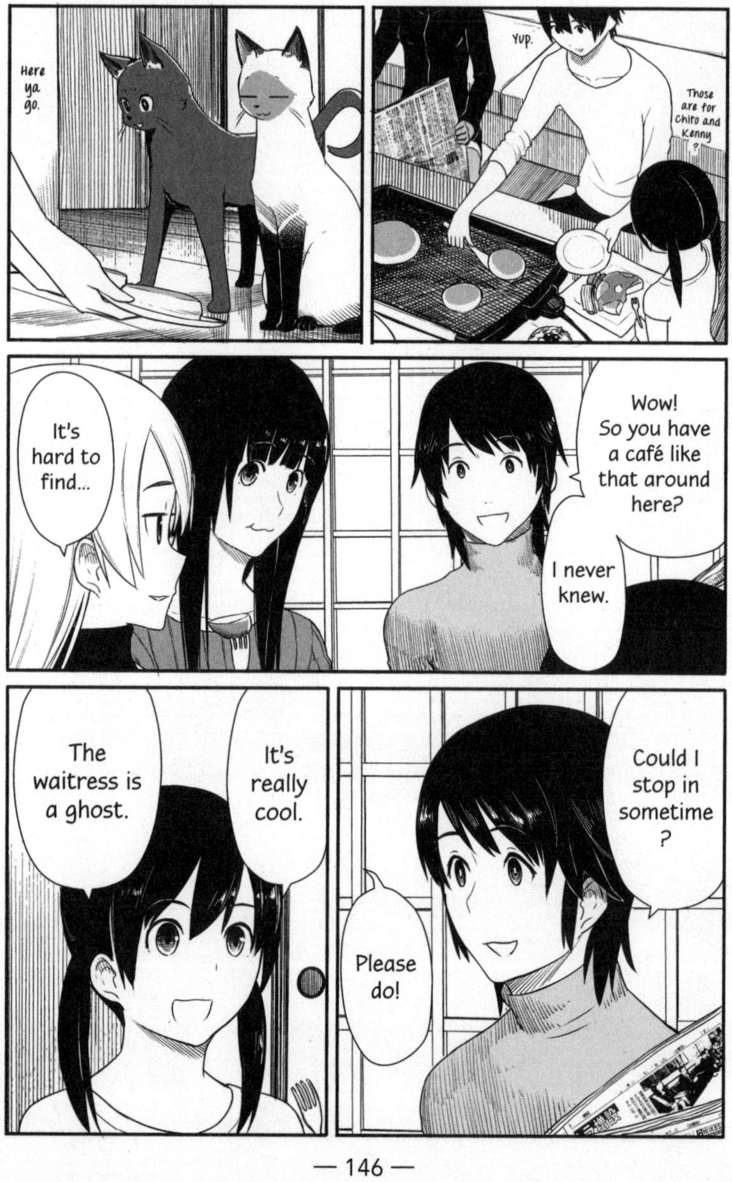
Those are for Chito and Kenny ?
Yup.
Here ya go.
Wow! So you have a café like that around here?
I never knew.
It's hard to find...
Could I stop in sometime ?
Please do!
It's really cool.
The waitress is a ghost.

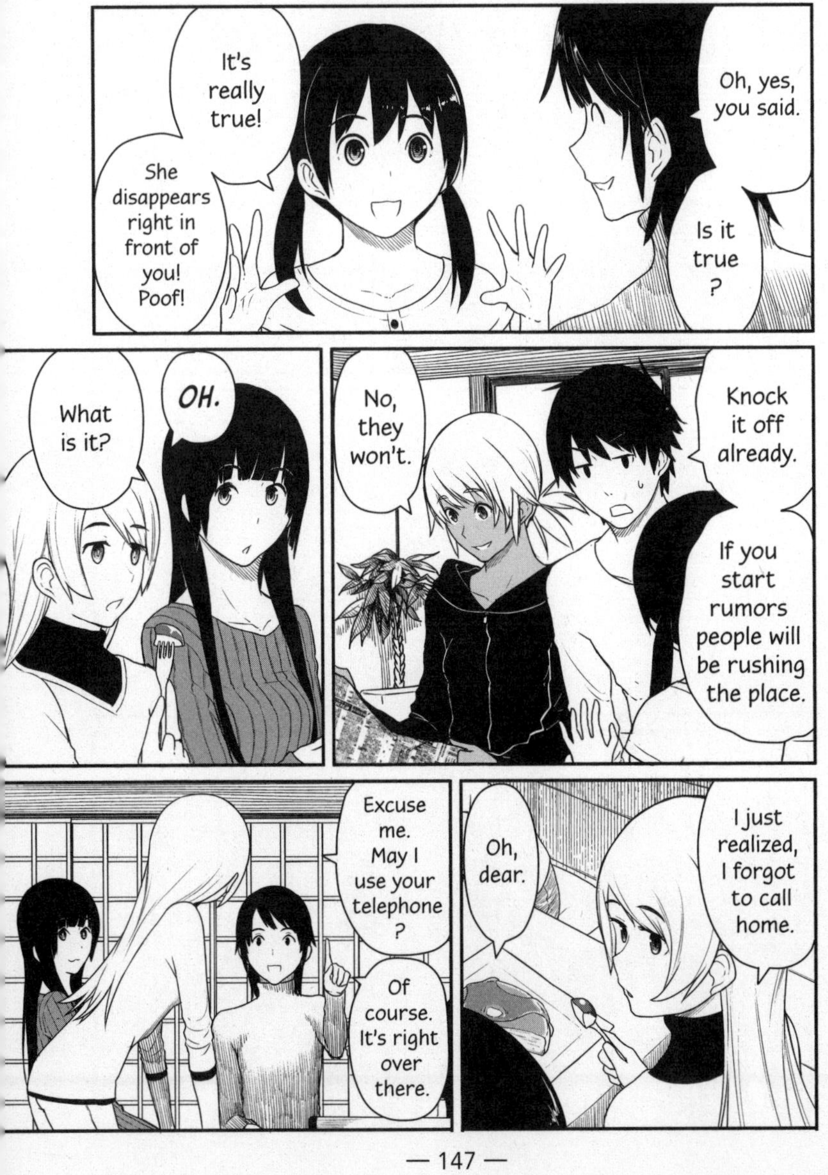
Oh, yes, you said.
Is it true?
It's really true!
She disappears right in front of you! Poof!
Knock it off already.
If you start rumors people will be rushing the place.
No, they won't.
OH.
What is it?
I just realized, I forgot to call home.
Oh, dear.
Excuse me. May I use your telephone?
Of course. It's right over there.

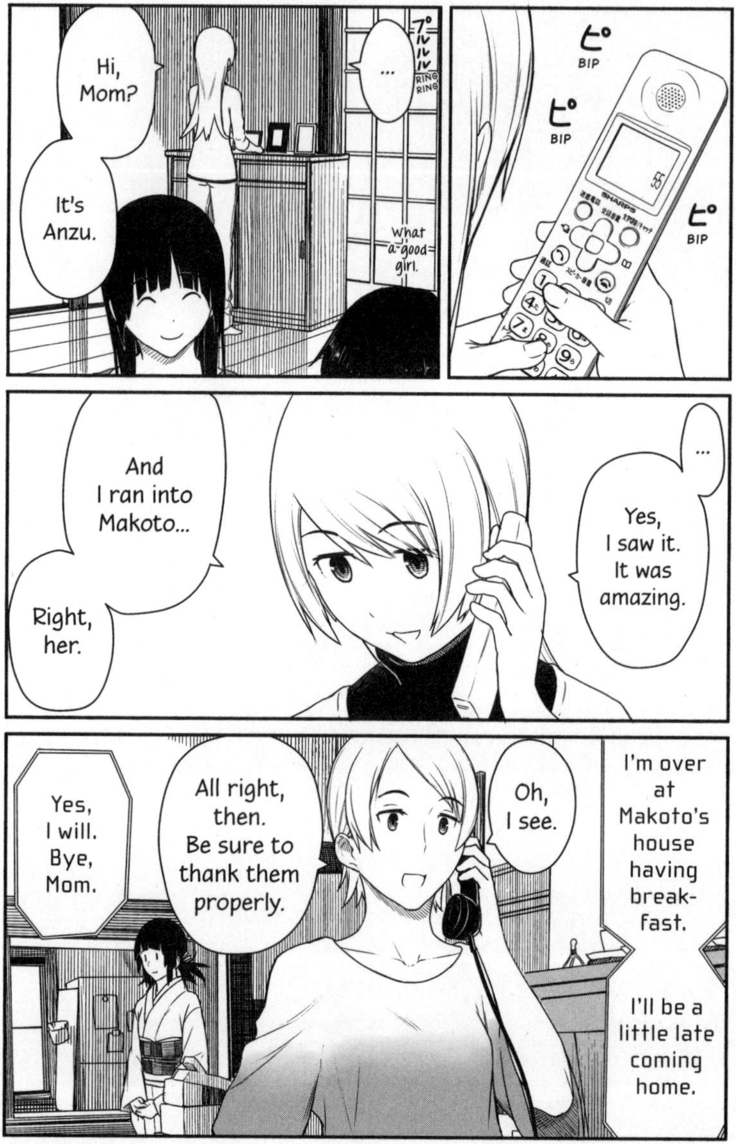
ピ
BIP
ピ
BIP
ピ
BIP
プルルル
RING RING
...
Hi, Mom?
What a good girl.
It's Anzu.
...
Yes, I saw it. It was amazing.
And I ran into Makoto...
Right, her.
I'm over at Makoto's house having break-fast.
I'll be a little late coming home.
Oh, I see.
All right, then. Be sure to thank them properly.
Yes, I will. Bye, Mom.

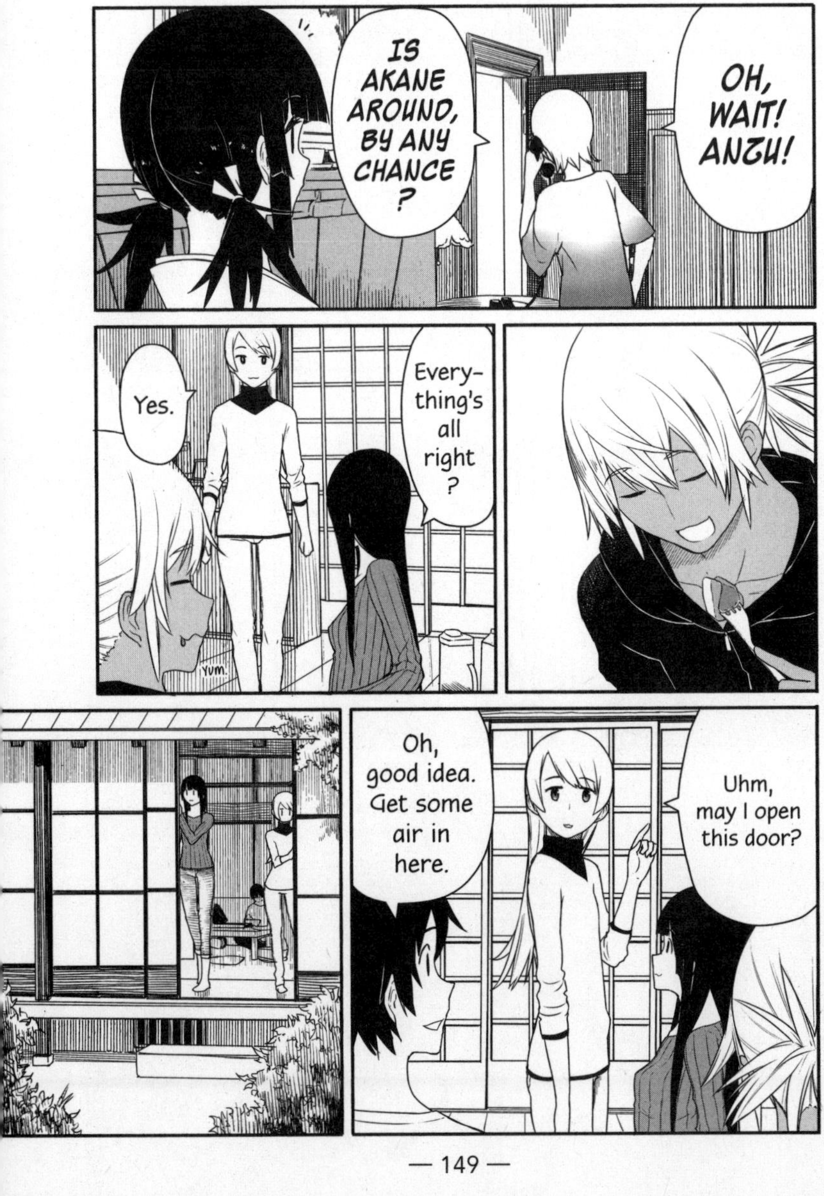
OH, WAIT! ANZU!
IS AKANE AROUND, BY ANY CHANCE?
Every-thing's all right?
Yes.
Yum.
Uhm, may I open this door?
Oh, good idea. Get some air in here.

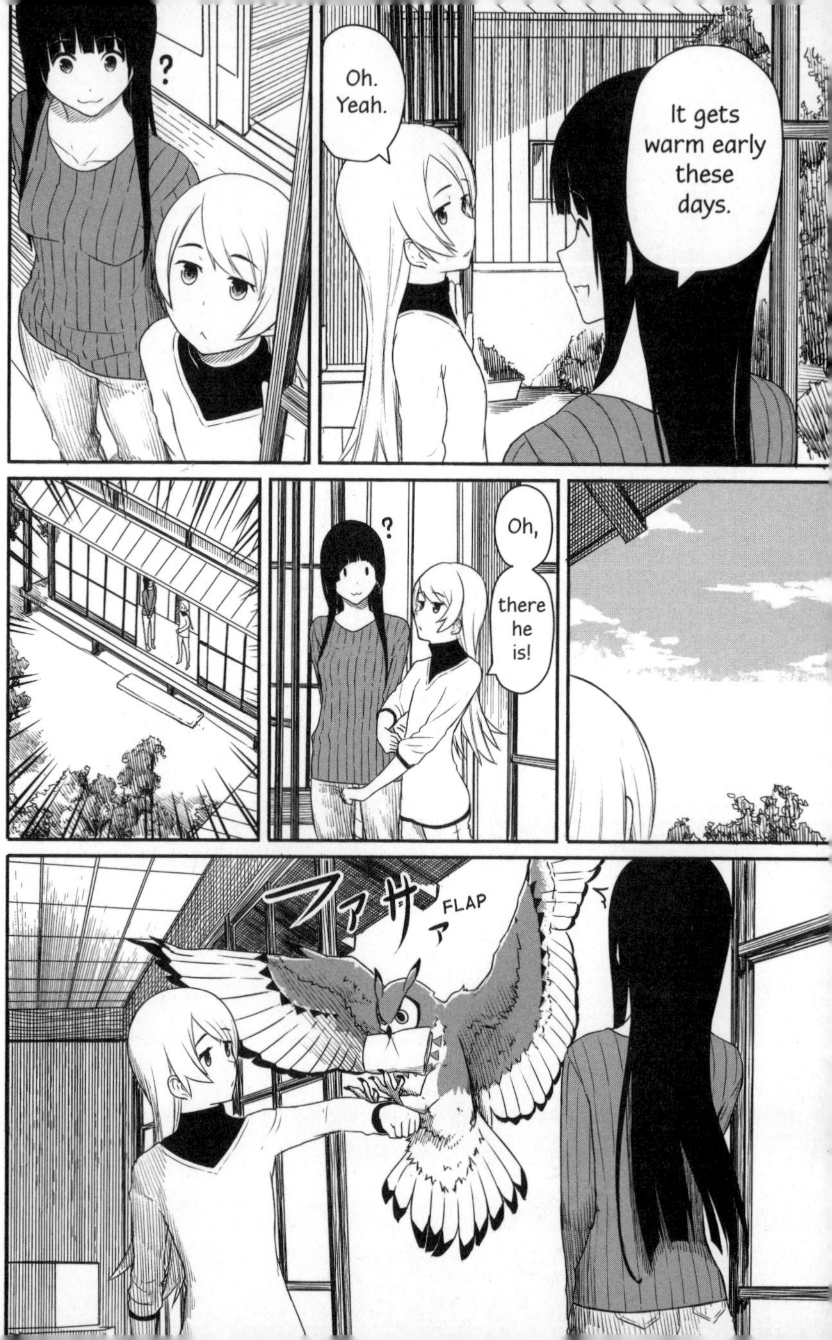
It gets warm early these days.
Oh. Yeah.
?
Oh,
there he is!
?
ファサァ
FLAP

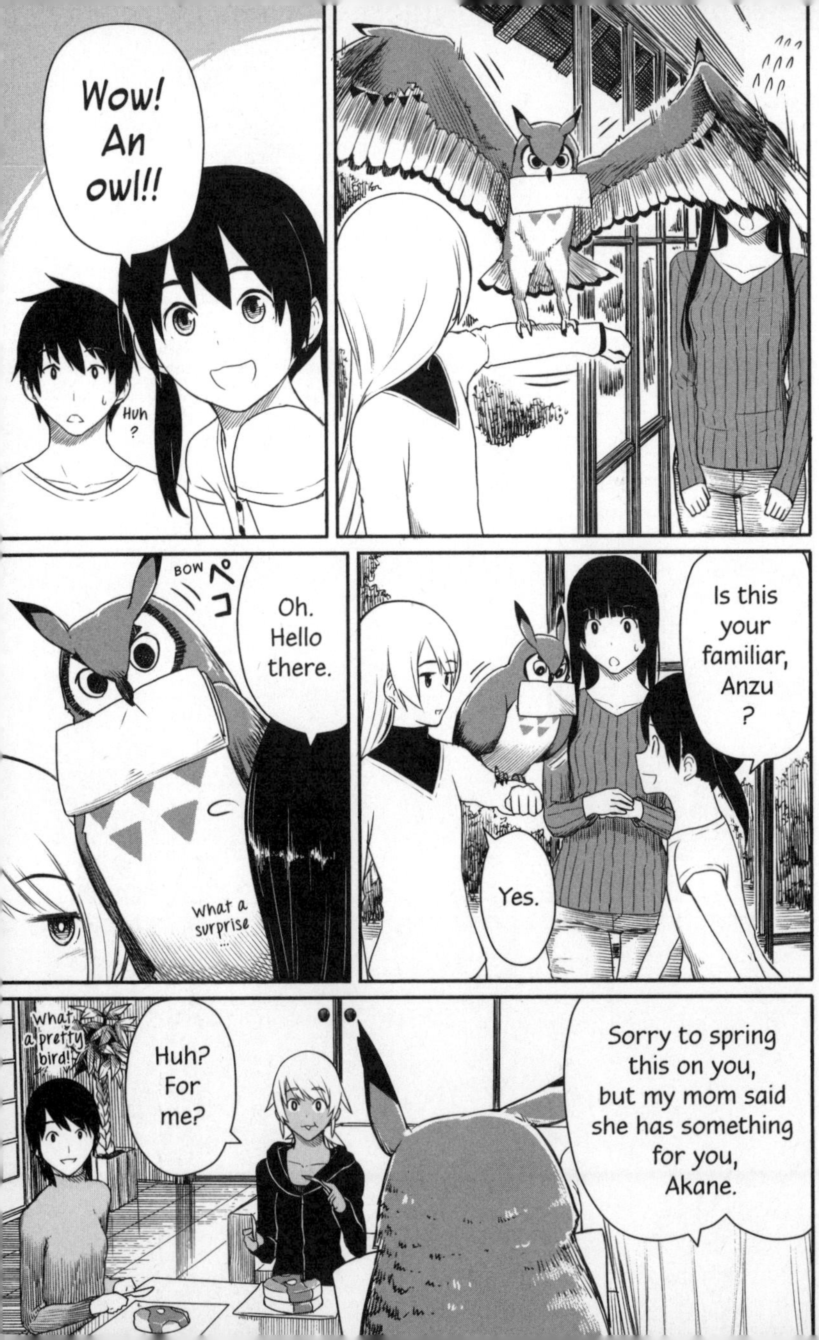
Wow! An owl!!
Huh?
Is this your familiar, Anzu?
Yes.
BOW
Oh. Hello there.
What a surprise...
Sorry to spring this on you, but my mom said she has something for you, Akane.
Huh? For me?
What a pretty bird!

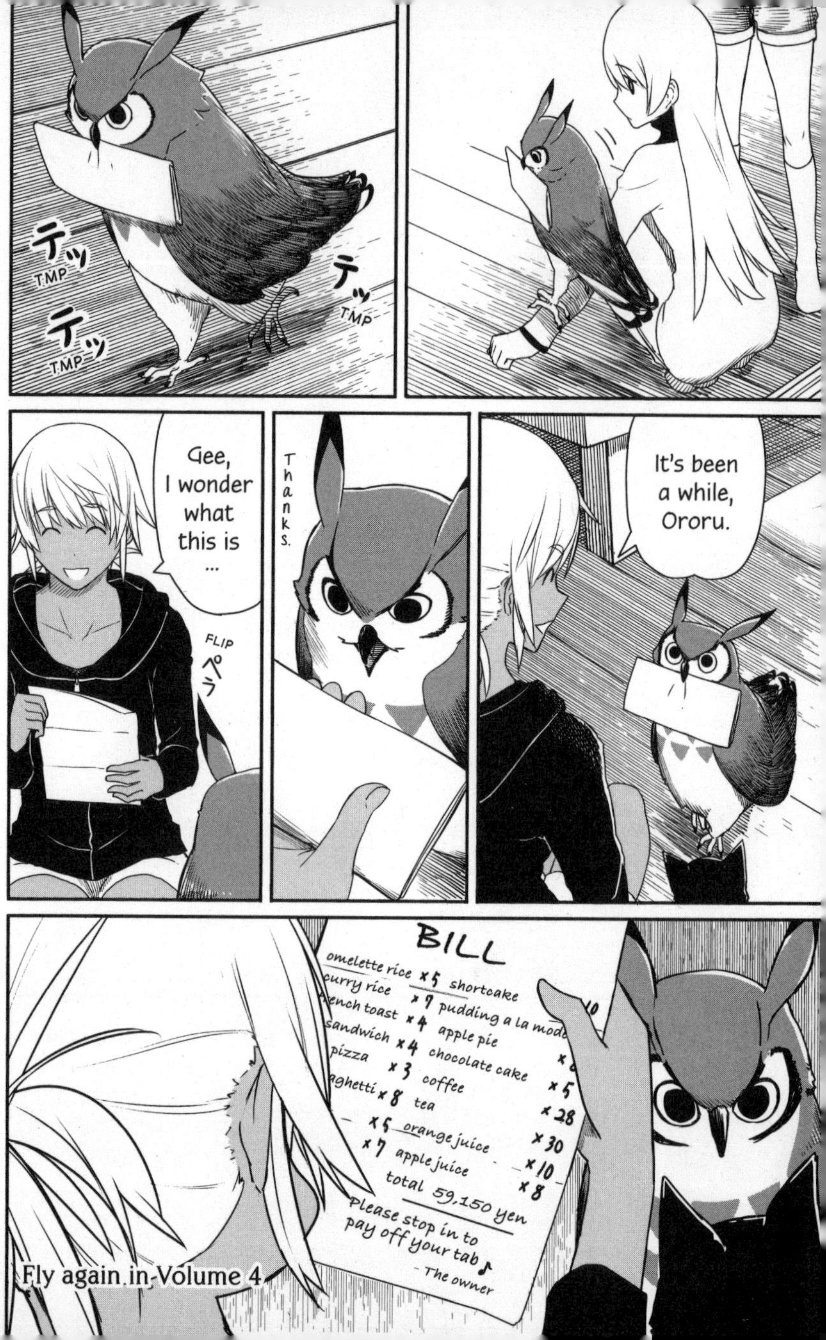
テッ
TMP
テッ
TMP
テッ
TMP
It's been a while, Ororu.
Thanks.
Gee, I wonder what this is ...
FLIP
ペラ
BILL
omelette rice ×5
curry rice ×7
ench toast ×4
sandwich ×4
pizza ×3
aghetti ×8
×5
×7
shortcake
pudding a la mode
apple pie
chocolate cake ×5
coffee ×28
tea ×30
orange juice ×10
apple juice ×8
total 59,150 yen
Please stop in to pay off your tab♪
- The owner
Fly again in Volume 4

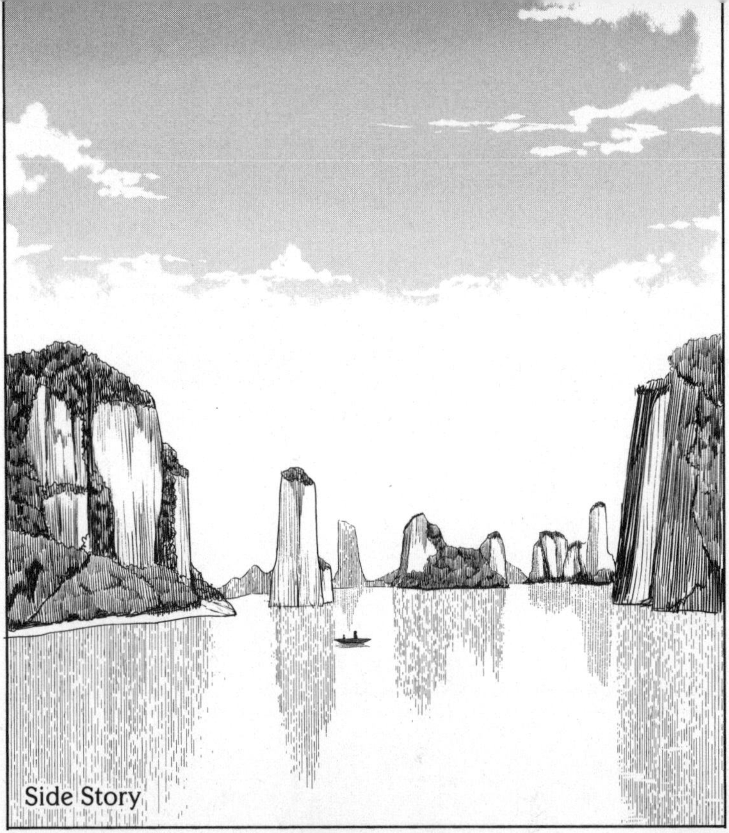
Side Story

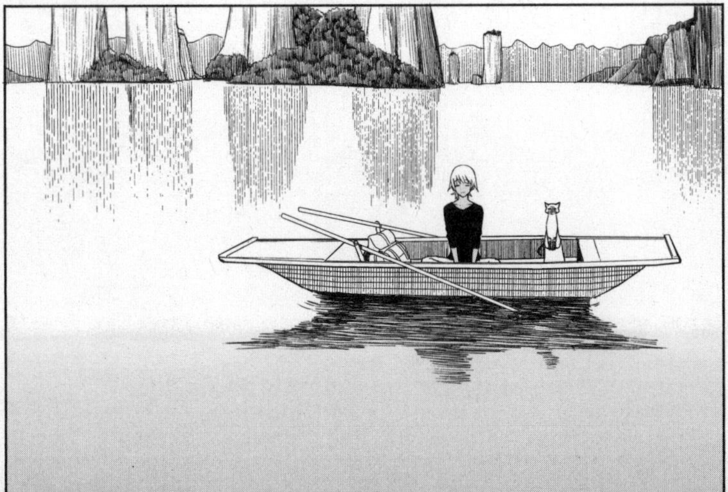

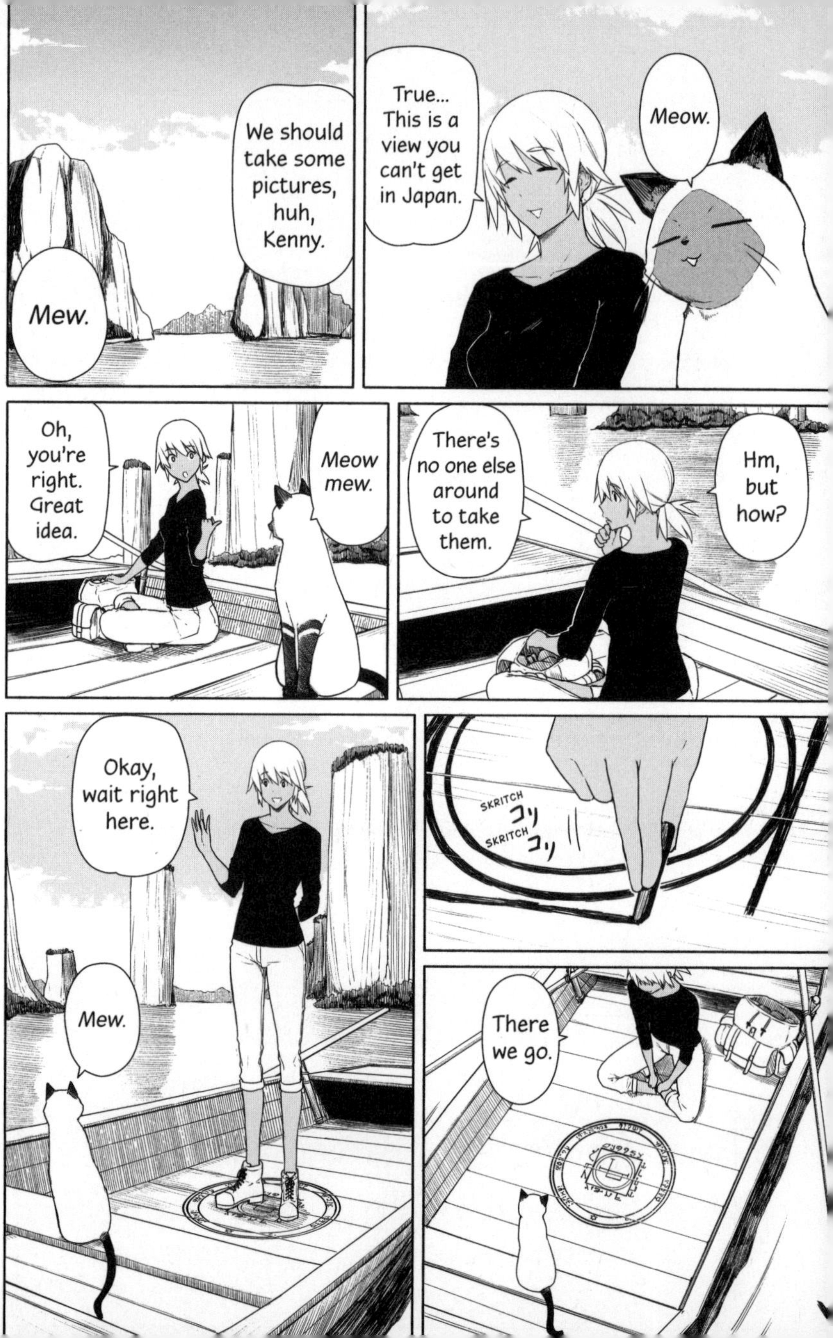
Meow.
True... This is a view you can't get in Japan.
We should take some pictures, huh, Kenny.
Mew.
Hm, but how?
There's no one else around to take them.
Meow mew.
Oh, you're right. Great idea.
SKRITCH コリ
SKRITCH コリ
There we go.
Okay, wait right here.
Mew.

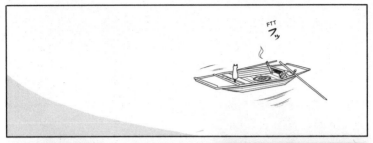

FTT
フッ

Mmf
...

Makoto.
Psst,
Makoto
...

I got
'er!

POOF
パッ

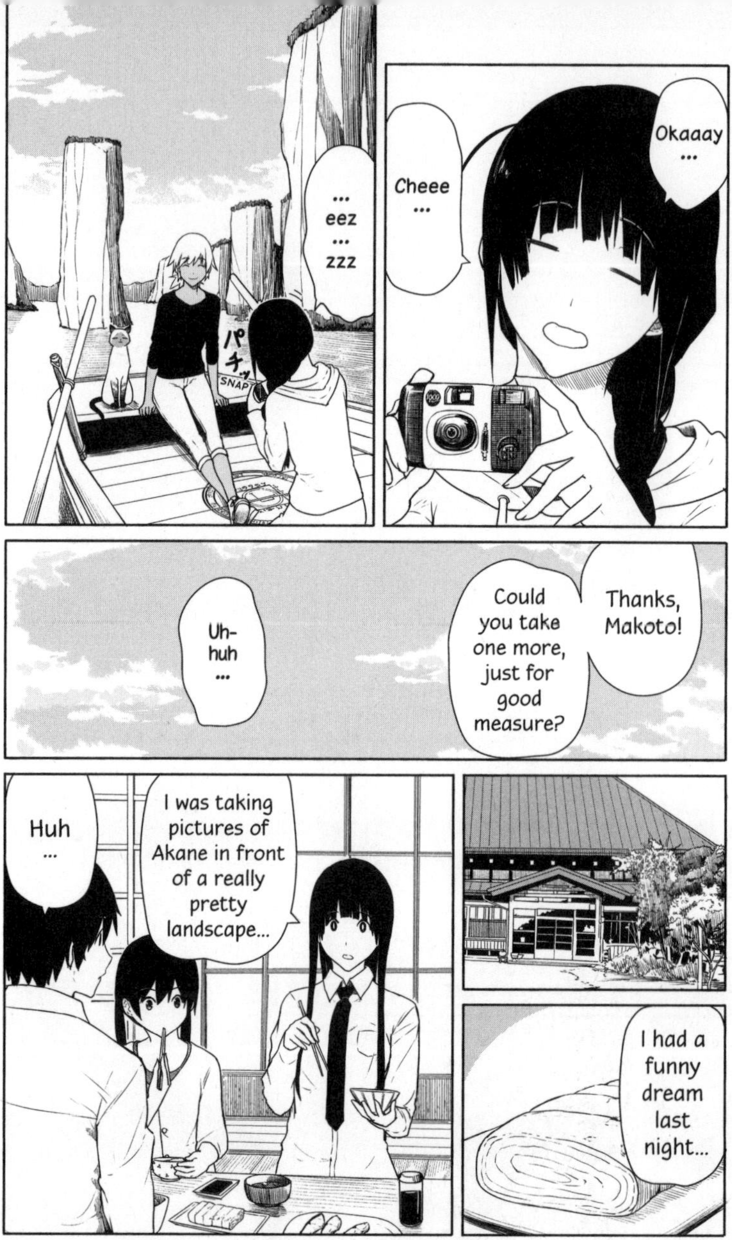
Okaaay ...
Cheee ...
... eez ... zzz
パチッ
SNAP
Thanks, Makoto!
Could you take one more, just for good measure?
Uh-huh ...
I had a funny dream last night...
I was taking pictures of Akane in front of a really pretty landscape...
Huh ...

Side Story ~ The End

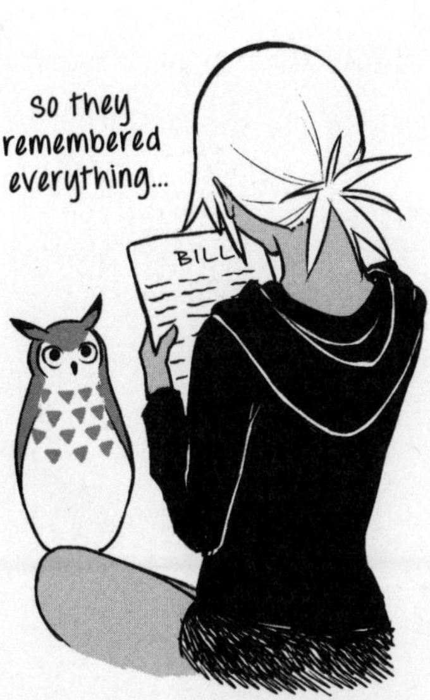
so they remembered everything...
BILL

flying witch ✳ kcm flying witch preview for next volume ✳

Volume 4 preview

Flying Witch 4 is coming soon, dear reader.

The days grow longer and the rainy season gives way to summer, when, in Aomori, there are fireworks, festivals and fireflies...

There's much to look forward to, so please keep reading!

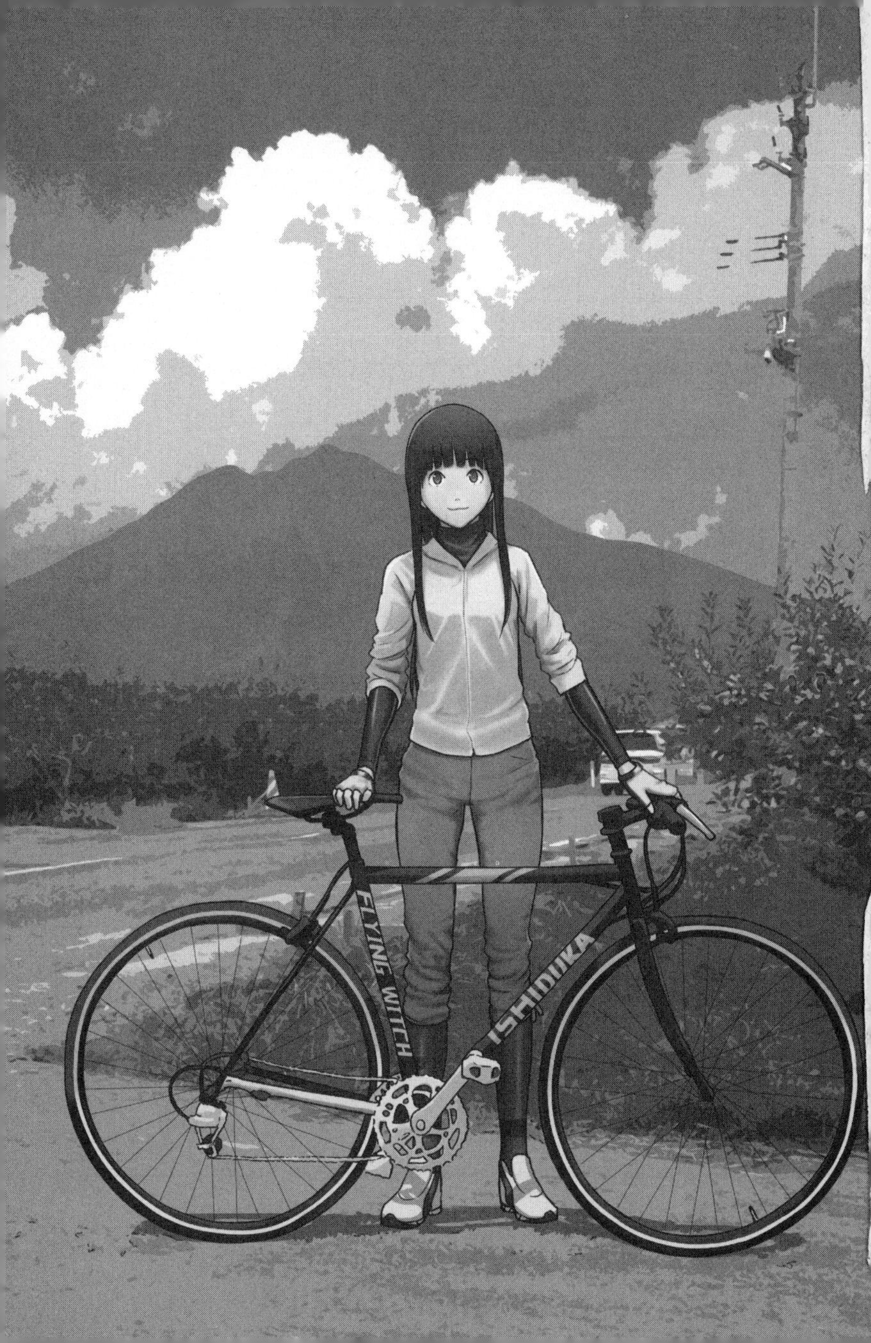
FLYING WITCH
ISHIDUKA

Flying Witch 3

Translation - Melissa Tanaka
Production - Grace Lu
            Tomoe Tsutsumi

First published in Japan in 2015 by Kodansha, Ltd., Tokyo
Publication for this English edition arranged through Kodansha, Ltd., Tokyo

Translation provided by Vertical Comics, 2017
Published by Vertical Comics, an imprint of Vertical, Inc., New York

Originally published in Japanese as *Flying Witch 3* by Kodansha, Ltd., 2015
Flying Witch first serialized in *Bessatsu Shonen Magazine*, Kodansha, Ltd., 2013-

This is a work of fiction.

ISBN: 978-1-945054-11-2

Manufactured in the United States of America

First Edition

Vertical, Inc.
451 Park Avenue South, 7th Floor
New York, NY 10016
www.vertical-comics.com

Vertical books are distributed through Penguin-Random House Publisher Services.